Sandplay

Sandplay is one of the fastest growing therapies. As yet there is no single volume that provides interested readers with a comprehensive account of the history, current practice and future direction of Sandplay. *Sandplay: Past, Present and Future* does just that.

Rie Rogers Mitchell and Harriet S. Friedman present the historical origins of Sandplay, biographical profiles of the pioneers and major innovators together with discussions of their seminal writings. The major current therapeutic trends are explored and the final chapter looks at the future of Sandplay through emerging issues. Each chapter has a list of references. A special feature is the comprehensive international bibliography of Sandplay citations and a listing of sand tray videotapes and audiotapes. Much of the Sandplay literature is not easily accessible and this special feature will provide a unique resource for the reader.

Sandplay: Past, Present and Future represents an important and much needed milestone in the development of this exciting field.

Rie Rogers Mitchell is a Professor of Educational Psychology and Counseling at California State University, Northridge. She is a member of Sandplay Therapists of America and the International Society for Sandplay Therapy. As a licensed psychologist she has been awarded a Diplomate in Counseling Psychology by the American Board of Professional Psychology.

Harriet S. Friedman is a Jungian analyst practicing in Los Angeles, California. She is a founding member of Sandplay Therapists of America and a member of the International Society for Sandplay Therapy. She is the former Director of the Hilde Kirsch Children's Center and a member of the Southern California Society of Jungian Analysts. A teacher on the faculty of the C.G. Jung Institute of Los Angeles, she has also lectured extensively on the integration of Sandplay and Jungian psychology.

Also available from Routledge:

Jungian Sandplay
The Wonderful Therapy
Joel Ryce-Menuhin

Chaos and Order in the World of the Psyche
Joanne Wieland-Burston

Changemakers
A Jungian Perspective on Sibling Position and the Family Atmosphere
Louis H. Stewart

Drawings from a Dying Child
Insights into Death from a Jungian Perspective
Judi Bertoia

Dance Therapy and Depth Psychology
The Moving Imagination
Joan Chodorow

Sandplay

Past, present and future

Rie Rogers Mitchell
and
Harriet S. Friedman

London and New York

First published 1994
by Routledge
11 New Fetter Lane, London EC4P 4EE

Simultaneously published in the USA and Canada
by Routledge
29 West 35th Street, New York, NY 10001

© 1994 Rie Rogers Mitchell and Harriet S. Friedman

Typeset in Palatino by LaserScript, Mitcham, Surrey
Printed and bound in Great Britain by
Biddles Ltd, Guildford and King's Lynn

British Library Cataloguing in Publication Data
A catalogue record for this book is available from the British Library.

Library of Congress Cataloging in Publication Data
Mitchell, Rie Rogers, 1940–
  Sandplay: past, present and future/Rie Rogers Mitchell and
  Harriet S. Friedman.
    p. cm.
  Includes bibliographical references and index.
  1. Sandplay – Therapeutic use. I. Friedman, Harriet, S., 1930–
  II. Title.
  RC489.S25M58   1993
  616.89'1653 – dc20   93-8079
                                                                  CIP

ISBN 0–415–10136–0 (hbk)
ISBN 0–415–10137–9 (pbk)

This book is dedicated to our husbands, Rex C. Mitchell and Richard E. Friedman, whose patient, loving friendship has been an endless source of inspiration, support, and help in this adventure.

Contents

Illustrations

Foreword

I am glad to write a foreword to this book on Sandplay by my friend, Harriet Friedman, and her colleague, Rie Rogers Mitchell. It pays close attention to a subject whose importance cannot be overlooked because of its universality not only in a geographical sense but also historically. In her book *Themis*, Jane Harrison writes, "A child's toys in antiquity were apt to be much more than mere playthings. They were charms inductive of good, prophylactic against evil influences." Thus play is recognized as having a social as well as a personal significance; indeed it can enter into all fields of mental activity, especially those that are creative. I think, however, I can best introduce this volume by considering the great importance that play took on, both in the field of psychotherapy and education during the first half of the present century.

It was Melanie Klein who grasped the significance of play and toys as depicting, referring to or symbolizing small children's profoundest emotions. It was she, already in 1926, who grasped their significance and introduced play into the psychoanalysis of small children. It was play with toys which revealed the primitive unconscious elements lying at the root of developments both in infancy, childhood and later adult persons as well.

A colleague of Klein, Susan Isaacs, was deeply impressed with her findings and studied children in The Maltinghouse School in Cambridge from Klein's position. The recordings were not only of children's play which was, however, given a prominent place in the form of spontaneous behavior, thought and feeling but included play as a part of the educational process. Her work gave impetus to educationists to include it more in their curriculum. Amongst them was Dr Margaret Gardner, a Lecturer in Education at the City of Leeds Training College for Teachers, and I cannot do better than quote from the Preface to her book, *The Children's Play Centre*.

When we first opened the Play Centre we could not help feeling some anxiety lest we could never do anything worth while for the children in the limited space and very limited time at our disposal. We need have had no doubts. The children had none. From the first moment when the playroom doors were opened to them, those two hours in the week appeared to become the loadstar of their lives. Their attitude towards all of us, to the College and to all the materials and experiences open to them, was direct and confident. They knew what they wanted. . . .

Later we realised that what we were encountering was not hunger for play, so much as hunger for experiences of all kinds, for creative and imaginative activities, for security and companionship, in short, for an expansion of the soul, a hunger for life itself.

In the meantime, apart from the enthusiasm engendered amongst many psychoanalysts, there had grown up a kind of therapy called specifically "play therapy." Toys were used and the therapist adopted a permissive and consequently passive attitude. The practice was quite widespread.

I think I have now given a sufficient glimpse into the source of the new knowledge that play was therapeutic and an impression of the widespread enthusiasm it created, especially amongst those engaged in child psychotherapy and education.

It was on this background that there grew up the vigorous and sometimes bitter conflict between Melanie Klein and Anna Freud, about the technique to be used in the psychoanalysis of children, which occupied much energy and left virtually none for considering Margaret Lowenfeld's work. That went on in the background. What was she achieving?

I consider it a valuable achievement to have invented a method of studying psychodynamic processes going on in children. Lowenfeld provided a small sand tray and an increasingly large number of toys as time went on. The children were invited to choose the toys they wanted and make "pictures" in the sand with them. The results were impressive and I made contact with her. Our contact could develop in a certain way because of her interest in archetypes. She had found, as I had too, that archetypal configurations appeared in children's play and she wanted to know what kind of toys should be used to help in detecting them. I was not keen on eliciting them so much as providing conditions under which children could express themselves archetypally or otherwise. Nevertheless I thought that the sand tray and toys for playing might facilitate the work I was doing and introduced it into my therapeutic efforts. I did so but eventually gave it up. I mention it to indicate that I formed quite a close relation with Margaret and that made it possible for me to arrange, at Emma Jung's request, for a meeting between her and Dora Kalff. That was one origin of the proliferation of "sandtray therapy" which has spread widely and which has been so successful in interesting Jungian analysts in the psychotherapy of children.

It may be of interest to state why I ceased my support for Margaret Lowenfeld, because it illustrates in rather a gross way why I no longer use a sand tray. Her method of child therapy involved a certain depersonalizing element. Most children's play is enacted in relation to others; first of all the breast expanding to other parts of his mother's and his own body, later father and siblings come into the picture to eventually include other persons outside the family. It is true that there is also solitary play like that which Jung engaged in as an initiation into his confrontation with the unconscious, but it is a mistake to diminish the personal nature of most play. This depersonalization went on into Lowenfeld's attempts to avoid the transference by not having a single therapist but switching the child between several. Also, if a child needed to make a mess he was removed to a special room where facilities were provided for him to do so.

In saying this I do not wish to claim that sand tray therapy, though I am critical of it, is not of value to children and that they get benefit from it as they do from all play. This special form of play has every right to be called therapeutic whilst in addition it can provide data of scientific importance.

Michael Fordham
Jordans, December, 1990

Preface

This book emerged much as the unfolding of the Sandplay process – organic and flowing – with more surprises than would have been expected at the outset. In the beginning, our initial interest was in writing an introductory handbook on Sandplay. In preparation and research for that work, we were impressed to find the richness of Sandplay's lengthy heritage expanding over approximately sixty-five years. As we read these historical works, we were struck by their relevance for contemporary therapists.

Sandplay is the term created by Dora Kalff to differentiate her Jungian-oriented technique from Margaret Lowenfeld's *World Technique*, while *sand tray* remains the generic term referring to the technique of using miniatures in a shallow box partially filled with sand. Unfortunately, much of the early work on the sand tray is difficult to access, except for the researcher who is willing to participate in the time-consuming task of finding the many out-of-print documents in many different languages that have been written on sand tray. With this realization, we put aside our writing of a Sandplay handbook so that we could bring to light the contributions of the leading pioneers of Sandplay, who pushed the boundaries of psychotherapy and research into the nonverbal realm.

We were fascinated with what we found out about these extraordinary pioneers. For some of them, the nonverbal approach grew from their own personal experiences and became a lifelong quest; others were interested for a short time, enlarging our knowledge through their research and then moving on to other pursuits. Still others were superb teachers who excited the imagination of clinicians who felt the need for a more symbolic, nonverbal method.

Many synchronistic events have occurred over the 65-year history of sand tray, each of these events has supported and advanced the growth and development of this medium. One of these early events was child psychiatrist Margaret Lowenfeld's recollection of H.G. Wells' book, *Floor Games*, and his use of miniatures in his play with his young sons. Drawing on this memory and observing that the use of language with children was a limited way of communicating, Lowenfeld was inspired to include miniatures in her therapeutic playroom for use by the children. In this setting the children spontaneously placed the miniatures in a small shallow box of sand to create scenes or patterns. Hence, in 1929, Lowenfeld's World Technique was born.

At that time, London was a fertile environment for many of the emerging ideas in child therapy. Melanie Klein had moved from Berlin to England in 1926 at the invitation of Ernest Jones. There she worked in the London Clinic for Psychoanalysis (Sayers 1991), developing her theories of child treatment based on Sigmund Freud's theories. She used toys to stimulate the child's imagination, and interpreted his/her play with emphasis on the internalization of early mothering (object relations) and its effect on the child/therapist relationship (transference). In 1939, Anna Freud moved to London and over time established both a day nursery and child treatment clinic. In the clinic she emphasized the interpretation of psycho-sexual developmental stages. In contrast to Klein, Anna Freud believed that the therapist/child transference with young children was irrelevant because they were in the process of developing mother–child relationships which precluded those feelings being transferred to the therapist. Michael Fordham, an English Jungian analyst, was also living in London and working with children. He pioneered a systematic, empirically-grounded developmental theory (based on infant observations and clinical studies) to substantiate the early development of the Self. Around this same time, Susan Isaacs and Donald W. Winnicott, two more prominent leaders in the field of child development and treatment, were also working in London. In this psychoanalytically oriented environment, Lowenfeld was a maverick and had her own independent ideas. She believed that theory should develop from observation of what emerged from children, rather than viewing the children's work from an established theory that may have been developed through analyzing adults. Therefore, her techniques were designed to facilitate the child's unencumbered communications with her in order to understand more clearly what was happening. It was out of this melting pot of ideas that a new therapeutic approach – the World Technique – was born.

About this same time in several parts of the world, the idea of using miniatures in a defined space for therapeutic or diagnostic purposes sprang up independently, demonstrating that the time was ripe for using this type of approach. A short time after Lowenfeld developed the World Technique in London, Erik Erikson developed the Dramatic Productions Test (DPT) at Harvard in the 1930s. Erikson first used the DPT to study the development and character formation of a group of Harvard students by examining how they placed miniatures in a defined space. Later in the 1940s, Erikson once again used the DPT to study the development of 100 youngsters over a three-year period who were involved in a twenty-year longitudinal study at

the University of California, Berkeley. Also in the 1940s, child psychotherapist Gerdhild von Staabs authored the Sceno-Test in Germany, a diagnostic technique designed for children in which they used human miniatures
to create a scene. Later in the 1950s, Lois Barclay Murphy developed the
Miniature Toy Interview, which used miniatures to assess the free play of
preschool and early latency aged children at the Sarah Lawrence College
Nursery School in New York State. The purpose was to assess a child's
needs, drives, problems, and ego structure in relation to his/her tempera-
ment and perception of life space. It was astonishing to realize that at the
beginning of their work, Lowenfeld, Erikson, von Staabs, and Murphy were
each unaware of the others' pursuits.

Another contributing factor in the growth of sand tray technique was that
it attracted therapists from many different theoretical orientations and backgrounds who were able to incorporate it into their work. Lowenfeld (1979)
herself believed that the technique was free from any theoretical bias:

> A psychoanalyst will find sexual themes, sometimes overtly, some-
> times symbolically represented there, for the reason that sexuality does
> play a part in a child's "World" picture. The Adlerian will undoubtedly
> find the power complex. . . . The "World" apparatus should appeal to
> the heart of the Jungian, seeing that the "World" cabinet is richly
> furnished with already completed archetypal symbols.
>
> (Lowenfeld 1979: 7)

Lowenfeld's belief that her method could be applied by therapists from a
variety of orientations was validated by the many people who integrated
the sand tray into their own frameworks. For example, Charlotte Bühler,
a faculty member at the University of Vienna and later associated with the
University of Southern California, observed Lowenfeld's work in London
during the early 1930s, incorporating the use of the World Technique into
her own research. She used it as a diagnostic instrument for cross-cultural
work and as a means of ascertaining the mental health of both children
and adults. Later, Bühler developed the "World Test" (later known as the
"Toy World Test"), which was used to generate normative data asso-
ciating certain types of trays with specific behaviors. In turn Bühler
influenced many other researchers and practitioners, including the
French clinician Henri Arthus, who developed the "Village Test" as a
diagnostic instrument in 1939. Subsequently, Arthus' work and writings
caught the imagination of several French psychologists, including Pierre
Mabille, who developed his own "Village Test" in 1945, and Roger
Mucchielli, who published his "Test of Imaginary Village" in 1960.

In Sweden, Lowenfeld's influence took yet another form. Gudrun
Seitz, founder of the Erica Institute in Stockholm, visited Lowenfeld in the
1930s and brought back the idea of using miniatures and sand with the
children at her Institute. In the 1940s Gosta Harding, psychiatrist at the

Erica Institute, used these materials to develop the Erica Method, which became a widely used diagnostic test in Sweden.

The connections extended yet even further – Lowenfeld also influenced Dora Kalff, a student and associate of C.G. Jung in Switzerland. In 1937, Lowenfeld had presented a case using the World Technique at an International Congress in Paris, which was attended by Jung. Some seventeen years later, when Kalff indicated her desire to work with Lowenfeld after attending one of her presentations in Zurich, Jung recalled the lecture he had attended and encouraged Kalff to study with Lowenfeld. Jung was personally aware of the healing powers of his own imagination. By uniting her Jungian background with Lowenfeld's technique, Kalff added another significant clinical dimension to the sand tray, joining a symbolic, archetypal orientation with Lowenfeld's perspective. Kalff emphasized the importance of using the tray in a free and protected space, enabling clients to contact the unconscious and express preverbal experiences and blocked energies. She found that the effect of this expression was the activation of regenerative and healing energies. This process enhanced the connection between the unconscious Self (the source of human spirit) and the ego (conscious awareness and choice), resulting in the restoration of the capacity to function normally and restoring the psyche to its natural functioning. Jung likened the healing tendencies of the psyche to that of the body. He said, "Just as the body reacts in a purposeful manner to injuries, infections or abnormal ways of life, so do the psyche functions react with purposeful defense mechanisms to unnatural or dangerous disturbances" (Jung 1960: 253). Kalff's Sandplay approach was based on this fundamental premise that the psyche can be activated to move forward in a purposeful and healing manner.

In the United States, psychoanalytically oriented clinicians Hedda Bolgar and Liselotte Fischer developed the "Little World Test" as a projective instrument for diagnostic use. In Britain, Ruth Bowyer, a faculty member at the University of Bristol and later at the University of Glasgow, developed norms for the World Technique, using it to determine the emotional adjustment of deaf children.

Although many diagnostic applications of Lowenfeld's World Technique were in use at one time, the projective/diagnostic emphasis has waned (even though the research findings remain sound and pertinent) in favor of its therapeutic application. Currently, its main use is as a therapeutic tool of self-expression and healing, as the sand tray allows an opportunity in therapy for a fuller expression of the joining of the mind, body, and imagination together. Even though there remain a sizeable number of practicing Lowenfeldians, as well as therapists who are attracted to using sand and miniatures in a tray within their own particular orientation, Kalffian Sandplay is currently the major approach worldwide.

The practice of Sandplay today usually includes two sand trays (one wet and one dry) of prescribed dimensions, painted blue on the bottom and sides to represent water or sky. After the therapist has introduced the procedure and given the client an opportunity to engage (touch, manipulate) the sand, miniatures on nearby shelves are selected by the client and placed in one of the trays to form a scene. During the creation of the Sandplay picture, the therapist becomes a "silent witness" to the process. Interpretation of the tray is delayed until a series of trays has been completed, over a period of time, so that the process can unfold naturally without interference from the intellect. A photograph is taken of each picture after the conclusion of the session. Some time later all of the photographs (or slides) may be reviewed by the client and therapist together. The joining of cognitive awareness to the deeply felt experience of Sandplay at this later time often brings a new level of insight.

The view of childhood itself has undergone dramatic changes throughout history. It is only recently that childhood has been recognized as the most formative period in the life of a human being. While the image of the child has historically evoked a universal archetype of caring and compassion, in reality it was not until fairly recently that infants and young children were considered valuable human beings whose lives were not expendable (Schorsch 1979). This was understandable as in earlier times the infant/child mortality rate was so high that parents could not afford to become bonded to a child until the child was old enough to survive. In contrast, today infancy and childhood are not physically precarious states as they were previously, and the child, as well as childhood, can be more wholeheartedly embraced. Childhood now is seen as a critically important period. Currently adults even look to children and their play for cues in studying imagination and creativity. A prime example is the use of the sand tray, a vehicle developed for the self-expression of children which is now benefiting adults as well as children.

The name "Sand*play*" can initially evoke a negative response from adults until the process itself is directly experienced. Even though it is recognized that children have played throughout history (Fordham 1993; Lowenfeld 1935), today there continues to be a lack of wholehearted acceptance of the benefits of play both in our society as well as in some therapeutic circles. This rejection of the spontaneous, creative, unfocused, and more feminine aspects within us is indicative of a widespread patriarchal attitude in society that values focused and rational thinking.

In the contemporary Sandplay community, play is recognized as one of the important ingredients in promoting healing, as it encourages the necessary transcendence of the thinking and cognitive realms. Kalff recognized that symbolic play creates a dialogue between the unconscious and the conscious mind (Dukes 1992). Stewart (1981) also reflects this view of play when he says:

... the child's symbolic play appears to serve the process of individuation in childhood ... through its dual functions of bridging between
ego-consciousness and the unconscious and making possible creative
imagination, it reveals ... ultimately an expression of the self. ... For
adults ... sandplay may provide that *rite d'entrée* which Jung described. By playing again like a child, with all the seriousness of a child
at play, the adult revives lost memories, releases unconscious fantasies,
and in the course of time, constellates the images of reconciliation and
wholeness of the individuation process.

(Stewart 1981: 35–6)

Besides play, Bradway (1987) cites other critical elements that promote
healing in Sandplay: the free and protected space created by the therapist
and the use of the elements of earth and water together promote an
experience of "coagulatio" (ie giving concrete reality to inner images and
experiences). The combination of these factors within a contained space
allows the playful and creative imaginative energies to unfold naturally.

Michael Fordham's foreword to this book gives a hint of the long-
standing ambivalence regarding the use of the sand tray. Fordham himself ultimately gave up the use of the sand tray because: (1) he felt that it
did not facilitate the transference between therapist and child in a personal way, and (2) because he objected to Lowenfeld's purposeful attempt
to avoid transference by regularly shifting a child from one therapist to
another therapist in her clinic. However, since that early time and with
the development of Kalffian Sandplay, which emphasizes the central
importance of the therapist establishing a free and protected space, there
has been a fundamental shift away from the early Lowenfeldian model.
Currently, there exists a recognition that therapeutic work at a depth level
is only possible when there is sufficient transference in the therapist–
client relationship, either appearing in the tray and/or in the relationship.
The issue of transference is discussed more fully in Chapter 8.

In *Sandplay: Past, Present and Future*, we have attempted to bring the
rich and diverse history of this special therapeutic approach to life for
clinicians, students, and teachers of Sandplay therapy. Indeed, anyone in
the healing arts who works with unconscious processes – whether
through art, dreams, movement, active imagination, or guided imagery –
will find inspiration in the histories of these extraordinary pioneers of the
nonverbal dimensions. In particular, this book will be valuable for practitioners working with clients in need of healing at the deepest preverbal
levels, for the use of Sandplay enhances understanding of the psyche even
as it helps to decipher communications from the unconscious. Those
working with verbally limited clients, such as young children, developmentally disabled individuals, and those whose primary language is
different from the therapist's, will also find this book helpful. In addition,

past and present research findings documented in this book will be of interest to scientifically oriented readers, and those interested in the history of psychology will find the path leading to the birth and development of Sandplay a fascinating and relevant story.

The first seven chapters of *Sandplay: Past, Present and Future* present an overview of Sandplay's historical origins, including biographical profiles of the innovators of this technique and discussion of their seminal writings and research findings. Chapter 8 explores five main therapeutic trends that have emerged from this diverse historical tapestry. The final chapter examines and explores the future of Sandplay by confronting emerging issues and concerns and suggesting how these can be better addressed in the future. At the conclusion of each chapter is a list of references for that chapter. At the end of the book is a comprehensive international bibliography of sand tray citations, as well as a listing of sand tray video- and audiotapes.

Since Sandplay is one of the few therapeutic techniques in which language skills are unnecessary for understanding the expressions of the psyche, it has truly become a cross-cultural method that is practiced worldwide. While use of Sandplay continues to grow, the art of Sandplay is at a crossroads of its history. The pioneers are gone. For Sandplay to continue growing and moving in increasingly meaningful directions, it is important that those using Sandplay have a broad understanding that encompasses both past and present. Only from this perspective can more thoughtful and conscious choices about the future direction of Sandplay be made.

Our hope is that this book will provide the practitioner and researcher with a basic foundation in Sandplay, established on the discoveries of the past as well as the flowing currents of present work. With a broad and firmly grounded perspective, future practitioners and researchers will be better equipped to understand the movement of the psyche as reflected in Sandplay.

Rie Rogers Mitchell
Harriet S. Friedman

REFERENCES

Bradway, K. (1987). "Sandplay: What makes it work?" In M.A. Mattoon (ed.) *The archetype of shadow in a split world: Proceedings of the Tenth International Congress for Analytical Psychology, Berlin, 1986*: 409–14. Einsiedeln, Switzerland: Daimon Verlag.

Dukes, S.D. (1992). "The significance of play." *Journal of Sandplay Therapy* 2(1): 53–7.

Jung, C.G. (1960). "General aspects of the psychology of the dream" in C.G. Jung *The Structure and Dynamics of the Psyche*: 237–80 (CW vol. 8). New York: Princeton University Press.

Lowenfeld, M. (1935). *Play in Childhood*. London: Victor Gollancz. Reprinted (1976) New York: John Wiley & Sons. Reprinted (1991) London: Mac Keith Press.

—— (1979). *The World Technique*. London: George Allen & Unwin.

Sayers, J. (1991). *Mothers of Psychoanalysis*. New York: W.W. Norton & Company.

Schorsch, A. (1979). *Images of Childhood: An Illustrated Social History*. Pittstown, New Jersey: The Main Street Press.

Stewart, L.H. (1981). "Play and Sandplay." In K. Bradway *et al.* (eds.) *Sandplay Studies: Origins, Theory and Practice*: 21–37. San Francisco: C.G. Jung Institute. Republished (1990) Boston: Sigo Press.

Acknowledgements

The path this book has taken has been made immeasurably easier by the extraordinary support and help, both professional and personal, of so many people. First, our thanks to Scott Mitchell who has grown up alongside this book. His forbearance allowed us the long hours necessary to work on this book while also bringing us laughter through his spontaneous and fun-loving nature. Endless support and interest have also come from Andy Friedman and Jodi Carlson, Ellen Friedman and Louis, Lucy and Jacob Blumberg, and Julie Friedman and Robert Kagon. The priceless gifts of enthusiasm, encouragement, and love of our families, friends, and associates have been essential: Lavaun Rogers, Florence Dearing, Irene Baron, Judy Broder, Jack Clarke, Joanne Cooper, JoAnn Culbert-Koehn, Allen Koehn, Edward Edinger, Ruth Halpert, Marcella Mitchell, Richard and Frances Rogers, Robert and Annette Rogers, Jeanine Auger Roose, Harriet Roth, and Eva Silver.

Vast amounts of detailed information and contributions of their accumulated wisdom were generously donated by: Ruth Bowyer Pickford, Kay Bradway, Hedda Bolgar, Michael Fordham, Peter and Martin Kalff, Bruce King, Fred Masserick, Robert Royeton, Andrew Samuels, H. Beric Wright, STA Council and members, and our Los Angeles Sandplay Group: Gloria Avrech, Joyce Burt, Faye Campbell, Betsy Caprio, Tom Hedberg, Ozma Mantele, Sachiko Reece, and Sheila Dickman Zarrow. Thanks also go to our colleagues at the Los Angeles C.G. Jung Institute and the Department of Educational Psychology and Counseling at California State University, Northridge.

Without the dedicated professionalism of experts in two libraries, this book could not have become a reality: Bobbie Yow, Lore Zeller and Linda Weidlinger at the Jung Institute of Los Angeles and Linda Keenan and her interlibrary loan staff at California State University, Northridge. Our deepest appreciation goes to the many researchers, writers, and clinicians, who have contributed to the sand tray literature over the last sixty-five years.

Superb manuscript editing has been provided by Margaret Ryan. Our translators have made heretofore inaccessible writings available to us: Carol Bare, Micheline Barkley, Tamara Mikalashevsky, and Yasuko Sakamoto.

We are indebted to the Margaret Lowenfeld Trust, Hedda Bolgar, Liselotte Fischer, Ruth Bowyer Pickford, W.W. Norton & Company, Random House Inc., Association of Humanistic Psychology, and *Quadrant* for granting us permission to use their photographs.

Chapter 1

H.G. Wells

Inspired the creation of the "World Technique"

The British author H. (Herbert) G. (George) Wells (1866–1946), writer of such renowned books as *The Time Machine* (1895) and *War of the Worlds* (1898), also wrote a little-known book in 1911, *Floor Games*, that would later inspire the creation of the field of sand tray therapy. In *Floor Games*, Wells described the spontaneous play he enjoyed with his two young sons, using miniatures and other small objects. Wells' portrayal of the creative games and play materials they used served as an inspiration to Margaret Lowenfeld in her development of the "World Technique" (Lowenfeld 1979). In his lifetime, Wells was unaware of the profound impact of his book. In fact, Wells considered *Floor Games* a minor work and did not even mention it in his autobiography (Wells 1934).

Floor Games was an unusual book for its time, reflecting a unique situation in the Edwardian 1900s – a father playing with his children! Not only was H.G. Wells an unconventional father, he was also an unusual thinker. His unorthodox viewpoints engendered considerable criticism by eminent and influential people, which began about the time *Floor Games* was first published in 1911 (G. West 1930), although that book was far overshadowed by the publication of two other books around the same time: *Ann Veronica* (1909) and *The New Machiavelli* (1911b). It was these two books that outraged certain segments of British society and triggered the heated verbal attacks that wounded Wells so deeply (Mackenzie and Mackenzie 1973; A. West 1984). Accused of being a radical and a feminist, and regarded as sympathetic to the Suffragette Movement, Wells' critics viewed him as more dangerous than the militant women, for he advocated not only the Vote, but also economic freedom and "an entire new system of relations between men and women, that will be free from servitude, aggression, provocation, or parasitism" (G. West 1930: 172, quoting Wells 1914). Wells' attitude toward his own children, together with his unconventional view of the equality of men and women, was perceived as representing a threat to the dominant patriarchal system. At the same time that Wells was being criticized by his peers, he served as a cult hero for some of the youth, who also felt an urgent need to break away from the old value system (Wells 1934).

The original edition of *Floor Games*, published in 1911, has large, primary-type printing (as though it were a book for a child to read), line drawings, and photographs of the actual play taken by Wells himself. The father–son play sometimes lasted for days at a time, and the many visitors to their home were drawn into the elaborate procedures (Mackenzie and Mackenzie 1973). The play took place in a contained area defined by boards and planks. From many boxes emerged small houses, people, soldiers, boats, trains, and animals, which transformed the floor of the nursery into a fantasyland of cities and islands. Two central games emerged from this play, which Wells described in his book: "The Game of Marvelous Islands" and "Games of the Construction of Cities." Wells also described in detail various historic scenes, barricaded castles, and little war games, as well as the play environment itself, the miniatures used, and the reasons why he encouraged this type of play with his young sons.

Wells harbored a deep, philosophical belief that play promoted a framework for expansive and creative ideas in adulthood. *Floor Games*, which emerged from his own personal experience, was his way of presenting this belief to the public. Even though Wells' idea that play facilitates optimum development is now central in the psychotherapeutic treatment of children, Wells himself was not aware of, or even interested in, the psychological meaning of the play. Psychological interpretations of his sons' spontaneous constructions were far from his mind, even when he observed that the children took "strange pleasure" in this kind of play (Wells 1911a). Years later, it was Margaret Lowenfeld's genius that seized Wells' idea, saw its psychological application, and developed it – all in one creative leap. Lowenfeld recognized the potential of using small toys to enable children to communicate their deepest, preverbal thoughts and feelings. At the same time, she recognized that the use of miniatures in a defined space could be objectively recorded and analyzed, independently of prevailing theories (Lowenfeld 1979).

Wells' interest in the development of the creative imagination shares some correspondence with C.G. Jung's formulation of the concept of the collective unconscious. In 1923, Wells spent a stimulating evening with Jung, who had come to England to give a lecture. Wells found that Jung's idea of the collective unconscious was compatible with some of his own views (Mackenzie and Mackenzie 1973). Wells himself held strong beliefs that "the immortal soul of the race" controls the direction of our individual lives. His writings urged reflection on this condition, and he encouraged increased human consciousness and societal evolution (G. West 1930). Wells also invoked Jung as an expert in his introductory soliloquy to *The World of William Clissold* (1926), and he quoted from Jung in his thesis for the D.Sci. degree, which he received from London University in 1942, when he was seventy-six years old (Smith 1986).

H.G. Wells was a complex man of many moods. In the Mackenzie and Mackenzie biography, Wells' at-home behavior was described by his sons' Swiss governess: "There are days when he goes skylarking about the house and garden like a schoolboy home for the holidays, and the next day everybody seems to get in his way and annoy him. So beware . . ." (1973: 230). What the governess "admired most about him was the enthusiasm he threw into his role as a father. His eyes twinkled with boyish gaiety when he talked to Gip and Frank: 'they assailed him with endless questions and how interesting were the answers which the learned man was ever ready to give them'" (1973: 230). The relationships between Wells and his boys were warm and loving, and he was deeply involved in their imaginative lives. "Whenever he was at home, bedtime was a ritual. H.G. would sit between the boys inventing stories and drawing endless 'picshuas' to illustrate them" (Mackenzie and Mackenzie 1973: 230–1).

When *Floor Games* was published, Wells' sons were eight and ten years old. It is interesting to follow the lives and careers of the two sons who engaged in the nursery games with their famous father. They did maintain close, lifelong relationships with him. The oldest son, Gip (George Philip, born in 1901 and later known as G.P.), became a zoologist at the University College in London. He married his father's secretary, Marjorie Craig, in 1927. She remained as Wells' secretary and, after his wife's death in 1927, became his manager, guide, and *alter ego* (Smith 1986). G.P. was also involved in his father's business as one of the collaborators on Wells' book, *The Science of Life* (1930). In 1968, G.P. wrote an introduction to *The Last Books of H.G. Wells* (Mackenzie and Mackenzie 1973).

Wells' younger son, Frank Richard (born in 1903 and named after Wells' brother), married Peggy Gibbons in 1927, a local girl whom he had known for many years. She later took over the management of Wells' beloved garden at his home in Hanover Terrace. When the critically acclaimed film *Things to Come* (1936) was produced, Wells spent a great deal of time on the set accompanied by his son, Frank, "who was the artistic limb of the Wells family and its chief film expert" (Smith 1986: 325). Frank also worked as an assistant on the set design for the film version of *The Man Who Could Work Miracles* (c. 1932), and he adapted three short comedies (*Bluebottles, The Tonic,* and *Daydreams*) for film that his father had written in 1928 (Mackenzie and Mackenzie 1973).

During his lifetime, Wells had a profound influence on many facets of contemporary life. He was described at his memorial service by William Beveridge as a "volcano in perpetual eruption of burning thoughts and luminous images" (Smith 1986: 484). He was a man who was internally driven to point the way to human progress. By some of his contemporaries he was viewed as the greatest intellectual force in the English-speaking world. He was given credit for shaping a new world view by giving voice to ideas that had never been expressed before (G. West 1930). His writings, which represent a remarkable achievement unequalled by any other author (G. West 1930), ranged from inquiry, criticism, and suggestion to entertainment and information.

Wells was aware of the impact of many of his ideas, but he was unaware of the rippling effect that his modest book, *Floor Games*, had on the subsequent development of child therapy. As with many ideas that are seen as relatively unimportant at the time, his notions about play have taken root in a particularly unique way, profoundly affecting the direction of psychotherapeutic treatment.

REFERENCES

Lowenfeld, M. (1979). *The World Technique*. London: George Allen & Unwin.

Mackenzie, N. and Mackenzie, J. (1973). *H.G. Wells: A Biography*. New York: Simon & Schuster.

Smith, D.C. (1986). *H.G. Wells: Desperately Mortal*. New Haven, Connecticut: Yale University Press.

Wells, G.P. (1968). Introduction in H.G. Wells, *The Last Books of H.G. Wells*. London: H.G. Wells Society.

Wells, H.G. (1895). *The Time Machine: An Invention*. London: Heinemann.

—— (1898). *The War of the Worlds*. London: Heinemann.

—— (1909). *Ann Veronica*. London: T. Fisher Unwin.

—— (1911a). *Floor Games*. London: Palmer. Reprinted (1976) New York: Arno Press.

—— (1911b). *The New Machiavelli*. London: John Lane.

—— (1914). *An Englishman Looks at the World: The Great State*. London: Cassell.

—— (1926). *The World of William Clissold*. London: Benn.

—— (1934). *Experiment in Autobiography: Discoveries and Conclusions of a Very Ordinary Brain (since 1866)*. New York: The Macmillan Company.

Wells, H.G., Huxley, J. and Wells, G.P. (1930). *The Science of Life: A Summary of Contemporary Knowledge about Life and its Possibilities*. London: Amalgamated Press.

West, A. (1984). *H.G. Wells: Aspects of a Life*. New York: Random House.

West, G. (1930). *H.G. Wells: A Sketch for a Portrait*. New York: W.W. Norton & Company, Inc.

Chapter 2

Margaret Lowenfeld
Originator of the "World Technique"

Margaret Lowenfeld (1890–1973), originator of the World Technique (a psychological technique used in communicating with children), was born in London and grew up in a large, lavish house in Lowndes Square. Her father, Henry (Heinz) Lowenfeld, was a descendant of a prominent Jewish family who had vast landholdings in the Polish part of Austria. By the 1880s his family had lost much of their wealth as a result of Poland's struggle for independence. This financial setback landed Henry Lowenfeld in England as a young man with only five pounds in his pocket. In an amazingly short period of time, he married a young English woman whom he had met at his family home in Poland, made a large personal fortune through buying and selling property, and bought back the family landholdings that had been sold previously for unpaid debts (Evans 1984).

Margaret's mother, Alice E. Evans, was the daughter of a naval captain. After she married the successful and eminent Henry Lowenfeld, she spent much of her energy becoming a prominent society hostess. Consequently, during their childhood years Margaret and her older sister, Helena, saw little of their mother, received little support or affection from her, and were relegated to the care of a nursemaid (Evans 1984).

Margaret described herself as an unhappy and delicate child. She spent a large part of her childhood ill in bed, enduring long periods of solitude. In her letters she recalled once hearing her mother say with exasperation, "Is that child ill *again*?" (Evans 1984: 24). She later recalled having "night terrors and screaming fits," and she was given to thumbsucking, a habit that was "very difficult to break." She also felt she had to compete with her gifted and successful elder sister, to whom interpersonal relationships and academic studies came so easily, while she herself found life difficult.

Margaret's early years were spent in both Poland and England. In Poland, she shared her long, free summer holidays with three Polish and eight German cousins, none of whom spoke English. At that age, Margaret spoke only English, which left her feeling powerless to make herself understood, an experience she found confusing and even frightening. She later learned to relieve her anxiety by learning to speak Polish and to understand German (Urwin and Hood-Williams 1988).

As a young child, Margaret both admired and idealized her father, who was an avid collector and a lover of the arts (Urwin and Hood-Williams 1988). The homes in which she was raised were full of interesting and colorful objects from faraway places (Lowenfeld 1979). Her father's friends were musicians, actors, writers, and artists; she and her sister were encouraged to meet these friends and listen to their multilingual conversation (Evans 1984).

At thirteen years of age, Margaret's life changed abruptly when her parents divorced. Her mother was left with custody of the two girls and a large financial settlement. Acrimonious contact between the parents ensued and her mother eventually succumbed to a series of illnesses. During these difficult times, she clung to her children. Both Margaret and Helena felt her neediness and attempted to compensate for her feelings of abandonment and emotional distress. Often her mother's illnesses were followed by bouts of illness in Margaret (Urwin and Hood-Williams 1988).

Despite the mother's many failings, she had progressive ideas regarding her daughters' education, providing both Margaret and Helena with exceptional educational opportunities that allowed them both to become physicians. Their choice of profession was strongly discouraged by their father, who wanted them to be conventional English girls and marry bankers. His hope was never to be realized by either of his daughters. Helena became a significant leader in the birth control movement and led the fight to gain acceptance from the Anglican bishops for the principle of contraception. With great determination and powers of persuasion, Helena was also able to change the opinions of the medical hierarchy. Through her considerable efforts, contraception was eventually made a medical specialty in its own right (Evans 1984).

Margaret graduated from medical school in 1918. She then served as a house surgeon at South London Women's Hospital before going to Eastern Europe in 1919 during the Russo-Polish War. In Europe, Lowenfeld served in a number of capacities. She was a medical officer with the British Typhus Unit in Poland and, with the American YMCA, worked alongside the Polish army and Prisoner of War Department. In both these capacities, she helped provide better conditions for prisoners in the war camps and for the troops along the 400-mile front. She also served as secretary of the European Student Relief, an organization that provided food and clothing for many thousands of Polish students and helped re-establish the universities after the war (Urwin and Hood-Williams 1988).

Following her military service, Lowenfeld remained as a land-owning citizen in the new state of Poland. Along with the population at large, she suffered from the famine, lack of fuel, and non-existent medical supplies that accompanied the war (Lowenfeld 1979).

These difficult war years, coupled with her unhappy childhood, formed the backdrop for Lowenfeld's thinking and facilitated her understanding of the inner life of children. The constant atmosphere of fear and helplessness which she confronted daily during the war reminded her of the experiences of unhappy children, while the dark misery of the prisoners-of-war she saw reminded her of the depressions of abandoned and neglected infants (Lowenfeld 1979).

Experiences in Lowenfeld's life left her skeptical of language as a primary tool of interpersonal communication. Having grown up in a complex and chaotic verbal environment in which several languages were spoken simultaneously, Lowenfeld had encountered many experiences in which language was a confusing rather than clarifying element. During her war years, she acted as a quadralingual interpreter – another experience that repeatedly thrust her into the conflicts and ambiguities of verbal communication. Through these varied influential experiences, she came to realize that language was a limited vehicle which did not allow the fullest expression of meaning; as a consequence she was left with a lifelong interest in the multidimensional aspects of nonverbal communication (Lowenfeld 1979).

In reflecting on her dramatic war experience, Lowenfeld said that it "did for me what the preliminary analysis does for the therapist-to-be, that is, it opened doors on to an interior world I would not otherwise have reached" (Lowenfeld 1979: 1). Although she later experienced two personal analyses, from which she felt she gained much, the analyses still did not answer two questions that continued to haunt her: Why do certain children and young adults, who are deprived of everything essential for health and development, nevertheless grow into healthy and creative adults? Why are some individuals capable of the most heinous crimes against other human beings? She felt that the answers to these questions could be understood by deepening her understanding of child development.

After her return from Poland, Lowenfeld encountered difficulty obtaining a medical position, since most available positions had been filled by men who returned from World War I. As a result, she decided to focus her time and energy on research in child development and completed her postgraduate work as a student at the Mothercraft Training Centre, which gave her experience in treating ill and poorly nourished infants (Urwin and Hood-Williams 1988). By the end of 1923, she had obtained a Medical Research Council scholarship and the Muirhead Fellowship to work at the Royal Hospital for Sick Children, Glasgow, on a study of the relations between acute rheumatism in children and home conditions. Her first publication, "Organization and the rheumatic child" (1927), was a report of her findings. In 1926 she became part of a medical team in pediatrics and biochemical research at the Royal Free Hospital, London, working on a project concerned with infant feeding and the functions of the mammary glands during the first ten days of life. Her article published with S. Taite, "Researches in lactation," was published in the *Journal of Obstetrics and Gynaecology of the British Empire* (1928).

In 1928 Lowenfeld embarked upon a major shift in her career emphasis that was to lead her into her pioneering work. She left an orthodox pediatric practice to found one of the first psychological clinics for children, located in "a district with small shops and identical brick houses mostly occupied by industrial workers" (Andersen 1979a: xi). An example of her charming leaflet, which announced the "Clinic for Nervous and Difficult Children," particularly appealed to the concerns of mothers:

> All children are difficult sometimes, but some children are difficult all the time. Some children seem always to be catching something and never to be quite well. Some children are nervous and find life and school too difficult for them. Some children have distressing habits. This Clinic, which is in charge of a Physician, exists to help mothers in these kinds of trouble with their children, and also to help the children themselves.
>
> (Lowenfeld 1979: xii)

Around this same time, Lowenfeld recalled Wells' *Floor Games* (1911), which had made a deep impression on her in young adulthood. Now Lowenfeld translated Wells' description into a therapeutic technique; she collected "a miscellaneous mass of material, coloured sticks and shapes, beads, small toys of all sorts, paper shapes and match boxes, and kept them in what came to be known by my clients as the 'Wonder Box'" (Lowenfeld 1979: 3).

When the clinic moved to another location (The Quest) in 1929, Lowenfeld was inspired to add two zinc trays to the playroom, one with sand and one with water (Bowyer 1970). Until this time, there had been no container or sand in the playroom; the toys were used mainly on the floor. The children responded naturally to having available small toys, sand, and water by combining them together in the sand tray: "Less than three months after a metal tray with mouldable sand placed on a table and a cabinet containing small miniature objects were included in the playroom equipment, a spontaneous new technique had developed, created *by the children themselves*" (Lowenfeld 1979: 280–1).

Early in 1929 the "Wonder Box Toys" were housed in a small cabinet, which was placed on a table. At this time, the cabinet and its contents were known as "The World." Not long after, the name "World" arose spontaneously from the children themselves while speaking of their sand productions (Andersen 1979b). By the summer of 1929, the constructions in the sand had come to be called "Worlds" by the therapists and children alike. With the emergence of the technique and its naming by the children, the World Technique was officially birthed in 1929. One of Lowenfeld's original goals in founding the clinic for children was "to find a medium which would in itself be instantly attractive to children and which would give them and the observer a 'language' as it were, through which communication could be established. Furthermore, once such a medium had been discovered and its use tested, it would be necessary to devise means for the study and evaluation of the material collected" (Lowenfeld 1979: 281). Here, in this child-created technique, Lowenfeld had found the instrument of her search. When children used miniatures in a shallow sand tray, their emotional and mental states of mind were communicated in a way that could be objectively recorded and analyzed. With the aid of this technique, she could now begin her work of exploring the child's mental processes.

By 1930 Lowenfeld's clinic, now known as the Institute of Child Psychology (ICP), was located in its own quarters. In addition to its emphasis on clinical work with children, the ICP was also a research and training center. As a training center the ICP granted certificates and/or diplomas to child psychotherapists from all over the world who studied from one to three years (Lowenfeld 1948a). The research centered on the study of those impressions and experiences of children that cannot be put into words and devising techniques through which these could be expressed. The World Technique and the Mosaic Test were the results (Lowenfeld 1948a).

The ICP had a multidisciplinary, holistic approach that integrated contributions from various fields such as pediatrics, neurology, social work, nutrition, and physical therapy. Compared to child guidance clinics that emphasized only the removal of symptoms in order to help children adapt to their environments, Lowenfeld believed that the ICP approach was unique. Its holistic approach helped children transcend some of the deleterious consequences of modern life by assisting them to become stronger within themselves both psychologically and physically (Urwin and Hood-Williams 1988).

The methods at the ICP well illustrated Lowenfeld's innovative ideas about child therapy. Children between the ages of one and eighteen were eligible for treatment. After intake, an intelligence test was administered by a worker unfamiliar with the child, and a careful case history was taken (mainly from the parents). (Children with below-average intelligence were usually referred elsewhere.) Ongoing contacts were established with both school and home. Each child client was treated two or three times weekly, each session lasting two and one-half hours. Parents were not admitted to the playroom on any account. Very little contact took place among the children themselves, though each child moved freely from room to room, or even outdoors, with his or her particular therapist of the day. Children were carefully observed by the clinic staff, whose observations were recorded on case sheets. Various types of play materials were available in the playrooms – construction materials; materials allowing movement and destruction such as clay, hammers, and punching toys; and materials for expression of fantasy such as blocks, dolls, and art materials.

Therapists (called workers) were randomly assigned to each child at each visit. Lowenfeld believed that the relationship of the therapist to the child should be "mostly that of a fellow-explorer and equal friend, who works together with the child at the study of the child and at the child's pace. In this way we find that the emotional experience of the child tends to be relived more in relation to the objects of play and to the whole building of the Institute than to the person of the therapist" (Lowenfeld 1948a: 30). This perspective differs markedly from that of Melanie Klein or Michael Fordham, who both emphasized the importance of the child's transference to the individual therapist.

For Lowenfeld, successful treatment would impart to the child a greater sense of harmony both within him/herself and in relation to the environment. In addition, the child would show increased curiosity and interest in learning as well as a greater aesthetic awareness (Urwin and Hood-Williams 1988).

BASIC TENETS OF THE WORLD TECHNIQUE

The equipment

Lowenfeld provided detailed specifications for using the World Technique. The height of the tray should be waist high, "so that the 'world' can be made in it with his hands" (Lowenfeld 1979: 6). Therapists should have several different heights of tables available to accommodate the different heights of children (Lowenfeld 1979). The inside of the tray should be painted blue to give the impression of water; the tray should be watertight and rust-proof. The sand tray, half-filled with sand of medium coarseness, should be smooth and flat when presented to the child. Water and implements for use with the sand (such as shovels, funnels, molds, a sieve) should be near at hand. The size of the tray Lowenfeld used was approximately 75 × 52 cm., with a depth of 7 cm. (29.5 × 20.5 × 2.8 inches), so that the child could view the entire tray without moving the head. Although the size of the tray was important to Lowenfeld, she was also practical in her specifications, acknowledging that "the exact optimum size and shape of the tray will probably be found to vary in different countries and should be in harmony with the proportions of notebooks, typing paper, etc., in general use" (Lowenfeld 1958: 327).

Usually only one sand tray was available; water was accessible in a pail nearby with a cup for pouring. Finally, a wide supply of miniatures should be made available for children with different needs and experiences. Her extensive list of miniatures is recorded elsewhere (Lowenfeld 1950, 1979). Lowenfeld's own miniatures were contained in a cabinet with multiple small drawers, which were labeled clearly and could slide out easily for viewing. Her original cabinet, first used by chance, was an old bird-egg collecting cabinet, which stood on one of the playroom tables (Andersen 1979b). This multi-drawered design (instead of open shelves or some other display arrangement) became an important part of her recommended sand tray equipment, because she believed that the child should not be overwhelmed with numerous miniatures displayed on open shelves. The contents of her special cabinet were seen only when the drawers were pulled out separately and thus could not be viewed all at one time.

Mucchielli, who visited the ICP in the 1950s, described the room in which the sand tray was housed:

> The room which is specially reserved for this apparatus is large, simple, bare, with a cement floor. It has two or three chairs, a little bench in wood, a sink of cement with taps and running water. Along the walls (are) sets of wooden shelves full of small toys of all kinds and a medley of bits and pieces. And further (along is) the material of "The World," as it should be called, with the sand tray and the large cabinet with drawers containing the items.
>
> (Mucchielli 1960: 6)

Introducing the World Technique

Lowenfeld's directions for introducing the World Technique to children reflected her view that the sand tray facilitates communication and helps the therapist better understand the child's mental processes. In her early use of the World Technique, children were expected to use the objects to make realistic scenes; however, it soon became clear that when "the workers refrained from expecting something realistic, and from interfering or suggesting to the children, then something new and excitingly creative grew out of the children's constructions" (Andersen 1979b: 280).

Lowenfeld introduced the sand tray to her child clients in two parts, which she named the Bridge and Picture thinking. In the Bridge part of the introduction, Lowenfeld suggested to the child that adults and children live on opposite banks of the river; they are here to work together at building a bridge over the river. In the Picture part, it was pointed out that many experiences cannot be expressed in words, but can be depicted in pictures and actions. She sometimes illustrated this point with advertisements and pictures from comics. Attention was then directed to the sand tray, as she explained that the sand could be left spread out for placing things on it or it could be heaped into masses; and the blue base of the tray could be used to represent sea, lakes, or rivers. Next the child was shown the content of the cabinet of toys and asked to "make a picture in the sand," using any or none of the objects in the cabinet. The child was told that s/he may use *any* object in the room, may do whatever is wished with the sand, and need not make a "real" picture; if an idea occurred to use the objects in an odd way, that would be just as interesting as using them in an ordinary way (Bowyer 1970). When the "World" materials were shown to adults, the introduction was modified into a general discussion of methods of symbolic representation in art, literature, advertisement, and satirical cartoons. Lowenfeld wrote that "once started on the work, introduction becomes superfluous; the interest of the creation itself is its own explanation" (Lowenfeld 1979: 5).

Therapist response

During the making of the tray, Lowenfeld instructed therapists to sit close to the child and to feel free to make observations about the scene being made, as though what was being created were a direct communication from the child's internal world to the therapist. After the scene was completed, the therapist might ask direct questions to clarify what a particular object meant to the child. "A running commentary is kept up as the child works, making him aware of what he is doing as he does it, but the deeper significance is not interpreted to the child until it emerges unmistakable from his work" (Lowenfeld 1946: 441). Lowenfeld's interest was focused primarily in why "objects appear at that time and place and [are] arranged in that exact way" (Lowenfeld 1946: 441). Sometimes information gleaned from a child's tray would be used to determine what activities the therapist would suggest in the following session.

Recording

In the early days, some "Worlds" were recorded in drawings, while others were described in text. Next, photography was tried, but Lowenfeld felt that it was too expensive and also distorted the perspective. Then in the late 1950s, the American artist Enid Kotschnig attended the ICP. After completing her own series of "Worlds," which familiarized her with the objects and the process, she developed a technique for depicting the serial "Worlds" in a simple, stylized way (Lowenfeld 1979).

WRITTEN WORKS AND PROFESSIONAL PRESENTATIONS

On March 25, 1931 Lowenfeld presented a paper before the prestigious Medical Section of the British Psychological Society. This was her first psychologically oriented publication and included her first explicit reference to the World Technique. In it she described her new clinic and the procedures she used in her treatment of children, clearly articulating three goals:

We first lessen his anxiety by the provision of security – that security being given by our acceptance of everything he produced, and our lack of reaction to it; secondly we draw off some of the excess of emotional energy which has become dammed up behind the neurosis, by giving it outlet in symbolic play. . . . Thirdly, we give him a framework of stability that reinforces the child's own struggles to achieve interior stability, and reassure him as to the non-reality of his own aggressive impulses.

(Lowenfeld 1931: 226)

In this presentation, Lowenfeld offered case studies of her work with children and, more importantly, differentiated her position from traditional child psychoanalysts, who emphasized transference and interpretation as the critical elements in treatment rather than the importance of the play itself. She pointed out how the productions that emerge in the play of children bear a striking resemblance to the dreams and unconscious fantasies of adults. She also emphasized her belief that interpretation of the play productions is unnecessary; the process of play itself, *without interpretation*, is therapeutic because it allows the expression of both acceptable and unacceptable feelings, thoughts, and other behavior.

In 1935 Lowenfeld published her first book, *Play in Childhood*, which was not available in the United States until 1967. Interestingly, in the Preface to the 1976 edition, Lowenfeld explained that she had decided against publishing *Play in Childhood* in the United States in 1935, because it was her view "that the focus of attention in psychological and educational circles in the USA was on aspects of childhood other than play." In 1967 she changed her position only because she believed that the situation in the United States had changed: "A vivid interest in the play of children had emerged in professional circles together with an attendant awareness of the need to make widely available detailed literature on the subject to stimulate and guide scholarly study."

Play in Childhood is a seminal book that continues to exert a strong influence on how play is viewed today. Play is described by Lowenfeld as "an essential function of childhood basically concerned with the adaptive process; related to that process which must continue throughout life and which profoundly affects man's ability to survive in his physical universe and ever-changing social environments." In Lowenfeld's view, play serves four purposes:

(1) It serves as the child's means for making contact with his environment. . . . Such play in childhood partakes of the nature of, and fulfils [sic] much of the same social purpose as work in adult life; (2) It makes the bridge between the child's consciousness and his emotional experience, and so fulfils [sic] the role that conversation, introspection, philosophy, and religion fill for the adults . . .; (3) It represents to the child the

externalised expression of his emotional life, and therefore in this aspect serves for the child the function taken by art in adult life . . .; (4) It serves the child as relaxation and amusement, as enjoyment and as rest.

(Lowenfeld 1935: Introduction)

In the conclusion of the book, Lowenfeld stated unequivocally that "without adequate opportunity for play, normal and satisfactory emotional development is not possible" (p. 321).

Play in Childhood is just as alive today as it was when first published in 1935. Honoring play as a healing modality was one of Lowenfeld's original contributions. Even though play was being used by child therapists when this book was written, play in and of itself was not recognized as therapeutic and healing. Rather, most therapists viewed it as peripheral to treatment or, at best, as an activity that could be interpreted from a psychoanalytic framework. Some therapists even viewed play as a defensive mechanism. *Play in Childhood* paved the way for an expanded view of the child's most natural impulse – play.

Lowenfeld demonstrated the World Technique for the first time at an international conference in Paris (Lowenfeld 1937a). C.G. Jung was present, and he interpreted one of the "Worlds" that Lowenfeld had shown. While a synopsis of Lowenfeld's presentation is available, Jung's analysis and commentary were not recorded. In Evans' biography (1984) of Helena Wright, the sister of Margaret Lowenfeld, there is some evidence that Lowenfeld had a continuing association with Jung, often visiting him in Zürich.

On April 18, 1937 Lowenfeld presented a paper to the British Psychological Society that her biographers have regarded as containing the most interesting and important developments of her theoretical concepts (Urwin and Hood-Williams 1988). In "A thesis concerning the fundamental structure of the mento-emotional processes in children," Lowenfeld described the World Technique apparatus in detail, presenting the technique as both a research and therapeutic tool that could bridge the gulf between scientific investigation and clinical application. From the pictures children make in the sand, she contended, objective data can be gathered and analyzed in a scientific manner. For Lowenfeld, sand trays reflect the preverbal, unconscious life of the child and provide an aesthetic experience that, while not translatable, is fundamentally satisfying and expressive of what the child needs to communicate to the therapist. One of the significant points in this paper was that Lowenfeld deliberately minimized psychoanalytic theory which saw the transference between the patient and therapist as essential, and she again noted how her approach differed from the psychoanalytic view in this regard. Also unique in this paper was the introduction of her "protosystem" theory which she used to replace the terms "unconscious/conscious" in referring to young children's thought.

Several years after her first presentation to the Medical Section of the British Psychological Society, Lowenfeld presented a second paper to the same group, which explored "The World pictures of children: A method of recording and studying them" (1939). In the audience were key figures in the psychoanalytic community such as Melanie Klein, D.W. Winnicott, and Susan Isaacs (head of the Child Development Department at the Institute of Education). From them she encountered considerable resistance to her ideas – which was a painful reminder of the chasm that had grown and continued growing between her and her professional community.

By this time both Melanie Klein and Lowenfeld had developed thera-peutic techniques for children independent of each other. Even though both used toys for therapeutic purposes, each approached child therapy from fundamentally different theoretical and clinical orientations. Klein was the first to use toys in the course of treatment, mainly in a play therapy mode, to stimulate the child's imagination and elicit associations. (Around 1925, Melanie Klein originated the idea of using play as a method for psychological investigation. In her consultation room, she arranged simple toys on a table: little wooden people, wagons, vehicles, cars, trains, animals, bricks and houses, as well as paper, scissors, and crayons. She believed that a child's general attitude and how s/he regarded the toys would give her an idea of her/his complexes (Mucchielli 1960). Anna Freud referred to the game used by Melanie Klein as "a little world in miniature" in her 1927 article, *Introduction to the Technique of Child Analysis.*)

Lowenfeld expressed her belief that Freudian child analysts adapted psychoanalytic principles to the treatment of children in such a way that all children's behavior and feelings were viewed solely through con-structs of that theory. The child psychoanalyst, according to Lowenfeld, "uses toys as a means of gaining contact with the child's mind in order that the mind may be dealt with on lines indicated by psycho-analytic theory: the child's use of toys is interpreted symbolically in harmony with that theory" (Lowenfeld 1939: 67). Her interest, by contrast, was to under-stand children's mental processes unencumbered by any theoretical bias. She wanted "to devise an instrument with which a child can demonstrate his own emotional and mental state without the necessary intervention of an adult by transference or interpretation" (ibid.).

Melanie Klein objected to Lowenfeld's position, stating that Lowenfeld sacrificed "the valuable possibilities inherent in the transference . . . (in order) to fit psychological science into the mold of physics" (ibid.: 82). Klein believed that transference feelings colored every relationship and were an integral component of the therapeutic interaction, including any of the play interactions and use of play equipment.

In her response to Klein, Lowenfeld reiterated her view that the trans-ference was to the *tray*, not to the therapist, and that to continue making interpretations only in relation to the personal transference interfered with the objective observation of the "World" production:

> In the psycho-analytic approach the analyst is the agent confronting the child with the "meaning" of his play by the interpretation given by her to it. In "Worlds" the child is confronted by a piece of his own feeling, thinking, remembering-life set out by himself for his own study. A transference situation, that is, a transference to the physician rather than to the material, is an intervention between the part of the child which made the "World" and the part that regards it. . . . There is an extraordinary force in this confrontation [when the child views his/her own sand tray scene]; the child having made the picture has to accept it as his own; the force of the statement brings home to him its reality.
>
> (ibid.: 87–8)

Klein also criticized Lowenfeld's description of psychoanalytic treatment as being too rigid. Klein stated that the "aim of the psychoanalytic play technique with children is to discover the child's emotional life, his wishes, phantasies and thoughts" (ibid.: 81). Klein went on to quote from a 1927 presentation she had given before the same professional group: "Slowly the analyst, by interpreting to the child what his play, drawings and whole behaviour means, resolves the repressions against the phantasies behind the play and liberates those phantasies" (ibid. 1939: 81).

Lowenfeld responded to these comments by stating that Klein's description of child therapy, which relied on words such as "repressions" and "phantasies," indicated a biased set of assumptions with which to approach a child. However, in conclusion she added a conciliatory note, saying that she did not wish to work in opposition, that she admired Klein's courageous and pioneering work, and that "our work can go side by side by different routes to a common goal" (ibid.: 67), later on adding that "it is not necessary to agree with a person to admire them" (ibid.: 89).

D.W. Winnicott, a disciple of both Freud and Klein, had objections of a different nature from those of Melanie Klein. He stated that he did not understand the aim of her work, and implied that Lowenfeld "was trying to prove something to someone" but he didn't know what she was trying to prove and to whom (ibid.: 84). He did not see the necessity of using a set apparatus instead of the personal freedom of play therapy. He believed that drawings would allow more individual expression than objects normally found in a "World" collection and that the variety of toys available would bewilder and overwhelm the child.

In response to Winnicott's criticisms, Lowenfeld explained that there was more flexibility in the use of the miniatures than was immediately apparent, for children used objects in a variety of ways, including creating their own special objects. To his objection regarding children being overwhelmed with the variety and number of objects, Lowenfeld explained that the toys were kept in drawers which, when opened, obscured all other objects in the cabinet; therefore, the child would not be visually overwhelmed. To Winnicott's first challenge regarding the irrelevance of the whole technique, Lowenfeld was silent. Later Winnicott came to believe that play is an end in itself for the child. This put him into alliance with Lowenfeld.

Other strong criticisms came from Susan Isaacs and Grace Calver regarding the lack of attention Lowenfeld gave to the age and developmental stage of the child when she observed the "Worlds." Lowenfeld acknowledged their criticisms and said that there was not enough time in this lecture to fully elaborate her observations about these important considerations. She indicated that her colleague, Charlotte Bühler, was currently engaged in research on this very subject.

After this painful presentation, Lowenfeld turned her attention away from the British psychoanalytic community and toward the interest in her approaches among many in the worldwide psychological community. The war years found her involved in safely re-establishing her clinic outside of London and continuing her research on the World Technique. During and after the war, she created and developed other techniques such as the Lowenfeld Mosaic Test (originated during the 1930s and standardized in 1951). From a mosaic tile design created by the child, this test gives information regarding the degree and type of disturbance (Lowenfeld 1954b). She also originated the Lowenfeld Poleidoblocs (designed during the 1940s and completed during the 1950s) and Kaleidoblocs (introduced during the 1960s), which are used today to introduce children to mathematics and logic (Andersen 1979b).

In 1948 Lowenfeld sponsored a conference at her Institute that was attended by child therapists from all over the world. Lowenfeld (as well as others) presented work illustrating the techniques and theory behind the World Technique and the Mosaic Test. The monograph, *On the Psychotherapy of Children*, is a collection of the papers presented at this conference.

The centerpiece of the 1948 monograph is a presentation by Lowenfeld on "The nature of the primary system," in which she stated her own formulations regarding children's thinking. This presentation was reprinted in 1964 under the title of "The non-verbal 'thinking' of children." Along with an article by Traill and Rowles, it can be found in a monograph entitled, *The Non-verbal 'Thinking' of Children and its Place in Psychotherapy* (1964). In this presentation, she voiced her strong belief that much of children's thought could not be expressed verbally nor understood logically by the therapist. This type of thinking, which she called "the Primary System," is "personal, idiosyncratic, massive and multidimensional, by its nature incommunicable in words to others" (Lowenfeld 1964: 45). According to Lowenfeld, the content of the Primary System is totally unavailable and inexpressible in Secondary System terms (i.e., in logical, reasonable, or verbal terms); the World Technique is a way to access the Primary System.

Lowenfeld also attempted to differentiate her views of the Primary and Secondary Systems from both the Freudian and Jungian views of the unconscious, stating that the Primary System was not developed through repression, as Freud stated, but was innate in the child. Her differentiation from the Freudian theory of the unconscious is clearly applicable. However, in reading this article today, her differentiation from Jung is unclear and her approach seems to be congruent with Jung's conceptualization of the collective unconscious as an inherent state that is beyond logical and verbal expression.

In this important article, Lowenfeld also addressed the question that had haunted her since her early war years in Poland: why do some individuals and some societies (e.g., Nazi Germany) become capable of heinous crimes against humanity? She hypothesized that such behavior could be understood in terms of the Primary and Secondary Systems. In the case of Nazi Germany, Lowenfeld pointed out that the Secondary System had been highly developed in Germany's populace prior to 1933, leaving little opportunity for individuals to play. Lowenfeld believed that:

> The lack of material in education and life for expression of the contents of the Primary System, and so for modifications to take place, kept it, in too many people, both at a primitive level and in a state of high tension. The loss of public confidence in the value of the Secondary System, consequent upon economic stress, led ultimately to a breakdown of the whole structure of the Secondary System. What then happened was a flooding of the personality of many individuals and groups with the disjointed elements of the Primary System. Within the Nazi movement, therefore, the Primary System, with its passion, cruelty, and unreality, came to take the place of the Secondary System, and then through the dynamic leadership of Hitler, the sort of stuff we find in the Primary System of neurotic children came to be taken for reality, and ultimately given actual expression in reality.
>
> (Lowenfeld 1948b: 47)

Interestingly, when this article was reprinted in 1964, this section dealing with Lowenfeld's concerns about the human capacity for evil was the only section omitted.

In 1950 Lowenfeld made her first trip to the United States to give lectures to groups that were involved in using her play therapy techniques. She was very interested in the work that had been conducted on her techniques in the United States by such researchers as Charlotte Bühler, Hedda Bolgar, and Liselotte Fischer. Much earlier, in the 1930s, Lowenfeld and Bühler had met and admired each other's work (see Chapter 4). Because of the war, regular contact during the early 1940s was impossible, and Lowenfeld was unaware of the direction of Bühler's work in developing norms for a test (Bühler called it the "World Test"), that was based on the World Technique. In her 1950 article, "The nature and use of the Lowenfeld World Technique in work with children and Adults," Lowenfeld stated her "considerable anxiety" about using the World apparatus as a test for personality and temperament. "It is not that I disapprove of batteries of tests or have any desire to restrict the use of any material that I have devised, but that I am anxious that my whole research and therapeutic method should not be misunderstood or distorted when part of the equipment is borrowed and adapted to a different purpose" (Lowenfeld 1950: 325). Clearly Lowenfeld did not want the World Technique to lose its therapeutic focus and become confused with a diagnostic instrument. History has proven that Lowenfeld's concerns were justified. Many sand tray therapists today still confuse the assessment techniques of Bühler with the therapeutic approach of Lowenfeld. They are, indeed, two different approaches.

In 1954 Lowenfeld attended the International Congress of Psychotherapy in Zürich, Switzerland. By this time Lowenfeld had been working with her World Technique for over twenty-five years and was firmly convinced that this tool could provide "the patient [with] a psychic experience as powerful as any known in the course of analysis in any of the standard schools" (Urwin and Hood-Williams 1988: 366). She also saw the use of this technique as appealing to both adults and children because it facilitated "the simultaneous presentation of different aspects of the personality at one and the same time and place . . ." (Urwin and Hood-Williams 1988: 366).

In her presentation before the Congress (which was later published in 1955 as "The structure of transference" in *Acta Psychotherapeutica Psychosomatica et Orthopaedagogica*), Lowenfeld attempted to clarify once again her point of view regarding transference, by defining it in broader terms than Freud's original view and by emphasizing that transference could take place outside of the therapist–client relationship. Lowenfeld saw transference in the "Worlds" of her clients when they displayed their early issues in the tray through their choice of miniatures, their spatial arrangements, and in the stories about their sand trays, rather than perceiving transference from a traditional psychoanalytic transference perspective – only between therapist and client.

Dora Kalff, the founder of the Jungian-based technique of Sandplay, attended this lecture and afterwards discussed it with Jung, who encouraged her to contact Lowenfeld personally. Perhaps it was Lowenfeld's more expansive view of the transference, as well as the potential for the symbolic approach, that caught Kalff's imagination and was the impetus for her interest in Lowenfeld's work.

Lowenfeld's second book, *The World Technique*, was published post-humously in 1979, six years after her death in 1973. The foreword was written by Margaret Mead, a close friend and admirer of Lowenfeld's work. (In fact, Margaret Mead adapted Lowenfeld's Mosaic Test for use in her work with "primitive" peoples.) Lowenfeld began this book in 1956, after receiving a grant from the Bollingen Foundation procured for her by Margaret Mead. The first part of the book was completed in three years, but was not published (Andersen 1979a). Lowenfeld's friend and companion, Ville Andersen, accumulated and edited the materials into book form.

In *The World Technique* (1979), Lowenfeld described her own early personal history and gave the background for the development of the World Technique. She also discussed the reasons why inhuman actions are carried out by individuals or by mass societies. She stated that, if children were given the opportunity to express their aggressive impulses through plasticine and sand, the acting out of these aggressive impulses in adulthood would be prevented. The major portion of the book is devoted to three detailed case studies, which contain information on therapist–child interactions. The children's trays are analyzed regarding a variety of objects, themes, patterns, and symbols, and the ways sand can be manipulated in the tray and the meaning of the sand configurations are discussed.

At the conclusion of the book, Lowenfeld observed that the subjective experience of an individual making a "World" is like

> meeting a slice of reality; almost as if unexpectedly meeting oneself in a mirror. It has the effect in well-balanced subjects of enlarging the boundaries of one's comprehension of oneself, and in patients of giving them a tool of expression which can present to their therapists and themselves aspects and subtleties of feeling and thought which both speech and gesture fail to present.

(Lowenfeld 1979: 270)

During much of Margaret Lowenfeld's working life, she lived in London with her close companion and colleague, Ville Andersen, who had originally come from Denmark to be a student at the Institute. As Lowenfeld became older, she spent more time at Cherry Orchards, a home she had bought at Cholesbury in Buckinghamshire. In 1972 she moved to a nursing facility near her sister's home; she died in February 1973, the day before her eighty-third birthday. She was buried in the graveyard of the church of St Lawrence at Cholesbury, where other members of her family were interred (Evans 1984).

CONCLUSION

Margaret Lowenfeld, one of the early pioneers in child psychology, left an indelible mark on the field. With her development of the World Technique, Lowenfeld had created a way to utilize children's natural inclination to play, helping them to reveal themselves and communicate their concerns nonverbally. It is interesting to note that, even though her contributions have been significant, and many other therapeutic and diagnostic techniques have been based on the World Technique, she has not always been credited for her creative and original insights. Indeed, many of today's practitioners are unaware of Lowenfeld's contributions. Her theories have been either overlooked or anonymously integrated into other systems. Nevertheless, her unique understanding of play and the development of the World Technique have caught the imagination of countless practitioners and researchers, who have absorbed her methods into their work, often without knowledge of her innovative contributions.

Lowenfeld's legacy has continued to be supported by a Board of Trustees, which administers the "Dr Margaret Lowenfeld Trust" (a research fellowship at Cambridge University in Child Care and Development Group in pediatrics), and maintains a collection of her written works and personal letters that is also housed at Cambridge. Particularly interesting is her correspondence with Donald Winnicott and Dora Kalff. A Lowenfeld seminar is held yearly in Cambridge, bringing together researchers and practitioners who share an interest in the relationship between emotions and nonverbal thought.

REFERENCES

Andersen, V. (1979a). "Historical note on the manuscript." In M. Lowenfeld, *The World Technique*: xi–xii. London: George Allen & Unwin.

—— (1979b). "Origin of the 'World'." In M. Lowenfeld, *The World Technique*: 278–81. London: George Allen & Unwin.

Bowyer, L.R. (1970). *The Lowenfeld World Technique*. Oxford: Pergamon Press.

Evans, B. (1984). *Freedom to Choose: The Life and Work of Dr Helena Wright, Pioneer of Contraception*. London: The Bodley Head.

Freud, A. (1926–1927). "Introduction to the technique of child analysis." In *The Psychoanalytical Treatment of Children*. New York: International Universities Press, 1955.

Lowenfeld, M. (1927). "Organization and the rheumatic child." *Lancet*, June 4: 1977. Reprinted (1988) in C. Urwin and J. Hood-Williams, *Child Psychotherapy, War and the Normal Child*: 147–55. London: Free Association Books.

—— (1931). "A new approach to the problem of psychoneurosis in childhood." *British Journal of Medical Psychology* 1(3): 194–227. Presented to the Medical Section of the British Psychological Society, March 15, 1931. Reprinted (1988) in C. Urwin and J. Hood-Williams, *Child Psychotherapy, War and the Normal Child*: 177–214. London: Free Association Books.

—— (1935). *Play in Childhood*. London: Victor Gollancz. Reprinted (1976) New York: John Wiley & Sons. Reprinted (1991) London: Mac Keith Press.

—— (1937a). "The value of direct objective record of children's phantasies with special reference to ideas of movement." *Proceedings of the International Congress of Psychology* 8: 396.

—— (1937b). "A thesis concerning the fundamental structure of the mento-emotional processes in children." Unpublished paper presented at the annual meeting of the General Section of the British Psychological Society in Manchester on April 18. Printed (1988) in C. Urwin and J. Hood-Williams, *Child Psychotherapy, War and the Normal Child*: 247–64. London: Free Association Books.

—— (1939). "The World pictures of children: A method of recording and studying them." *British Journal of Medical Psychology* 18 (pt. 1): 65–101. Presented to the Medical Section of the British Psychological Society, March, 1938. Reprinted (1988) in C. Urwin and J. Hood-Williams, *Child Psychotherapy, War and the Normal Child*: 265–309. London: Free Association Books.

—— (1946). "Discussion on the value of play therapy in child psychiatry." *Proceedings of the Royal Society of Medicine* 39: 439–42.

—— (ed.) (1948a). *On the Psychotherapy of Children*. London: E.T. Heron & Co. Ltd.

—— (1948b). "The nature of the primary system." In M. Lowenfeld (ed.) *On the Psychotherapy of Children*: 31–48. London: E.T. Heron & Co. Ltd. Reprinted (1988) in C. Urwin and J. Hood-Williams, *Child Psychotherapy, War and the Normal Child*: 325–45. London: Free Association Books.

—— (1950). "The nature and use of the Lowenfeld World Technique in work with children and adults." The Journal of Psychology 30: 325–31.

—— (1954a). *The Lowenfeld World Technique*, Memorandum from the Institute of Child Psychology, 6 Pembridge Villas, Bayswater, London.

—— (1954b). *The Lowenfeld Mosaic Test*. London: Newman Meane.

—— (1955). "The structure of transference." *Acta Psychotherapeutica Psychosomatica et Orthopaedagogica* 3: 502–7. Paper presented at the International Congress of Psychotherapy, Zürich, July 20–24, 1954. Partially reprinted (1988) in C. Urwin and J. Hood-Williams, *Child Psychotherapy, War and the Normal Child*: 363–7. London: Free Association Books.

—— (1958). "La Tecnica del Mundo: un metodo objetivo para el estudio de la personalidad de ninos y adultos." *Revista de Psiquiatria y Psicologia Medica: IV Congreso Internacional de Psicoterapia*, Barcelona: 509.

—— (1964). "The non-verbal 'thinking' of children." In M. Lowenfeld, P. Traill and F. Rowles (eds) *The Non-verbal 'Thinking' of Children and its Place in Psychotherapy*. London: Institute of Child Psychology Ltd.

—— (1979). *The World Technique*. London: George Allen & Unwin.

Lowenfeld, M. and Taite, S. (1928). "Researches in lactation." *Journal of Obstetrics and Gynaecology of the British Empire* 35(1): 114–30. Reprinted (1988) in C. Urwin and J. Hood-Williams, *Child Psychotherapy, War and the Normal Child*: 157–70. London: Free Association Books.

Mead, M. (1979). Foreword. In M. Lowenfeld, *The World Technique*. London: George Allen & Unwin.

Mucchielli, R. (1960). *Le Jeu du Monde et le Test du Village Imaginaire* (The World Game and the Imaginary Village Test). Paris: Presses Universitaires de France.

Traill, P. and Rowles, F. (1964). "Non-verbal 'thinking' in child psychotherapy." In M. Lowenfeld, P. Traill, and F. Rowles (eds) *The Non-verbal 'Thinking' of Children and its Place in Psychotherapy*. London: Institute of Child Psychology Ltd.

Urwin, C. and Hood-Williams, J. (1988). *Child Psychotherapy, War and the Normal Child*. London: Free Association Books.

Wells, H.G. (1911). *Floor Games*. London: Palmer. Reprinted (1976) New York: Arno Press.

Chapter 3

Erik Homberger Erikson
Originator of the "Dramatic Productions Test" (DPT)

Psychoanalyst Erik Erikson also saw the potential of using small toys in a defined space to access the human psyche as had other innovative clinicians and researchers during this time period, such as Margaret Lowenfeld and Charlotte Bühler. Although Erikson would not be considered one of the founders of the sand tray movement, he is included in this history because he developed the Dramatic Productions Test (DPT), which used miniatures in a defined space as a means of understanding human development.

Erikson's work on the Dramatic Productions Test began about the time that Lowenfeld published her book on *Play in Childhood* (1935) and was actively lecturing about her recent development of the World Technique. Bühler had also begun to use Lowenfeld's world materials in her research. However, Erikson was unaware of both Lowenfeld's and Bühler's use of these materials. Indeed, it is interesting to note how many people worldwide began to use small toys for research and therapy at about the same time. Clearly, this was a synchronistic moment in history, capturing the energy and resonance around this new use of age-old materials.

Erik Erikson (also known as Erik Homberger) was born in 1902 of Danish parents. His parents were separated before his birth and he was raised by his mother in Germany, who married his pediatrician, Dr Homberger, when Erikson was three years old. He grew up in a solid and comfortable home in a town near Stuttgart, where he had ample space to explore. From his room he could view a nearby castle and grounds. In Erikson's home, he watched his step-father treating ill and hurt children. His mother entertained many artists of the region. At the time Erikson grew up, "Germany presented to its citizens a rich tradition of culture, solidly transmitted by the educational system" (Coles 1970: 14). Despite a strong formal education, Erikson was not a good student.

Upon graduating from high school, Erikson felt at a loss and alienated. For this reason instead of going on to college, Erikson traveled through Europe – a searching young adult. Eventually he settled in Vienna, where he secured a position as a teacher in a small progressive school run by close friends of Sigmund Freud's youngest daughter, Anna. Erikson soon became part of the child psychoanalytic circle and had a training analysis with Anna Freud. He was also trained by several other prominent analysts (among them Aichhorn, Hartmann, and Federn). After his training experiences, he was accepted as a psychoanalyst in the International Psychoanalytic Association, despite his lack of a formal college education (Stevens 1983).

In 1929 Erikson married a young woman of mixed Canadian and American background, Joan Serson. Four years later they left Vienna with their two young sons because of the Nazi threat. After a short time in Denmark, the Erikson family arrived in the United States and Erikson established a practice in Boston as one of the first child analysts on the East Coast. Because of his unique training and background, he was invited to do research with the Harvard Psychological Clinic, where he had the opportunity to exchange ideas with some of the most prominent psychologists and anthropologists in the country. It was in the context of this rich collegial atmosphere that the Dramatic Productions Test was developed (Coles 1970).

It was around this time that Erikson changed his surname from "Homberger" to "Erikson" to denote his Danish ancestry, while keeping Homberger as a middle name out of respect for his step-father. His early writings on the Dramatic Productions Test are under the name "Homberger."

In 1939 the family, with two sons and new infant daughter, moved to California where Erikson worked with a team at the University of California, Berkeley, which was engaged in a longitudinal study of child development. Here, again, he used the Dramatic Productions Test in his research. Later, when he was offered a teaching post at Berkeley, Erikson joined several other academics in refusing to sign the controversial Loyalty Oath on point of principle. Because signing the Oath (later declared unconstitutional by the Supreme Court), which was a statement of non-affiliation with the Communist Party, was mandatory for employment at that time, he and his family returned to the East Coast, where he worked at a clinic specializing in psychoanalytic training and research. In 1960 he was appointed Professor of Human Development and Lecturer in Psychiatry at Harvard University. Since his retirement in Northern California, he has continued to write, lecture, and travel extensively (Stevens 1983).

THE DRAMATIC PRODUCTIONS TEST

Erikson's Dramatic Productions Test (DPT) reflected the profound influence of Freud (Coles 1970), as well as Erikson's own belief that visual and sensory experience precede the ability to verbalize (Stevens 1983). Freud had suggested that people could be understood by how they seek expression in the drama of their everyday lives, whether it is in their daydreams, in their life style, or in some other expression. Erikson viewed children's play as a series of visual and sensory images that expressed their lives; only later could these images be put into words. It was from this perspective that Erikson developed the Dramatic Productions Test. Erikson believed that he could study human development and character formation from the way in which the miniatures were used by adults (i.e., the way the images expressed a dramatic scene).

The Dramatic Productions Test was presented on a table and included an assortment of miniatures (figures of people, animals, furniture, cars, and building blocks). In introducing the DPT to adult subjects, the examiner told the subject that s/he "was interested in ideas for moving picture plays and wished him to use the toys to construct on a second table a dramatic scene" (Homberger 1938: 553). After answering a few typical questions (for example, "Do I have to use all the toys?"), the observer left the room for fifteen minutes, but watched the behavior of the subject through a one-way screen. When the time was up, the observer returned, wrote down the subject's explanations, and sketched the scene. Erikson then analyzed the DPT by looking at the dynamic use of space, shapes, sizes, and distances in the scenes.

RESEARCH WITH THE DPT

Erikson initially used the Dramatic Productions Test in a study of twenty-two men at Harvard College (Homberger 1938). One of his most striking findings was that, even though the Harvard students were all English majors, they did not build scenes representing themes from literature, cinema, or theater. Instead, what emerged were scenes (expressed in symbolic form) that could be connected to traumatic events they had experienced in their own childhoods. These traumatic childhood memories, while apparently repressed, exerted so strong an influence that the students could not consciously override them to respond to the instructions to build a "dramatic scene." Erikson noted that "the specific conflicts appearing in the constructions indicate that the subjects when confronted with toys, continued where they had left off in their childhood play with the attempt to overcome passive traumatic experiences by active repetition in play" (Homberger 1938: 581).

In the early 1940s Erikson again used the Dramatic Productions Test for part of a twenty-year longitudinal study conducted by the Guidance Study at the Institute of Child Welfare of the University of California in Berkeley. He tested more than 150 youngsters once a year for three years, aged eleven through thirteen (Erikson 1951, 1963, 1964, 1968). His instructions to the children were similar to those given to the Harvard group, which asked them to make a "dramatic scene." He felt that this type of instruction would help pre-adolescent youngsters reconcile the use of toys that seemed appropriate for much younger children.

Contrary to the Harvard experiment, however, the observer remained in the room, sketching the various stages of the scene being constructed and noting the child's behavior. When the scene was completed, the child was asked two questions: "What is it all about?" and "What is the most exciting thing about this scene?" Later, the scene was photographed.

Erikson (1951) was particularly interested in how space was used, not only in the scenes, but also in how the child him/herself moved in the space. He considered such factors as:

1 the child's approach (e.g., was it first to the shelves and then to the table, and how did the child bridge the space?);
2 the relationship of the play construction to the table surface (how much of the table was used, where were the toys placed, and what was the alignment of the toys to the shape of the table?);
3 the gestalt of the scene (what was the relationship of the parts to the whole and the parts to one another?);
4 the original quality of the scene, including the presence of unique details.

Erikson also observed the quality and character of the child's approach to the play situation. Was the child's behavior:

1 calm, careful, and consistent;
2 fast and energetic;
3 quiet, followed by sudden determined action;
4 quick, with spurts of enthusiasm that quickly ran their course?

He noted spontaneously revealing remarks such as, "I don't know what to do." He also emphasized the importance of the final stage of construction, which was often characterized by repeated new beginnings, a tendency to let things fall or drop, irrelevant conversation, perfectionistic tendencies, inability to finish the scene, or a sudden loss of interest. (Interestingly, these early observations of Erikson's are similar to those made by contemporary sand tray therapists.)

When Erikson examined the scenes of these pre-adolescents, he found themes of early traumas (as in the Harvard study), as well as scenes depicting difficulties in the family, physical or hypochondriacal concerns, and psycho-sexual conflicts. When his findings were analyzed statistically, they showed distinct gender differences. Boys' constructions used more blocks and vehicles at all ages; the blocks were used to erect structures such as buildings and towers and to build streets. Boys' stories often revolved around the dangers of collapse. Their scenes also tended to involve more physical movement and the boys therefore preferred toys that moved or represented motion. A common activity was moving cars and animals around the streets, usually under the control of the toy policeman (the figure boys tended to use most).

Girls employed blocks less frequently than boys, using them primarily to enclose a structure and to mark rooms in a house. Girls were more likely to use furniture and family figures in greater numbers than did the boys; their scenes tended to emphasize relationships among people, mainly family members. Less trauma occurred in the scenes; sometimes an animal intruded to upset things in a slightly threatening but humorous way.

Considerable controversy was generated by Erikson's interpretation of the differences he found between boys and girls, especially those findings regarding girls' concerns with closed or open interiors of structures and boys' concerns with action (almost all of it outside) and with height ("up" and "down"). Erikson regarded these differences between the sexes as being rooted in the experience of being male or female and he likened them to the physical, biological, and functional differences of the sexes. His research later became the target of vigorous feminist attacks. Erikson responded to these attacks by stating that, although somatic processes may certainly establish predispositions, these can then be shaped and given meaning by the society (Stevens 1983). In other words, cultural attitudes toward the different styles of behavior ultimately determine their value.

CONCLUSION

Erikson's use of the Dramatic Productions Test has long been over-shadowed by his theory of the Life Stages, which continues to attract interest from both professional and lay people alike. Neither Erikson nor any of his fellow researchers continued the use of the DPT, even though it was considered a valuable instrument (Honzik 1951). After this important research with the DPT, his interest shifted from classical research to viewing the world from a broader perspective. It is unfortunate that today many contemporary sand tray therapists are unaware of the role that Erikson played in developing such a test and interpreting the scenes in a way that is enlightening as well as congruent with current thinking.

REFERENCES

Coles, R. (1970). *Erik H. Erikson: The Growth of his Work*. Boston: Little, Brown & Company.

Erikson, E.H. (1951). "Sex differences in the play configurations of pre-adolescents." *American Journal of Orthopsychiatry* 21: 667–92.

—— (1963). *Childhood and Society*. New York: Norton.

—— (1964). "Inner and outer space: Reflections on womanhood." *Daedalus* 93: 582–97.

—— (1968). *Identity: Youth and Crisis*. New York: Norton.

Homberger, E. (1938) (a.k.a. Erik Erikson). "Dramatic productions test." In H.A. Murray (ed.) *Explorations in Personality*: 552–82. New York: Oxford University Press.

Honzik, M.P. (1951). "Sex differences in the occurrence of materials in the play constructions of preadolescents." *Child Development* 22(1): 15–35.

Lowenfeld, M. (1935). *Play in Childhood*. London: Victor Gollancz. Reprinted (1976) New York: John Wiley & Sons. Reprinted (1991) London: Mac Keith Press.

Stevens, R. (1983). *Erik Erikson: An Introduction*. New York: St Martin's Press.

Chapter 4

Charlotte Bertha Bühler
Originator of the "World Test"

Charlotte Bertha Bühler (1893–1974) deserves an important place in the history of Sandplay because she recognized the potential of using miniatures in a designated space as a diagnostic and research instrument. Using Lowenfeld's World Technique to develop norms for individual assessment and diagnosis, she created the World Test (later known as the Toy World Test). She also compared how children from various cultures used miniatures within a defined space.

Charlotte Bühler (a.k.a. Buhler, Buehler) was born in Berlin in 1893. Her father, Hermann Malachowski, was of Slavic Jewish background and enjoyed a position of affluence and prominence, despite the anti-Semitic feelings rampant in Germany at the time. As a talented and innovative architect, he helped build the first department store in Germany. Although Bühler's mother was an elegant and beautiful woman who lived an upper-class life, she felt frustrated and resentful that her social class hindered her from pursuing a career as a singer. Her mother poured into Bühler her own aspirations and career frustrations. Bühler was the oldest of two children. She had a brother five years younger with whom she was very close; they enjoyed music and hiking together (Allen 1980). Her deep interest in the aesthetics of culture was nurtured by both parents.

As a child, Bühler was baptized a Protestant, which was a common practice at that time among upper-class Jewish families trying to avoid discrimination. Bühler followed a more intellectual path than many of the young women of her class. She became interested in psychology early in her teenage years after a period of intensive religious study, which was followed by a period of painful religious doubt. The study of metaphysical and religious philosophers had led her to an intense questioning of the existence of God. Her conclusion was that religion could not solve metaphysical problems. She then turned to the study of the nature of human thought processes in hopes of finding answers to her urgently felt questions.

After attending private schools, Buhler's philosophical pursuits led her to the University of Freiburg in 1913. Here she studied medicine, philosophy, and psychology. She later attended the University of Kiel and completed her undergraduate studies at the University of Berlin in 1915 under Carl Stumpf, a pioneer experimental psychologist. Dr Stumpf offered her a graduate assistantship – unprecedented for a woman at that time. In her highly independent manner, she characteristically refused his offer in order to follow her own intellectual pursuit – the study of thought processes. Despite her refusal, Dr Stumpf continued to support her interest and referred her to the leading investigator of thought processes, Oswald Kulpe, at the University of Munich.

Shortly after her arrival in Munich she met Kulpe's chief assistant, Karl Bühler, a physician and psychologist, who had just returned from the War. The two were drawn to each other, fell in love, and were married in 1916. This was a creative union that produced not only two children (Ingeborg, born 1917, and Ralf, born 1919), but over the next twenty years also generated new developmental research techniques that incorporated direct observation of children's growth. The couple worked together at the University of Vienna and soon became leading investigators in the field of child development. Their research opened the way for a kind of sophisticated but common-sense view of childhood that differed greatly from the psychoanalytic orthodoxy prevalent in Europe at that time (Massarik 1974). The methods of infant observation they developed were unique and innovative, setting new standards that are still used today. Based upon their observations of normal children, the Bühlers produced developmental norms. Indeed, Gessell's pioneering work was built on the Bühlers' research methods (Allen 1980). Later these studies of normal child development took Charlotte Bühler into the field of mental health, with the aim of demonstrating the appropriateness of psychology's increasing contribution (specifically developmental norms) to psychiatry.

Charlotte Bühler had been in close correspondence with Margaret Lowenfeld since 1933, sparked by an immediate, mutual, professional attraction between the two women (Bowyer 1970). Lowenfeld admired Bühler's original methods of infant observation and Bühler was impressed with Lowenfeld's development of the World Technique, seeing it as yet another method for assessing cognitive thinking and child development.

Bühler and Lowenfeld began their professional association in 1935 when Bühler proposed a research program to validate some of Lowenfeld's observations (Bühler 1951a). Lowenfeld had observed that children with emotional problems made different types of Worlds than children without emotional difficulties. For example, emotionally disturbed children tended to fence in large parts of the world, place wild animals where they did not belong, place objects in unusual surroundings, and use the same objects frequently. Lowenfeld had never statistically compared her patients' "Worlds" with those made by an unselected group of normal children. It was Bühler's idea to validate and standardize Lowenfeld's observations. As head of the psychology department of the University of Vienna, Bühler had the resources and opportunity to develop an instrument that would reliably assess differences between individuals as well as cultures. The first research study was completed by a graduate student at the University of Vienna, Margaret van Wylick (1936), under the direction of Käth Wolf and Charlotte Bühler. This original study marked the beginning of Bühler's research on the World Test.

The World Test (also known as the Toy World Test) consisted of 160 tiny miniatures (called elements) contained in a box of 60 × 30 × 25 centimeters (23½ × 12 × 10 inches) with interior compartments for each of the ten categories: people, domestic animals, wild animals, houses, vehicles, enclosures (eg fences), constructions (eg bridges), nature, war implements, other objects (Bühler 1951b). Included with these materials were an instruction book and record sheets (Mucchielli 1960). Bühler also used a larger set of 300 miniatures for therapy sessions. Her use of a prescribed number of miniatures contrasted with the approach of Lowenfeld and that of contemporary sand tray therapists, neither of whom saw the benefit of restricting the number or type of miniatures.

Bühler's research, as well as her personal life, was interrupted by world events. In 1938, while traveling abroad, she learned that her husband had been detained in Austria by the Nazis because of her Jewish background. All their possessions were confiscated and they were stripped of their influential positions, becoming just another refugee family moving from country to country, seeking asylum.

The Bühlers first went to London, where Charlotte quickly returned to the research world by founding an Institute for the study of normal children with the aim of training students in clinical observation (Bowyer 1970). Bühler also observed children making "Worlds" at Lowenfeld's Institute (ICP) and Lowenfeld, in turn, was supportive of Bühler, encouraging her own students to attend Bühler's Institute for further training in clinical observation.

Bühler later became interested in comparative research. From 1935 to 1940 she traveled and lived throughout Europe, collecting data for her World Test by using teams of researchers in Vienna, London, Oslo, Eindhoven (Holland), and the United States. This odyssey gave her research an added dimension. The results of this research were published in her 1952 article, "National differences in World Test projective patterns" (see p. 35 for results of this research).

Bühler's World Test research continued to have an impact internationally through the 1960s. Two French clinicians, Dr Henri Arthus and Guy de Beaumont, saw the World Test being administered for the first time in Utrecht, Holland, at the Institute of Professional Guidance in 1939 and were so intrigued by it that they brought it back to France (Mucchielli 1960). Arthus (1949) developed a unique variation on it which he named the "Village Test" (i.e., similar materials were used but clients were requested to "make a village"). In 1950, Pierre Mabille (1950) proposed a standardization of both the Village Test equipment and interpretation.

After visiting Bühler in the 1950s, the French researcher Roger Mucchielli (1960) wrote a book on the use of miniatures in diagnosis and therapy with children and adults. Mucchielli's book also described his own creative derivative called the "Imaginary Village."

After the Bühlers moved to the United States in 1940, they took a succession of posts as they moved from place to place. In 1945 Bühler became a United States citizen and settled in Los Angeles. She became chief clinical psychologist at the Los Angeles County General Hospital (1945–53). She also was an assistant clinical professor of psychiatry at the University of Southern California (USC) School of Medicine. Despite the difficulties due to lack of research funds and facilities available to her, she persevered in her research. It was at this time in Los Angeles that she published her research findings and standardized the World Test (Allen 1980).

During the 1940s, Bühler and Lowenfeld were out of contact because of the War. In 1950 they met to talk about their work. Lowenfeld found Bühler's World Test to be quite alien to her own approach. She was concerned that it would be confused with the therapeutic approach of the World Technique. After their meeting, Bühler still continued to use miniatures for assessment and diagnosis, but attempted to differentiate it from the World Technique by naming her test the "Toy World Test."

Bühler continued her research and writing on the World Test until other pursuits eclipsed this long-time interest of hers. Later in her life, she collaborated with Abraham Maslow, Carl Rogers, and Viktor Frankl in organizing what later became known as the Old Saybrook Conference, which in 1964 gave birth to the Humanistic Psychology movement (Massarik 1974). In the early 1960s, she was President of the Association for Humanistic Psychology.

Physically incapacitated in 1972, Bühler returned to Germany, but "this neither ended her productivity nor did it put a halt to her active collaboration with scholars throughout the world" (Massarik 1974: 6). She maintained a vibrant level of activity until she died in her sleep on February 3, 1974 at the age of 80.

BASIC TENETS OF THE WORLD TEST

Fundamental differences between the World Test and Lowenfeld's World Technique are quickly apparent. Not only are the goals different (diagnosis versus therapy), but the materials and space are used differently. For the World Test, Bühler did not use a tray filled with sand. Instead, she recommended that the tiny miniatures be used on a table or on the floor. She did not specify the size of the table or floor space to be used, but did recommend that a minimum of six feet of floor space was necessary to enable the client ample room to walk around and view the work (Bühler 1951a). Bühler's omission of sand was probably based on van Wylick's (1936) study, which found that the use of sand seemed to make no difference in the outcome of children's therapy. It is interesting to note that Bühler sometimes did provide her child clients with a box full of sand when she was conducting play therapy sessions (Bowyer 1959).

As would be expected, Bühler's omission of sand and a traditional tray evoked a controversy between the followers of Lowenfeld and those of Bühler. As a result of this controversy, Bowyer (1959), a colleague of Lowenfeld, conducted a study, with a larger sample size than that used by van Wylick (1936), to determine if sand contributed to the therapeutic process. (See Chapter 7 for more details regarding this study.) Contrary to van Wylick's earlier findings (1936), Bowyer found that the use of sand by the client added a critical dimension to the experience and afforded another important diagnostic indicator of accessible imaginative resources as well as the capacity for perceiving ways of enlarging one's perspective. Bowyer's study was conducted after Bühler had completed her major work on the World Test.

Introduction to the World Test

It is interesting to note that, even though Bühler's test was standardized, the instructions given to the subjects were open-ended and very similar to those used by Lowenfeld and contemporary sand tray therapists. Her approach was to present miniatures and other equipment to subjects with an invitation for them to create freely whatever they wished.

Examiner response

The World Test manual prescribed that the examiner follow specific steps during the testing. After five or ten minutes, the subject was asked, "What are you making?" The examiner would ask leading questions periodically and make casual remarks of encouragement and praise in order to elicit as much information as possible. Further, the examiner was supposed to appear occupied with other work and only casually interested. After the end of 20 to 30 minutes, the examiner was to ask what the subject was doing and whether they were finished. If the subject desired, the examiner could allow the work to continue.

RESEARCH ON THE WORLD TEST

From the late 1930s to the mid-1950s, Buhler continued to conduct research on the World Test writing several publications on her findings. Some of these articles were written in collaboration with students and colleagues (Bühler and Carrol 1951; Bühler and Kelly 1941; Lumry 1951; Michael and Bühler 1945); others she wrote independently (Bühler 1941; Bühler 1951a; Bühler 1951b; Bühler 1952). Her research had two aims: First, she wanted to develop scientific guidelines that could be used in understanding trays. Specifically, she wanted to develop an instrument that could assess the differences between clinical and "normal" Worlds. Second, she was interested in determining if groups of people had similar projective patterns. She used the World Test to determine if there were national differences between the creations of children from five different countries.

Bühler's (1951b) article, "The World Test: Manual of directions," is part of a larger monograph, written in collaboration with B. Lumry and J. Carrol and published in the *Journal of Child Psychiatry*. This larger monograph is a survey of the studies which standardized the "World Test." In her article, Bühler presented the results of her research findings regarding clinical and normal "Worlds." She described what she called "signs" – indicators of emotional disturbance and/or mental retardation. According to Bühler, one sign is usually found in almost all subjects, whether or not there is emotional disturbance. Two signs, particularly when one is a CRD sign (defined later), seem to indicate a fairly serious emotional disturbance.

The signs Bühler identified as having relevance were:

1 *A-signs: Aggressive World Signs* (soldiers fighting, animals biting or wild animals present, accidents, people getting hurt, falling, and storms raging). Bühler found that aggressive signs were normal in children and were most often manifest in those creations subsequent to the initial creation. The presence of A-signs in first creations suggested the possibility of a more intense aggressiveness. She also noted that accidents were depicted more frequently in the sand trays of children who were somewhat disturbed, and the depiction of a number of accidents suggested deep resentment. Bühler interpreted violence in "Worlds" as a possible projection of aggression; she also noted that the instruments of aggression could be viewed in a positive role of protection and defense as well as of destruction.

2 *E-signs: Empty World Signs.* In order for a World to be designated as "empty," Bühler had rather stringent requirements, which may limit the relevancy of this sign for the contemporary Sandplay therapist. It is her clinical observations about the meaning of empty worlds that are the most interesting and may be applicable. Bühler's criteria for an empty world were as follows: (1) less than fifty elements; (2) elements from less than five of her possible twelve categories; and (3) major groups of people omitted (e.g., no adults, only children, or only soldiers and police.)

According to Bühler, the worlds of children under eight years old are normally quite empty. She suggested that this could be a reflection of their more undeveloped psychological state. For older children and adults, the empty world expressed either intellectual retardation and/ or emotional aridity, although most empty worlds indicated emotional rather than intellectual deficiency. An empty world suggested interior emptiness, feelings of loneliness or, conversely, a need to be alone. It could also suggest resistance to the task, an emotional fixation on certain objects, or blocked creativity. The complete omission of people could have a two-fold meaning, reflecting either the desire to escape from people or to defy them.

3 *CRD-signs: Distorted Worlds* ("closed," "rigid," and "disorganized" worlds). Closed worlds were defined by Bühler as partially or completely fenced-in; rigid worlds had unrealistic rows of animals, people, or things lined up in a fixed, stiff manner; and disorganized worlds showed miniatures in disparate and disconnected places and chaotic arrangements of the items or groups. CRD-signs were more significant symptoms of emotional disturbance than either A- or E-signs. Bühler found that: (a) all emotionally disturbed subjects she tested had at least one of the CRD-signs in their worlds; and (b) each of the CRD-signs was symptomatic of a similar disturbance. For example, subjects often used the CRD-signs interchangeably, first creating a closed world and then creating a rigid world. CRD-signs could be indicators of insecurity, need for enclosures, rigidity, and confusion.

Bühler interpreted the use of enclosures as signifying either an attempt to define oneself or to imprison an enemy. She saw closed worlds as indicating a desire for protection for those individuals who are insecure or need to resort to self-protective devices to conceal their emotions. She observed that, if a client set up fences before any other materials were used, this indicated an unusual need for protection. Rigid worlds indicated varying degrees of compulsive orderliness, perfectionism, and excessive fears. Disorganized worlds did not necessarily indicate deep emotional disturbance for young children, but could indicate varying degrees of confusion and dissolution of the personality structure for older children or adults. The retarded individual had significantly more empty and distorted worlds. Bühler observed that, in some cases, the memory of a traumatic experience that is triggered by the handling of the miniatures can be so overwhelming that no construction takes place.

Bühler's publication in 1952, "National differences in World Test projective patterns," was a review of the research she had conducted over a five-year period on national differences. In this original and innovative piece of research, she examined the worlds of 264 children from five different countries – United States, Austria, England, Holland, and Norway – using the five "signs" of emotional disturbance identified earlier. Analysis of the children's constructions suggested, for Bühler, the following national tendencies. The American group showed very aggressive traits and highly populated worlds, which Bühler interpreted as demonstrating the conflict between competition and cooperation in the culture. Austrian children were found to be more aggressive and rigid than any other group, as well as somewhat disorganized, suggesting a conflict between rigid aggression coupled with a confused, open, defenselessness and disorganization in the culture. The English children showed a strong defensiveness and a closing off from others, along with aggressive tendencies, supporting England's long history of defending its vulnerability to the outside world by creating a strong military. The Dutch children, who were the least aggressive, tended to make small worlds with rigid structures. Congruent with their cultural identity, their worlds were characterized by orderliness and rigidity, along with a lack of imagination and a tendency toward withdrawal rather than aggression. The Norwegian children produced rather unpopulated, unaggressive, and empty worlds. The open, unpopulated spaces seemed to point to a defenseless, nonaggressive, withdrawing, unorganized, and quite individualistic response to life in Norwegian culture.

Bühler presented case studies of children from different countries to illustrate her findings on national differences, as well as to indicate the different ways children defend against anxiety. This was a clear departure from her previous approach in which the World Test was used solely as an aid to diagnosis.

Bühler's cross-cultural findings are important for sand tray therapists because they emphasize the importance of considering the profound national/ethnic as well as individual differences in viewing the creation of a sand tray. Remaining alert to the subtle or overt manifestation of the client's cultural background in the tray brings a fuller understanding of what is being expressed from a deep layer of the psyche.

CONCLUSION

Charlotte Bühler's considerable contributions need to be viewed in a larger perspective that encompasses more than just her work on the World Test. With Bühler's prestige, knowledge, and research background, the possibility of applying the scientific method to the sand tray became a reality for the first time. As a theoretician and a thoughtful researcher, Bühler was clearly the one best suited for this task. Her scientific mind was able to discern meaning from the multitude of patterns presented in the trays, from which she then standardized a system for interpretation of the Worlds.

Bühler's unique combination of abilities thus brought the World Technique to the attention of a new audience – that of the scientific community. Her structured and formalized body of work influenced many researchers who followed her. Currently, a number of studies are being conducted by researchers, some of whom are Jungian-oriented, who are using her diagnostic signs.

It is unfortunate that contemporary sand tray therapists tend to undervalue Bühler's contributions. Many are unaware of her research. Others find her work too academic, with an excessive emphasis on rational factors. Some say her work is not applicable to current sand tray approaches because she valued the scientific rather than intuitive approach. She also did not use sand, and she emphasized diagnosis of only the first one or two "worlds" rather than examining a series of pictures. While these criticisms may have some validity, they tend to be overshadowed by the clarity and insight that her keen thinking brought to the understanding of the sand tray, a clarity that can be well joined to the intuition that is necessary for a full understanding of the sand tray process.

REFERENCES

Allen, M. (1980). Bühler, Charlotte Bertha. In B. Sicherman and C.H. Green (eds) *Notable American Women: The Modern Period: A Biographical Dictionary.* Cambridge: The Belknap Press of Harvard University Press.

Arthus, H. (1949). *Le Village: Test D'activité créatrice.* Paris: Presses Universitaires de France.

Bowyer, L.R. (1959). "The importance of sand in the World Technique: An experiment." *British Journal of Educational Psychology* 29: 162–4.

—— (1970). *The Lowenfeld World Technique.* Oxford: Pergamon Press.

Bühler, C. (1941). "Symbolic action in children." *Transactions of the New York Academy of Science* 17: 63.

—— (1951a). "The World Test: A projective technique." *Journal of Child Psychiatry* 2: 4–23.

—— (1951b). "The World Test: Manual of directions." *Journal of Child Psychiatry* 2: 69–81.

—— (1952). "National differences in World Test projective patterns." *Journal of Projective Techniques* 16(1): 42–55.

Bühler, C. and Carrol, H.S. (1951). "A comparison of the results of the World Test with the teacher's judgment concerning children's personality adjustment." *Journal of Child Psychiatry* 2: 36–68.

Bühler, C. and Kelly, G. (1941). *The World Test: A measurement of emotional disturbance.* New York: Psychological Corporation.

Lowenfeld, M. (1950). "The nature and use of the Lowenfeld World Technique in work with children and adults." *The Journal of Psychology* 30: 325–31.

Lumry, G.K. (1951). "Study of World Test characteristics as a basis for discrimination between various clinical categories." *Journal of Child Psychiatry* 2: 14–35.

Mabille, P. (1950). *La Technique du Test du Village.* Paris: Presses Universitaires de France. (Reprinted: Dufour, 1970.)

Massarik, F. (1974). "Charlotte Bühler: A reflection." *Journal of Humanistic Psychology* 14: 4–6.

Michael, J.D. and Bühler, C. (1945). "Experiences with personality testing in a neuropsychiatric department of a public general hospital." *Diseases of the Nervous System* 6(7): 205–11.

Mucchielli, R. (1960). *Le Jeu du Monde et le Test du Village Imaginaire*. (The World Game and the Imaginary Village Test.) Paris: Presses Universitaires de France.
van Wylick, M. (1936). *Die Welt des Kindes in seiner Darstellung*. Vienna: Josef Eberle. (Summarized in Bowyer, L.R. [1970]. *The Lowenfeld World Technique*. Oxford: Pergamon.)

Chapter 5

Hedda Bolgar and Liselotte Fischer
Originators of the "Little World Test"

In the mid-1930s Hedda Bolgar and Liselotte Fischer, close friends and both psychodynamically oriented clinicians living in Austria, collaborated to develop the "Little World Test" (also known as the "Bolgar–Fischer World Test"). They were familiar with Lowenfeld's work and were also aware that Charlotte Bühler, living in Vienna, was using Lowenfeld's materials for research purposes.

Both Bolgar and Fischer were interested in developing a nonverbal cross-cultural test for adults that would assist in clinical diagnoses, similar to the Rorschach Ink Blot Test or the Thematic Apperception Test (TAT). For their test, they chose universally familiar small toys and objects that had been used by children for generations (personal communication, Hedda Bolgar, October 27, 1991). Rather than using small toys in a play therapy mode, as Klein had done, Bolgar and Fischer developed their test using materials similar to those used by Lowenfeld (Fischer 1950a). They also attempted to standardize the method in a manner similar to Buhler's work, but with a different approach to scoring.

Bolgar and Fischer's goal was to develop a nonverbal projective instrument through which they could observe symbolic representations of human motivation, selection, and creative behavior. They believed that they could watch the creative process unfold by observing how small elements (miniatures) were brought into relationship with one another, so that a whole construction (in the Gestalt sense) was produced (Fischer 1950a). They also believed that their approach to the World material was unique, for it allowed direct observation of how adults visualized their view of the world within a standardized setting. In contrast to Lowenfeld, they believed that the World materials were more than just a means of communication in therapy; they were "a medium of approach of highly projective value" (Fischer 1950a: 66).

In 1938 both women left Vienna because of World War II. Hedda Bolgar went to the United States and joined the faculty at the University of Chicago, receiving her analytic training in Chicago. While in the Midwest, she gave training workshops in the use of the "Little World Test," where it was enthusiastically received by her colleagues. Later she moved to Los Angeles, California, to work on a grant with Franz Alexander.

Liselotte Fischer first went to Brazil, then Sweden, finally arriving in the United States. She eventually established a practice as a child psychologist on the East coast.

It was Bolgar and Fischer's intention to market their test in the United States, but they soon encountered unexpected obstacles. First, they had difficulty obtaining the toys during the war. Then they were surprised by Buhler's strong territorial feelings about using miniatures as a standardized test, even though Buhler's test was aimed at children, while Bolgar and Fischer's test was for adults, and differed in equipment and types of miniatures used. Buhler did not object to their doing research, but did not want them to market their test materials.

BASIC TENETS OF THE LITTLE WORLD TEST

As with Buhler's Toy World Test, the Little World Test contained a specified number of miniatures and categories (232 miniatures in 15 categories: houses, fences, trees, people of identifiable appearance and individualized human figures, soldiers, domestic and wild animals, dogs, cars, boats, airplanes, a train, a bridge, and a few items such as an icecream wagon, a semaphore, etc., classified as "details"). The miniatures were colorful but almost schematic, made of either wood or metal (Bowyer 1970). They were offered in open boxes placed on a large octagonal table, approximately five feet in diameter (personal communication, Hedda Bolgar, October 27, 1991). They chose an octagonal table as a compromise between round and square. Subjects created their productions on this same table. Sand was not used because Bolgar and Fischer thought it was inappropriate for adults and that their test could be better standardized if sand were not used. Subjects were instructed to do whatever they liked with the materials and to use as much or as little as they wanted. There was no time limit on this test. A complete record of behavior and verbalizations was kept. All questions were answered by the examiner, but conversation was not encouraged. The work was followed by a brief question period to elicit the subject's spontaneous explanations, observations, and comments. At the conclusion of the test, a schematic drawing of the construction was made by the examiner.

WRITTEN WORKS AND PROFESSIONAL PRESENTATIONS

The Bolgar and Fischer standardization of World material was formally introduced in a short presentation by Dr Bolgar at the American Psychological Association meeting in 1940 and more fully described in an article in the *American Journal of Orthopsychiatry* in 1947. The standardization was based on a group of 100 normal adults, 50 men and 50 women, from 18 to 70 years of age, with varied socio-economic backgrounds, spontaneously recruited from the multi-national population in Austria before the war (Bowyer 1970).

In 1950 Fischer wrote two articles: one was an overview of the Little World Test published in a book on personality assessment (Fischer 1950a); the other was first presented as a paper at the 1949 Orthopsychiatry annual meeting and then published in their journal (Fischer 1950b). Both articles discussed the use of the Little World Test to distinguish a normal profile from a clinical one (i.e., mentally retarded, alcoholic, neurotic, organic dysfunction, psychopathic, and schizophrenic).

Scoring categories

The six scoring categories developed by Bolgar and Fischer offered a valuable method for observing clients' behavior as well as for understanding sand tray productions. Their observational categories were: *choice, quantity, form, contents, behavior,* and *verbalizations*.

1 *Choice* (the types of miniatures chosen by the subject). The first miniature chosen by a subject was given particular weight because Bolgar and Fischer believed that this object would often determine the character of the entire construction. They found that a house or bridge was most frequently used as the first object.
2 *Quantity* (the number of pieces, the variety of the construction, and the amount of space used). In their standardized collection, the number of pieces used extended from 35 to 120. Inner richness and expansiveness of personality was deduced from the variety of the construction (by the ratio between the number of items used and the number of categories) and by the amount of space used (the amount of the available space actually occupied by the construction).
3 *Form* (the geometric shape of the production, the view or perspective from which the subject built the construction, the use of the foundation/table, the direction each construction was capable of moving, and the symmetry/balance of the production). Bolgar and Fischer's findings for each of these five aspects of form are delineated below:

   (a) *Geometric Shape*. Squares or rectangles, either by themselves or in combination with other forms, were most prevalent. Round forms and combinations of round and linear forms appeared only occasionally.
   (b) *View*. Most constructions were open on all sides and could be viewed from all angles. Scenes having a definite front and rear view, as though they were on a stage, were rarely depicted.

(c) *Foundation*. The table was mostly used as a foundation; its shape or wood grain was seldom considered as part of the construction.

(d) *Direction*. For the most part, objects moved freely in various directions with no preference for one direction. A few productions had all objects pointing or moving toward or away from the subject.

(e) *Symmetry*. The great majority of all constructions were not symmetrical.

4 *Contents* included what was constructed with the relative emphasis on the following factors: practical use (P), logical construction (L), social factors (S), vitality and fun (V), and aesthetic factors (E). Most subjects built realistic scenes of towns, villages, and rural settlements complete with bushes and trees; they rarely tried to recreate an actually existing place. Almost every construction, however, contained some unrealistic elements, such as a tree placed in the middle of a street or a bridge that served no function. Further, the miniature people were depicted realistically, working and playing, as in real life. Individual differences in the constructions were reflected in the varied emphases. Some subjects emphasized the practical problems (P) of arranging animals in a barnyard or houses on a street; others were more interested in abstract structural problems (L), such as the interrelationship of boats in a harbor. Still others concentrated on the social organization (S), while some gave prominence to nature and the natural drives of humans and animals (V). A few subjects stressed the aesthetic aspect (E) of style, shape, and color.

5 *Behavior* (willingness, work-method, speed, and certainty). Reluctance to participate was unusual; enthusiasm and immediate absorption in the task was the most common response. Two distinct styles of work emerged: the most popular approach was characterized by careful planning of a whole scene, into which details were fitted as the construction grew; the other was to proceed with no organized plan. Medium speed and medium certainty was characteristic of the average performance. (The styles of work evidenced by adults coincided with van Wylick's findings (1936) with children: young children add small units of miniatures together haphazardly making a large construction, while school-age children mainly use a general blueprint-like "layout," into which details are inserted. Interestingly, the approach of some adults is similar to the pre-school child.)

6 *Verbalizations* (type and amount of spontaneous comments). Completely nonverbal behavior was quite unusual. Most subjects asked at least one question, prompted by their need for some specific object or category. At least one spontaneous comment was found in most records and what was said often added to the personality picture.

Research findings

Bolgar and Fischer (1947) developed a scoring sheet, which was used to evaluate the performances of their 100 adult subjects. Based on these evaluations, a "normal" performance (a performance observed in not less than 50 per cent of all cases) was established for theme and type of construction, choice and motivation, form, quantity, realism of representation, and relative emphasis on the five selected aspects of life in the American culture. A normal performance began with the subject selecting a house or bridge. Then:

> . . . subsequent choices would follow the lead of the material rather than being motivated from within. The subject would build a free creation which would be a town or a village. He would use houses, including a church, but not necessarily any other public building. His construction would contain trees, fences, common people, special people, dogs, farm animals, automobiles, the bridge, and at least one detail such as a horse-and-buggy or a soft-drink stand. There would be a road somewhere in the construction. He would take 35 to 120 pieces and distribute them over eight to ten of the categories just mentioned. The construction would be square or contain mainly square elements. It would be wide open on all sides; the table would be used as a foundation only; all figures would move freely in different directions; arrangement would be asymmetrical. This miniature town would be realistic; people, animals and objects would be represented as the subject sees them act in real life.
>
> The subject's behavior would be characterized by enthusiasm or at least good cooperation. He would approach his task analytically and work rather slowly but with considerable certainty. He would not talk much but would explain what he was doing and occasionally ask questions about the material and inquire for an object he would like to use but could not find.
>
> (Bolgar and Fischer 1947: 123)

In order to determine if their scoring approach was influenced by cultural factors, Bolgar and Fischer administered the Little World Test to between 25 and 75 subjects in each of four geographic areas: Central Europe, Scandinavia, Brazil, and the United States. They found that the differences were negligible and mostly related to minor details of content. This significant finding differed from Buhler's (1952) work on cultural differences, which indicated that children from various countries saw their worlds quite differently.

Fischer (1950b) conducted research on the "Little World Technique" to determine if their method of scoring would show differences between normal and clinical groups. She found that the scoring system did, in fact, differentiate clinical groups from non-clinical groups. The clinical groups had a significantly greater number of dysfunctional signs (see below), although many normal subjects made "Worlds" that included one clinical sign. She also found, however, that the scoring system was unable to differentiate clearly between specific clinical groups (e.g., alcoholics from schizophrenics), because too many of the same signs were found in each of the diagnostic groups.

Fischer's overall findings were in agreement with Lumry's research. Lumry (1951) used Buhler's World Test to evaluate four categories of children (between the ages of 6.5 and 9.5 years) in the United States and Europe: normal (non-clinical), retarded (I.Q. below 75), withdrawing, and stutterers. She found that the World Test could differentiate normal children from the children in the other three groups ($p < .01$), but could not discriminate between the three clinical groups.

Although the Bolgar and Fischer scoring system did not significantly differentiate between diagnostic categories, several interesting trends emerged:

1 Compared to the normal group, the clinical group showed a tendency to create "Worlds" that were characterized by emptiness or disorganized overcrowding, lack of general drive (too few items used), lack of balance in relation to others (too many or too few human figures used), and significant deviations in the shape of constructions.
2 In the alcoholic group, an unusually small number of objects was used, but the objects were selected from many categories, giving the impression of buried or unused capacities. Their "Worlds" tended to be unrealistic and unpopulated by people, and their willingness to cooperate was low.
3 The neurotic group appeared more adjusted than the alcoholic group. Both the number of objects and categories used, as well as the realistic use of individual items, were similar to the non-clinical group. However, the Worlds of the neurotic group were more diffused with deviations of shape and a lack of organization.
4 The mentally retarded group (I.Q.s ranging from 29 to 73) did not begin working spontaneously; they needed more direct instruction and encouragement to proceed. This group built their "Worlds" mainly in rows and in a repetitive manner – for example, there was a house with a person in front, another house with a person in front, and so on. Their constructions appeared unrealistic and made only sparse use of objects.
5 The manic group used many items and categories, and their constructions had a particular richness that appeared overdone and somewhat confused.
6 The schizophrenic group deviated most from the non-clinical groups. They used individual items unrealistically, made oddly shaped

"Worlds", and built empty-looking constructions with too many items from too few categories. Some of their "Worlds" were without people and some had many people.

CONCLUSION

By 1947 Bolgar had lost interest in pursuing further research on the Test. She later became a training analyst at the Los Angeles Institute for Psycho-analytic Studies and a founder of the Wright Institute in Los Angeles. Fischer continued research and publication until 1950 (personal communication, Hedda Bolgar, October 27, 1991), when she turned her focus entirely on her child practice in New York until her retirement in the 1980s.

Bolgar and Fischer moved the "World" materials into yet a wider arena by developing a scoring system and normative standards for adults. They had hoped to develop a nonverbal test that would take its place beside the Rorschach and other commonly used projective instruments. Coming from a psychodynamic background, their particular interpretation of the test results added the possibility of yet another theoretical dimension to the World materials. However, in the decades that have followed the development of the "Little World Test," this considerable body of work has not caught the attention or imagination of contemporary clinicians interested in projective testing or of Sandplay therapists. We believe that their scoring categories convey a similar approach to that used by con-temporary Sandplay therapists and, if known, could add a more struc-tured and organized understanding to the analysis of sand trays.

REFERENCES

Bolgar, H. and Fischer, L.K. (1940). "The toy test: A psychodiagnostic method." *Psychological Bulletin* 37: 517–18.
—— (1947). "Personality projection in the World Test." *American Journal of Ortho-psychiatry* 17: 117–28.
Bowyer, L.R. (1970). *The Lowenfeld World Technique*. Oxford: Pergamon Press.
Buhler, C. (1952). "National differences in World Test projective patterns." *Journal of Projective Techniques* 16(1): 42–55.
Fischer, L.K. (1950a). "The World 'Test'." In W. Wolff (ed.) *Personality Symposia on Topical Issues: Projective and Expressive Methods of Personality Investigation ("Diagnosis")*: 62–76. New York: Grune & Stratton.
—— (1950b). "A new psychological tool in function: Preliminary clinical experience with the Bolgar–Fischer World Test." *American Journal of Ortho-psychiatry* 20: 281–92.
Lumry, G.K. (1951). "Study of World Test characteristics as a basis for discrimina-tion between various clinical categories." *Journal of Child Psychiatry* 2: 14–35.
van Wylick, M. (1936). *Die Welt des Kindes in seiner Darstellung*. Vienna: Josef Eberle. (Summarized in Bowyer, L.R. [1970]. *The Lowenfeld World Technique*. Oxford: Pergamon.)

Chapter 6

Dora Maria Kalff
Originator of "Sandplay"

Dora Maria Kalff, originator of the Jungian Sandplay method, was born in Switzerland on December 21, 1904. She grew up in Richterswil, a small village on Lake Zürich some twenty kilometers from Zürich. Kalff's father, August Gattiker, was a traditional family patriarch for whom she had great veneration and with whom she maintained a close bond. With a deep love for all his four children, Kalff's father was remembered as strict, yet fair and generous. He was a textile merchant and an important politician in Switzerland. He served as mayor of his town many times and was elected as a national counselor (comparable to a United States senator or congressional representative). During World War II he took a strong stand against the Nazis and, consequently, was blacklisted and targeted for extermination in the event of Switzerland's occupation. Because of his influential position and ability to maintain business connections with other textile merchants throughout the world, he was able to help supply Switzerland's textile needs during the war years (Martin and Peter Kalff, personal communication, 1990).

Kalff's mother, Lilly Gattiker-Sautter, also Swiss, came from a family that had lived in Richterswil for many generations. Dora Kalff was the third of four children (she had two sisters and one brother). Kalff remembered her mother as a warm, gentle, and supportive woman who enjoyed music, the arts, and drawing – interests which she fostered in all her children (Montecchi and Navone 1989). According to Dora Kalff's sons (personal communication, 1990), their experience with their grandmother was suffused with warmth, love, and acceptance. Indeed, her maternal qualities were well recognized by others outside of the family; she was chosen to be godmother to thirty-two of the town's children (Johnson 1990).

Delicate health plagued Dora Kalff throughout her childhood and youth, preventing her from participating in physical activities and fostering a natural introversion that allowed a rich inner life to flourish (Montecchi and Navone 1989). Luckily her fragile health was not to trouble her throughout her life; during most of her adult years she enjoyed good health, and by far outlived her three siblings (Peter and Martin Kalff, personal communication, 1990).

Because it was believed that the climate would be beneficial for her respiratory problems, Kalff was sent as a teenager to a boarding school high in the Alps near St Moritz. There she attended the prestigious Girls School of Fetan, graduating from the Humanistic Gymnasium in 1923. Her course of study was equivalent to completing two years of college in the United States. At the gymnasium, she was recognized by her teachers as an exceptional student and was encouraged to pursue her interests in esoteric studies and foreign languages. She studied Latin, Greek, and Sanskrit, nurtured her deep interest in the Orient, and developed a fascination for exotic ideas, people, and places (Martin and Peter Kalff, personal communication, 1990). These diverse interests were destined to play an important role in her future personal and professional life.

Following her graduation, Kalff pursued her own educational, artistic, and spiritual interests (a traditional choice for women of that era and social class) rather than following a career-oriented path. She attended Westfield College in London, majoring in philosophy. Then, because of her musical talents, she left London and went to France to take advantage of the opportunity to study music with the renowned pianist, Robert Casadesus. Under his tutelage, she received a concert diploma.

Kalff's creative path next led her to Italy, where she learned artistic bookbinding. At a friend's home in Florence, she met and fell in love with an Italian man. However, because of religious differences (the Kalff family was Protestant and he was Catholic), Kalff's father was opposed to the union and ordered his daughter back to Switzerland. She returned, deeply wounded and disappointed, contemplating following her sister's vocation by entering a convent (Montecchi and Navone 1989). Convent life was not to be her fate, however.

At one of the many social outings that Kalff's older sister arranged, she met Leopold Ernst August (L.E.A.) Kalff, a younger son and junior member of his family's private Dutch bank, Jon Kalff & Co., Amsterdam (Johnson 1990). In 1934, at the age of twenty-nine, she married L.E.A. and moved with him to Holland. Her ample dowry was merged with the Kalff family funds. The couple led a comfortable life and shared many interests, especially in the Orient, where L.E.A. Kalff had previously lived for several years.

In 1939, Kalff returned to Switzerland for the birth of their first son, Peter. After returning to Holland, the threat of Nazi invasion and illness of her infant son precipitated her decision to leave after only six months, while her husband remained in Holland (Johnson 1990). She and her baby were in the lucky group that was able to get space on the last train leaving Holland before the war engulfed that country.

When Kalff returned to Switzerland, she was treated as a foreigner in her own land, for she had lost her Swiss citizenship because of her marriage. Remaining unrecognized as a Swiss citizen during the war years caused her great hardship; she received no food stamps or other privileges granted to citizens. The opulence of her life with her husband had suddenly vanished. The Nazis had confiscated the Kalff family business (the bank) and financial resources in Holland. Although her father in Switzerland repeatedly offered help, Kalff refused it, preferring to remain independent. About this period she remarked, "Everything depended on me. Everything was on my shoulders. I was responsible for everything" (Montecchi and Navone 1989: 395).

In 1944, Kalff moved to the little village of Parpan, because her son suffered from a respiratory illness. This village, high in the mountains of Grigioni, was primarily a ski holiday retreat. Peter, a gregarious and outgoing youngster, easily made friends with the children of the families who came to the village on a regular basis. Often these friends played at Kalff's home. One day the mother of several of these children phoned Kalff, requesting a get-together, because she had observed that, when her children returned from playing at Kalff's home, they always seemed so relaxed and happy. She was curious about this woman who created such a positive atmosphere for children. Their meeting ignited a lifelong friendship as well as a new direction for Kalff's life: the woman was C.G. Jung's daughter, Gret Jung-Baumann (Kalff 1982).

Kalff's introduction to Gret Baumann proved to be fortuitously synchronistic on many levels. By 1948 Kalff's father had died and, because of financial setbacks due to his efforts in the war, he left only a small inheritance. There was just enough money for Kalff to finance a new pursuit and Baumann suggested that, since she was so gifted with children, she should study psychology. Baumann also introduced Kalff to her father, C.G. Jung, who after meeting her agreed that Kalff's natural abilities with children indicated a psychologically oriented career.

After the war, Kalff's husband visited her from time to time in Switzerland and in 1946, their second son, Martin, was born. However, the marriage was not to survive their war-enforced separation and they were divorced in 1949. In this same year, Kalff began her six years of study at the C.G. Jung Institute in Zürich. By 1950 she had decided that she needed to live closer to the Institute and, through an acquaintance, heard about an old farm house that was for sale in the nearby town of Zollikon. It was a centuries-old country-style home, built in 1485 with walls two to three feet thick, with a fountain in the courtyard. Immediately upon seeing the house, Kalff intuitively knew that this would be the ideal setting for her future life and work. It exceeded her requirements of "three bedrooms, a living room with windows, vines growing in the garden, and a Madonna" (Chambers 1988–9). She immediately hired Jung's son, Franz, an architect, to undertake the renovations for the house. Upon completion, the Jungs visited her restored home and liked it so well that Dr Jung jokingly suggested that they trade houses.

In 1954, while still studying at the Jung Institute, Kalff attended a lecture given by Margaret Lowenfeld in Zürich. Deeply impressed by Lowenfeld's World Technique and intrigued with pursuing it further, Kalff told Jung about the new approach. Jung himself remembered attending a 1937 conference in France where he had formally responded to a presentation given by Lowenfeld. He encouraged Kalff's interest in pursuing this technique, recognizing the potential of the World Technique to act as a symbolic tool for children.

By 1956 Kalff had completed all of the studies required for certification as a Jungian analyst, including personal analysis with Jung's wife, Emma. At the final interview prior to certification, much to her surprise she was told that, without a traditional university degree, she would not be certified. This was a new rule of the Institute that had not been established when she had begun her studies, nor had she heard about it as her training proceeded. Both C.G. Jung and Emma Jung intervened on her behalf, but to no avail. Although deeply disappointed, Kalff coped well and did not allow the lack of formal certification to deter her from her goal to work with children from a Jungian perspective (M. Kalff 1990). Many years later she was officially recognized as an analyst because of her significant contributions, and became a member of the International Association for Analytical Psychology.

Almost immediately a new path came into sight. When Kalff contacted Lowenfeld about the possibility of working with her, Lowenfeld replied, "If you are interested, you must come to London and study at the clinic for three years" (Montecchi and Navone 1989). However, upon learning that Kalff had studied with C.G. Jung, she agreed to a shorter period of time.

In 1956 Kalff went to London and studied for one year. At the request of Mrs Jung, Michael Fordham, who was the first Jungian child therapist living in England, acted as Kalff's mentor in London. He was able to facilitate the contact between Kalff and Lowenfeld as he was a leader in the emerging psychological community in which Lowenfeld participated and was interested in her work (personal communication, Michael Fordham, October, 1990). In addition, Kalff also studied with D.W. Winnicott. Her rich and stimulating experience in London helped solidify the direction of her future development of Sandplay (Weinrib 1983).

Returning to continue her practice in Switzerland, Kalff now began the creative process of attempting to integrate her Jungian-based approach with what she had learned from her work with Lowenfeld. During this period of incubation, when her own ideas were crystallizing, she had little contact with Lowenfeld or with others in the Swiss psychological community. Isolated by the simple fact that she was the only Jungian analyst working with children in Switzerland at that time, ironically she found Jung to be a willing listener and supporter of her work, giving her encouragement, advice, and friendship (Weinrib 1983).

Jung himself had experienced a long period of isolation following the "parting of the ways with Sigmund Freud," when he was thrown into a state of chaos and uncertainty that neither analysis of his dreams nor re-examination of his life could alleviate. It was then that he personally discovered the healing powers of play: he regularly submitted himself to playing a building game with earth and stones on the shores of Lake Zürich, which released a flow of fantasies from his unconscious and aided him in his own "self analysis," of which he speaks so movingly in his autobiography, *Memories, Dreams, Reflections* (Jung 1961).

Integrating her many years of Jungian training with her contemplations of the World Technique, Kalff now began to synthesize her own personal theory. She named her approach "Sandplay" in order to differentiate it from Lowenfeld's World Technique. Kalff recognized that Sandplay provided a natural therapeutic modality for the child, allowing the expression of both the archetypal and intra-personal worlds, as well as connecting the child to outer everyday reality. The blending of all of these dimensions within the safe and protected space created by the therapist encouraged images of reconciliation and wholeness and re-established the vital connection between the ego and Self. Once the ego–Self axis was reactivated, Kalff theorized, the child would function in a more balanced and congruent manner. After many years of observing this process in children, she also realized that Sandplay could be equally beneficial for adults.

In the late 1950s, after Kalff had consolidated her own Jungian-based theory, Lowenfeld and Kalff exchanged letters (now stored in the Lowenfeld Archives in Cambridge). In this correspondence, Kalff expressed her appreciation to Lowenfeld and agreed to give her credit for originating the technique. They also agreed that Kalff would use the term "Sandplay" to describe her work, so as not to confuse it with the World Technique.

Intimately connected with her interest in developing Sandplay as an analytical tool was Kalff's long-standing attraction to Asian philosophies. During her time of redirection and change, her interest in Asia was brought into clearer focus through two dreams. According to her son Martin, her first dream was set in Tibet, where she was approached by two monks who gave her a golden rectangular instrument. Implicit in this gift was the understanding that she was to swing the instrument and, as she did so, an opening appeared in the ground that cut through to the other side of the world, the West, where she saw the light of the sun. The dream was later interpreted by Emma Jung, who helped Kalff understand that, through her knowledge of the Orient, she might also serve the Occident. Kalff's work in bridging these two opposite cultures of East and West ultimately brought her great fulfillment.

The second significant dream came the night of Jung's death. In the dream Jung invited her to dinner. In the middle of the dinner table was a big mound of rice. Pointing to the rice, Jung indicated that Kalff should continue her exploration of the East.

The interconnections between East and West unfolded in many ways throughout Kalff's life. Not long after the Dalai Lama and his followers were banished from Tibet in 1959, she took in as a boarder a Tibetan Lama, Geshe Chodak, who had become a refugee. Kalff gave him safe haven in her home with her own family for eight years. This personal connection opened contacts between Kalff and many other Tibetan monks, including one of the Dalai Lama's personal tutors, Trijang Rinpoche, who visited Switzerland in 1966 and stayed in Kalff's home. This exchange in turn led to several meetings between the Dalai Lama and Kalff and encouraged visits from many spiritual leaders, including the heads of all four branches of Tibetan Buddhism. Through Kalff's efforts, a home adjacent to her own was purchased in the mid-1970s as a Tibetan teaching and religious center.

Another bridge between East and West began to form when she met the renowned Zen Buddhist scholar, D. Suzuki, at an Eranos Lecture. Kalff later traveled to Japan to meet with him and exchange ideas. In describing her practice of delaying the interpretation of sand trays, Suzuki recognized a parallel with the Zen practice in which the pupil, as seeker-after-wisdom, is not given a direct answer to his/her question, but is rather thrown back on his/her own imagination and inner resources. The meeting with Suzuki reinforced Kalff's feeling that her approach was respectful of a profound universal truth (Weinrib 1983).

Kalff's association with Suzuki, along with her contacts in the Jungian community in Japan, provided the opportunity for her to teach Sandplay there. (Professor H. Kawai, a noted Jungian analyst, was particularly instrumental.) From her initial trip in 1966 (Kalff 1971) until her death, her work was received with enthusiastic and wholehearted acceptance. Sandplay resonated well with Japanese culture for several reasons. For one, the Japanese had a similar artistic tradition called "Hakoniwa," which involved creating a miniature landscape in a box. Another reason may be that Japanese therapists were greatly influenced by the symbolic perspective of C.G. Jung as well as the non-judgmental, person-centered approach of Carl Rogers (personal communication, Sachiko Reese, November, 1989); Sandplay, with its symbolic and non-judgmental emphasis, could be easily incorporated. In addition, the nonverbal method of Sandplay meshed well with Japanese customs that emphasized nonverbal communication of feelings, perhaps softening the verbal aspects of the Jungian and Rogerian approaches. And finally, there was the pervasive resonance of Dora Kalff's spiritual attitude with the ancient philosophies of Japan. Kalff felt close to the Japanese and Tibetan

Buddhist traditions, which she was able to communicate in her presentations of the Sandplay process. These traditions were integrated as well in her daily life; she meditated daily and participated in Chung Long breathing, which she felt gave her energy.

Sandplay is currently among the major psychotherapeutic approaches in Japan. A yearly conference attracts hundreds of interested Sandplay practitioners. A professional journal, *The Archives of Sandplay Therapy*, is published regularly by the Japan Association of Sandplay Therapy, with Hayao Kawai and Yasuhiro Yamanaka serving as editors.

Kalff's ability to speak German, Italian, French, Dutch, and English enabled her to communicate with audiences throughout the West in their native languages. In this way, she carried the spirit of her work in a most personal manner, igniting the imagination of her audiences and infusing the images and stories of Sandplay experiences with immediacy and relevance. Sandplay apparently spoke to the unmet needs of therapists throughout the world who were seeking to find nonverbal methods that could circumvent or complement the traditional verbal approaches to facilitate a more balanced expression of the psyche.

As a result of Kalff's considerable travels, many psychotherapists and Jungian analysts have integrated Sandplay into their work. Strong interest in Sandplay has emerged in Europe (particularly in England, Germany, Italy, and Switzerland) and in North America (particularly in California, Florida, Hawaii, Minnesota, New York, and Ontario, Canada).

Dora Kalff died on January 15, 1990, at her home in Zollikon, Switzerland. Only a few months earlier, she had taught a three-week Sandplay seminar in her home; shortly thereafter she suffered a stroke that left her physically disabled but mentally alert. In the several months before her death, her strong connection to her unconscious, that had guided her in both her life and work, appeared to be preparing her for a future journey. Her son, Martin, wrote of this time:

> She was talking about her death about a month before she actually left us. To speak had already become difficult, but in special moments her words became clear and understandable. Thus she spoke clearly about a journey she was going to undertake. Although she felt that the journey was to be by ship, she also said that it was a journey into another life. For her this was so real, that at one moment she said to me: "I have to go through some sort of a tunnel, don't you sense it, too?" One morning she seemed amazed and said: "It is really strange, but this room has no walls anymore." From the atmosphere one could feel that the ordinary room had opened up and had become transparent for another dimension. When she spoke about these things, she appeared to be in a joyful and happy mood.
>
> (M. Kalff 1990)

Ten days after her death, a memorial service was held at the Protestant church in Zollikon. Kalff's connections with people throughout the world continued after death as in life. Memorial services were held in many communities around the globe in recognition of her contributions. A particularly large commemoration was held in Bodega Bay, California, in February of 1990, and included a Tibetan Bell Concert.

The worldwide tapestry of connections Kalff wove continues to grow through the work of the International Society for Sandplay Therapy (ISST), which she founded in 1985 to provide training and certification in Sandplay. Archives containing in-depth case studies from each of the ISST members are kept in Zollikon, Switzerland (see Bibliography of ISST Case Studies). Duplicate copies of many of these case studies can be found at the C.G. Jung Library in San Francisco.

BASIC TENETS OF SANDPLAY

Kalff has presented the basic tenets of Sandplay in her numerous public presentations, writings, and video- and audiotapes. An overview of her approach, written in German (1978) and later translated into English by Kalff, has been published in the *Journal of Sandplay Therapy* (Kalff 1991).

Physical guidelines for the work

Kalff considered sand to be an extremely important and natural thera-peutic material because it consists of tiny grains that give it plasticity and softness. Sand provides varying tactile sensations, depending on whether the sand is dry or moist. Sand, like the earth, contains the natural, primordial elements.

Kalff's recommendation that Sandplay therapists have two trays avail-able, one with moist sand and the other with dry sand, was in contrast to Lowenfeld's approach that used only one tray filled with sand, with water available nearby, and with Buhler's approach that positioned miniatures on a table without sand.

Kalff's trays were constructed in dimensions similar to those used by Lowenfeld (28½ × 19½ inches with a depth of 3 inches standing at a height of approximately 30 inches) and were both painted blue on the inside to give the impression of water or sky. The miniatures were placed on open shelves so that the client could easily view them without opening and closing drawers, as in the Lowenfeld approach. "Hundreds of small figures of every conceivable type are provided" (Kalff 1980: 31) to repre-sent a cross-section of all animate and inanimate images encountered in the external world as well as in the inner imaginative world.

Introducing the tray

Normally, Kalff would not suggest that a Sandplay be created during an introductory session, preferring to establish a personal connection first that would serve as a foundation for future work together. At an appropriate time, she might ask the client, "Would you like to do a Sandplay?" However, she also recommended that a more involved introduction might be appropriate when adults are in ongoing therapy, when there is a reluctance to participate in Sandplay, or when verbal therapy is not advancing. At this time, it could be helpful to talk about the importance and value of play in accessing the imagination and providing a sense of balance and wholeness while reassuring the client that play is not just a regression to childhood. Kalff herself was known to quote J.C.F. von Schiller's statement that a human being is only complete when at play.

After the client touched the sand, Kalff would explain that the blue background was meant to bring to mind images of water and concluded her brief introductory remarks by suggesting that the client "put in what speaks to you."

Therapist's role and attitude

It is necessary for the therapist to have an understanding of the work as it proceeds, as well as to be a silent witness to the Sandplay creation. This nonverbal collaboration takes place on a level of consciousness that is outside the ordinary conscious, rational modes. During the making of the tray, Kalff recommended that the therapist sit off to one side of the client so as not to intrude on the experience, yet remaining near enough to be available when needed. As the tray is assembled, the therapist sketches, quietly takes notes, and acts as a witness to the drama that is unfolding, connecting to the feeling atmosphere of the process as well as to the individual scene. Interpretations and explanations of the trays are not offered at the time the scenes are completed. It is crucial that a free and protected space be created in order to enable the client's imagination to emerge. The therapist creates this "free and protected space" by functioning as both a physical and psychological container: the client feels free to explore and yet is also protected from going beyond his/her limits. Thus the therapist must have the ability to hold two qualities: to be (1) non-judgmental and (2) a limit-setter.

Recording

In addition to the sketch made by the therapist while the Sandplay is in progress, a photographic slide is taken of it after the client leaves. Sometime later, perhaps months or even years, when the client and therapist agree that the time is right, a retrospective of the Sandplay slides are shown, helping the client make the connections between the symbolic images and his/her outer life (delayed interpretation).

WRITTEN WORKS AND PROFESSIONAL PRESENTATIONS

Dora Kalff's published writings on Sandplay are sparse and do not adequately reflect the fullness of her spiritual and humanitarian legacies. Nevertheless, her influence has been great, thanks in part to her publication, *Sandplay* (1980), and because many of her workshops have been chronicled by widely available audio- or videotapes (Kalff c1972, 1979, 1988b).

Kalff's first published work was not directly about Sandplay. Nevertheless, it reflected her strong interest in symbolic imagery and her knowledge of the numerous meanings that symbols have evoked over time and which still remain in the collective unconscious. In this work, "The significance of the hare in Reynard the fox," Kalff (1957) discussed images of both the fox and the hare and their early significance in universal literature and folklore. This article provided the basis for some of her later writings and lectures, which reflected her conviction that symbols, such as these, hold a universal power through time and touch a deep level of the unconscious.

Kalff's earliest workshop in the United States was conducted in San Francisco in March, 1962, at the invitation of the Society of Jungian Analysts of Northern California. Her presentation was received with enthusiasm and an informal group was established "to keep in touch with developments in Sandplay and facilitate the use of Sandplay in clinical practice" (Stewart 1981: 1). Following this presentation, she accepted yearly invitations to speak in the Bay Area to increasingly large and interested audiences.

In 1966, Kalff presented a series of lectures in Southern California, sponsored by the Footlighters' Child Guidance Clinic at the Hollywood Presbyterian Hospital (Kalff 1966b). Here she articulated the theoretical foundation of Sandplay as providing an opportunity for the manifestation of the Self, which is the necessary precondition for the healthy development of the ego. For Kalff, Sandplay was an effective means of evoking and nurturing the vital bridge between ego and Self. The importance of the connection between the Self and the ego is a central concept in Jungian psychology: when the ego and the Self are in relationship, then the individual is living closest to his/her totality and is moving toward the most actualized state. Jung perceived the ego to be the center of consciousness but less than the whole personality. The ego has its own role, maintaining a sense of personal identity and mediating between the conscious and unconscious realms, yet it still needs to be directed by the larger Self, which is the ordering principle of the entire personality.

Kalff, who was profoundly influenced by noted Jungian analyst and developmental theorist Erich Neumann, integrated his stages of development with her theory of Sandplay in this 1966 lecture. According to Neumann (1973), during the first year of life the totality of the personality (the experience of the Self) is contained for the infant by the mother. Neumann called this stage of life the "mother–child unity." After the first year, the normal child is sufficiently developed to begin separating its Self from the mother. During the second and beginning of the third years, the Self begins to consolidate within the child's unconscious, which allows the child to be more independent and to experience a personal relationship with the mother. During the stage of separation from the mother and consolidation of the Self, the child begins to create symbols of wholeness (circles and squares) in his/her drawing and painting. These numinous symbols are the energy-laden images of the innate potentials of the human being and, when expressed, influence activation of the Self. As these symbols of the Self become manifest, their numinous contents can be felt, the experience of which is a necessary precondition for the development of a sound ego.

Kalff made the assumption that, for a child who is having problems, the manifestation of the Self has failed to appear because of too little maternal protection, overanxious motherly care, and/or external traumatic influences such as war, illness, or other environmental disturbances. However, the constellation of the Self that was not possible in the early years, Kalff believed, could be activated at any juncture of life.

The child's Self has the possibility of constellating and manifesting in Sandplay if the therapist is able to establish a "free and protected space" that recreates the original mother–child unity and "establishes an inner peace which contains the potential for the development of the total personality, including its intellectual and spiritual aspects" (Kalff 1966a: 5).

As the child creates the Sandplays, the therapist witnesses the use and placement of the emerging symbols. The connection between the child and the therapist re-establishes the mother–child unity and produces the healing influence when the therapist is attuned to the meaning of the emerging symbols. This therapeutic effect takes place even when the therapist's insight is not shared with the child through words. In some situations another approach may be indicated and "the pictures are interpreted to the child in an easily understood way that is connected with his life situation. This leads to a knowledge of a correspondence between the inner and outer problems, which in itself produces the next step in development" (Kalff 1966a: 8–9).

Kalff published her first article on Sandplay in 1966, "The archetype as a healing factor." Here she emphasized that the first tray provides the therapist with a guide to treatment, for it often gives information hidden in the symbols about the nature of the problem, the prognosis, and how the healing will occur. In citing one case, Kalff describes a nine-year-old boy's first tray and subsequent movement in his trays. Kalff sees the nature of the boy's problem as his perception of the world that, to him, is filled with insurmountable problems which keep him from realizing his talent. This problem is illustrated in the lower left of the tray, where the boy fences in both a house and a boy swimming nearby. This restriction indicates that he feels detached from his own unconscious resources (as represented by the green tree and the filling station) that are placed outside the fence. Kalff perceived the possibility of a positive prognosis for this boy as his unconscious resources (from which the healing energies would emerge) were nearby and potentially available.

After about four months of slow progress in therapy, during which time Kalff was able to establish a secure environment for the child, a Self-symbol appeared in the sand represented by a circus ring. Three more pictures followed, which Kalff noted as corresponding to three developmental stages as defined by Neumann (1973): the animalistic or vegetative stage, the phase of struggle, and adaptations to the group. Thus, this child followed a process which progressed from consolidation of the Self to strengthening the ego as he moved through these three archetypal stages as defined by Neumann. At each step, he experienced increasing strength in meeting outer world challenges.

In this article Kalff also integrated a diagram by a Chinese philosopher, Chou-Tun-Ye, with her own view of the manifestation of the Self in childhood and adulthood. The diagram traces the life process from birth to death. The first diagram indicates that at birth the infant is in a primal state. A second diagram shows that the developing child encompasses both Yin and Yang energies as it begins to integrate both forces. From the dynamic interaction of the opposites, the manifestation of the Self becomes possible, followed by an integration of all aspects of the personality (represented as fire, water, earth, wood, and metal). The diagram then indicates that during the second half of life, the tendency is toward the development of the Self and the movement toward individuation. According to the law of transformation, the final diagram shows the moment leading from life to death, containing the seed of new life.

Dora Kalff's only book was originally written in German and published under the title of *Sandspiel* in 1966 by Rascher Press, Zürich. It was translated into English by Hilde Kirsch, a founding member of the Society of Jungian Analysts of Los Angeles. This translation was published in 1971 by Browser Press, San Francisco, as *Sandplay: Mirror of a Child's Psyche*. It was translated anew and reprinted in 1980 under the title of *Sandplay: A Psychotherapeutic Approach to the Psyche* by Sigo Press in Santa Monica, California. The 1980 reprint of *Sandplay* is essentially the same book as the 1971 edition with the exception of name changes for some of the presented cases, slight translation differences, and an addition of a short epilogue. There is an error in the 1980 edition with regard to the dimension of the sand tray. The correct dimensions are given in the 1971 edition: 19½ × 28½ inches with 3 inches in depth.

In this book, Kalff lays the foundation for her Sandplay approach. Kalff's first chapter is devoted to a theoretical overview of Sandplay in which she emphasized that the role of symbols was to influence human development and to serve as vehicles for expressing the wholeness of the personality. Kalff describes her playroom, located in her historic and inviting home, containing traditional play materials in addition to the sand trays and miniatures. Her home was built over hundreds of years, and evolved according to its own natural tendencies. Kalff says, "the house offers an atmosphere which corresponds to the natural tempera-ment of young people" (Kalff 1980: 38). This distinctive house provided a temenos for her work throughout her lifetime.

Each of the remaining nine chapters in her book deals with a case study. Seven of these cases are children and two are adult cases. Her case studies show how blocks in psychic development can be released so that normal development can proceed. Kalff's understanding of the sand trays is discussed, specifically that, when new forces, energies, and powers are freed, a connection between the conscious and unconscious can then be established. Following this, there is a possibility that a centering process will unfold, signifying movement toward healthy psychic development and a greater harmony between inner and outer experience.

To explain her approach, Kalff cites the case of twelve-year-old Kim, who is experiencing a learning inhibition. He begins therapy with an overly adapted, "good boy" persona. His initial sand tray suggests a fragile psychic foundation and blocked energies (possibly as a result of early maternal loss). Subsequent trays contain defensive walls (of sand) and aggressive elements (e.g., tanks, military airplanes). Through Kalff's understanding of the trays and her intuitive capacities, she sees that his newly awakened energies need to be expressed in an active physical way. Thus, she facilitates his play with darts, bows and arrows, air guns, and even a blowtorch! Through these activities, Kim's energies are caught, focussed, and led into constructive paths where the negative aggressions can be adequately expressed. In later sessions, Kim returns to the sand tray, expressing himself in a markedly different manner. His trays are now filled with colors, people, trees, and even four Indian women with children (the mother–child unity), signifying that the inner feelings of security that he had lost in early childhood are now beginning to emerge. A short time later, Kim creates a tray in which the manifestation of the Self is exhibited. Kalff recognizes that, in this important moment of the mani-festation of the Self, Kim has achieved the starting point of a healthy ego and the unfolding of his inherent personality. Kalff warns that, despite his powerful expression in the tray, therapy continues to be indicated; she knew that protection and care of his new growth would be necessary at this time. At the conclusion of therapy, Kalff realizes that Kim has gone through three psychological stages: expression of the aggressions; manifestation of the Self; A positive use of the energy sources. Kim has achieved the goal of being able to live from his natural self. In addition, he is able to complete his work at school in a confident manner, have many friends, and maintain a close and loving relationship with his father.

In the case of Kim, it is apparent that Kalff used a variety of play therapy approaches along with Sandplay. In fact, Kalff viewed nonverbal play as working "hand in hand" with Sandplay to access the Self (Kalff 1969). Yet, Sandplay still remained the centerpiece of the therapy, helping her to determine the direction of the therapy as well as helping clients access, express, and integrate neglected aspects of their psyche. For Kalff, Sandplay was not an adjunctive technique, but was in and of itself enough for healing. In fact, on the publication of the 1980 edition of her book, she was distressed (Kay Bradway, personal communication, January 23, 1993) to read the back cover (which she did not write), which states: "Sandplay is *not* [italics added] a method of therapy in and of itself." That same year (1980), Kalff herself wrote in the foreword to *Sandplay Studies* (Bradway et al. 1981): "I personally have never considered it [Sandplay] an adjunct to verbal analysis" (p. ix). Later, in her foreword to Weinrib's (1983) book, Kalff clarified her view by stating that, in the beginning phase of Sandplay therapy, she prefers "to create an open space for the unconscious inner impulses to manifest without the interference of premature conceptualization. When the process has proceeded to a point well after the constellation of the Self, the verbal and analytical work becomes more important" (p. xvi). Thus, Kalff emphasized the nonverbal techniques of Sandplay and play therapy at the earlier stages of therapy, while seeing the value of verbal and analytical approaches in later therapy stages (after the constellation of the Self).

Kalff's ability to recognize the psyche's creative seeds enabling necessary development and change is impressively demonstrated in this book. Her broad therapeutic approach, in conjunction with her depth of learning in Asian and Western philosophies, is clearly illustrated in these cases from her practice.

Sandspiel (c.1972) is the most widely viewed of Dora Kalff's videotapes. Here the viewer has the rare opportunity to enter Kalff's picturesque home in Zollikon, Switzerland, and listen to her discuss and articulate her beliefs and theories about Sandplay. The video begins in her garden with a child arriving for therapy, playing next to the fountain. Kalff greets the child and invites him into her Sandplay room. Later, several children are chronicled in their process of selecting miniatures, making a Sandplay, and freely interacting with her.

In this videotape, Kalff particularly emphasized the importance of creating the "free and protected space." She observed that children in modern society lack the feeling of internal security as a result of being disconnected from their own natures. She does not blame parents for this condition, but noted simply that our overly rational and mechanistic society does not nurture this important aspect of the personality.

In discussing the advantages of Sandplay, Kalff noted that the child has the opportunity to access the deepest part of the Self and express it symbolically in Sandplay. This can bring about an experience of totality which engenders a feeling of calmness and centeredness. Another advantage is that the Sandplay picture can be viewed prognostically and can give indications for treatment.

The most moving aspect of the videotape is Kalff's work with an insecure child, whose series of trays are viewed in relationship to her theory. She analyzes both the symbols that the child uses as well as his process of transformation as it is manifested in the trays. His series of sand trays dramatically illustrates the unfolding of his natural Self from a condition of isolation and insecurity to one of more confidence and finally to a position of strength, expansion, and security in his everyday world.

"Beyond the shadow" was initially presented at the 1986 Tenth Congress of the International Association for Analytical Psychology. Unfortunately, Kalff's presentation was not included in the published proceedings of this conference. However, it was subsequently published as one of eight articles by The Japan Association of Sandplay Therapy in the first edition of their journal, *Archives of Sandplay Therapy* (Kalff 1988a), and later videotaped at the 1988 International Transpersonal Conference. Kalff presented twenty-four trays from different clients in order to depict the constellation of the Self. According to Kalff, many images and shapes can reflect the connection with the Self, such as those in the shape of a mandala, those depicting new birth, or symbols showing the integration of opposite forces.

This article strikingly illustrates and clarifies Kalff's major premise that the original Self can be accessed through Sandplay. She notes that, when the Self is expressed symbolically in the tray, it can be experienced as a deeply personal and numinous moment, often mysterious and enigmatic. This moment can be similar to the "peak" experience (Maslow 1968). In another article, Kalff (1971) states: "The manifestation of the Self is experienced by the patient as an inner harmony which impresses itself upon the patient's daily life" (p. 56). Further, it is at this time, as well, that the dark and destructive energies also have the possibility of becoming transformed and experienced in a constructive way. Kalff emphasizes that it is the transformative experience of creating a sand picture that contains the healing, not merely the client's conscious observation of the pictures. However, during this period of transformation, time and support are needed for it is "as delicate as a newly sprouting blade of grass" (Kalff 1980: 48). Thus, she emphasizes that it is important to protect this new potential as it emerges.

In a paper presented at the Fourth International Congress for Analytical Psychology, Kalff (1971) stated that the step *after* the constellation of the Self was the *unfolding* of the Self. During this period, the inherent potentials of the personality begin to come alive on the vegetative level, as described by Neumann (1973). "This stage is often indicated in the sand pictures by representations of landscapes, inhabited only by animals. In addition, the number five in various forms appears *almost invariably* during the unfolding process" (Kalff 1971: 56). Kalff relates the number five to the physical body (as in the five extremities, head, arms, and legs, the five fingers, five toes, and the five senses) and the five basic elements (earth, wood, metal, fire, and water). She posits that the number five symbolizes the body–mind relationship and "seems to signal the transformation of physical energy into spiritual experience, and that the body is somehow vital in the achievement of spiritual experience" (p. 57).

In Kalff's preface to *Studies of Sandplay Therapy in Japan* (1982), she emphasized the importance of providing a "free and sheltered space" in order to facilitate a renewed flow of energies. She points out that freedom is inherent in this approach for the client is free to select any of the numerous figures available in a Sandplay collection. "This large variety of figures . . . corresponds on an outer level with the inner creative many-foldness which is hidden in every person. This is, so to speak, an invitation for the patient to open up and to be free to express his inner wealth" (Kalff 1982: 227).

Kalff explains that Sandplay also provides the opportunity for the many symbols (miniatures) to be "channeled into a concentrated form of self-expression. This 'channel' is represented by the limited size of the sandbox. . . . If there would be no limits to the activities it could well happen that either destructive energies take over or that the person gets too dispersed . . . the limits function as a protection or a shelter" (Kalff 1982: 227–8).

In addition, Kalff stresses the importance of the therapist's preparation to be free and loving on an inner level, in order to create an atmosphere of freedom and empathetic acceptance. The following portion of her foreword is included here in its entirety as it reflects not only Kalff's humanitarian concerns but also her personal convictions:

One important aspect of this freedom is to become void of judgmental concepts and to become free to accept the patient as he is. This could also be described as a state of receptive openness. In this state one does not judge prematurely what is created by the play to be either negative or positive. The attitude should be such that if something positive is about to happen that this has the force in itself to break through and express itself. There is no need for the therapist to label it as good because it is not the explanation that counts but the experience the patient is going to have. Likewise it would be a mistake to label something as negative because we never know ahead of time what good may come out of darkness. The state of freedom the therapist is to aim at should be such that by his mere presence this freedom can be communicated also non-verbally to the patient. In such a situation the patient may slowly also discover within himself the transformative power of freedom.

Besides an inner state of freedom the therapist should also attempt to develop his own capacity to love. Love means in this context to sincerely wish that the patient may become free of his suffering. It is a quality which allows the therapist to see the patient not only as a patient but as another human being. If the patient experiences that he is accepted in that way it will also enable him to look with love at those sides within himself which previously he found to be unacceptable and negative. In that way the capacity to love works as a shelter or protection for that which is still weak within the patient. It allows that to grow which otherwise might be repressed by a non-caring attitude. This love expresses itself also in taking serious[ly] what is done or said by the patient.

This is only a brief indication of one of the many aspects which I have found through my experience to be essential in the process of healing.

(Kalff 1982: 228–9)

CONCLUSION

With the blending of Jungian theory with Margaret Lowenfeld's World Technique, Kalff created a unique method for accessing the healing energies of the unconscious. Stewart (1981) appraises her influence when he says:

It is impossible to capture in words the qualities of Dora Kalff that captivated and inspired so many now-enthusiastic sandplay therapists. In addition to her free and protected space, her persuasive impact resides in the sand worlds themselves. Even when frozen in the static images of slides projected upon a screen, they still retain some of the magical quality of the living worlds which were animated by the imagination of client and therapist alike, and which spring to life once again for all who can see them with the inner vision of imagination.

(Stewart 1981: 3)

Because of her Jungian insights, Kalff had the vision to see the emerging symbols in the sand tray as objectifying the energy of the unconscious. This unique foresight allowed her to understand that the symbols were expressions of both the inner and outer worlds, mediating and connecting both universal and personal meaning.

Kalff infused a new depth and direction to Lowenfeld's sand tray approach by adding both Jungian and Eastern spiritual dimensions. Differing from popular verbal therapies, her approach embraces the non-verbal and irrational elements that are missing from our currently one-sided technological society. When these heretofore repressed elements are available, then it is possible for creative and healing energies to be released making life experience richer and more satisfying. Through her many long years of inspired teaching, there now exists a growing group of dedicated professionals throughout the world who are committed to continuing Sandplay work.

REFERENCES

Bradway, K., Signell, K.A., Spare, G.H., Stewart, C.T., Stewart, L.H. and Thompson, C. (1981). *Sandplay Studies: Origins, Theory, and Practice.* San Francisco: C.G. Jung Institute. (Republished (1990) Boston: Sigo Press).

Chambers, L. (1988–9). Transcript of audiotaped interviews with Dora Kalff.

Johnson, F.C. (1990). "In memoriam: Dora Kalff (1904–1990)." *Quadrant* 23(1): 103–13.

Jung, C.G. (1961). *Memories, Dreams, Reflections.* New York: Random House, Inc.

Kalff, D. (1957). "The significance of the hare in Reynard the Fox." *Journal of Analytical Psychology* 2(2). (Reprinted (1992) in *Journal of Sandplay Therapy* 1(2): 13–26.)

—— (1966a). "Symbolism and child analysis." Unpublished transcription of seminar conducted at Footlighters' Child Guidance Clinic, Hollywood Presbyterian Hospital, Hollywood, CA.

—— (1966b). "The archetype as a healing factor." *Psychologia* 9: 177–84. Originally printed (1962) in German in A. Guggenbühl-Craig (ed.) *The Archetype: Proceedings of the 2nd International Congress for Analytical Psychology*: 182–200. Basel, Switzerland: S. Karger.

—— (1969). "Das Sandspiel: Ein Beitrag aus der Sicht C.G. Jungs zur Kinderpsychotherapie" [The Sandplay: A contribution from C.G. Jung's point of view on child therapy]. In G. Bierman (ed.) *Handbuch der Kinderpsychotherapie*: 451–6. Munich/Basel: Ernst Reinhardt Verlag.

—— (1971). "Experiences with far eastern philosophers." In J.B. Wheelwright (ed.) *The Analytic Process: Aims, Analysis, Training*: 56–67. (The Proceedings of the Fourth International Congress for Analytical Psychology.) New York: G.P. Putnam's Sons.

—— (c1972). *Sandspiel.* (Videotape.) Directed and produced by Peter Ammann. Available from the C.G. Jung Institute, San Francisco, CA.

—— (1979). "Sandplay: Mirror of the child's psyche." (Audiotape). Los Angeles: C.G. Jung Institute.

—— (1980). *Sandplay: A Psychotherapeutic Approach to the Psyche.* (W. Ackerman, trans.) Santa Monica: Sigo Press. Originally published (1966) in German as *Sandspiel.* Zürich: Rascher. First published (1971) in English as *Sandplay: Mirror of a Child's Psyche.* (H. Kirsch, trans.) San Francisco: Browser Press.

—— (1981). Foreword. In K. Bradway *et al.*, *Sandplay Studies: Origins, Theory and Practice.* San Francisco: C.G. Jung Institute. Republished (1990) Boston: Sigo Press.

—— (1982). Preface. In H. Kawai and Y. Yamanaka (eds) *Studies of Sandplay Therapy in Japan* I: 227–9. Tokyo: Seishin-Shoboh.

—— (1983). Foreword. In E.L. Weinrib, *Images of the Self: The Sandplay Therapy Process*. Boston: Sigo Press.

—— (1988a). "Beyond the shadow." *Archives of Sandplay Therapy* 1: 87–97.

—— (1988b). *Beyond the shadow . . . Sandplay therapy.* (Videotape.) Recorded at the International Transpersonal Conference. Produced by Conference Recording Service.

—— (1991). "Introduction to Sandplay therapy." *Journal of Sandplay Therapy* (1) (1): 7–15. Originally published (1978) in German as "Eine kurze Einführung in die Sandspieltherapie." *Praxis der Psychotherapie* 23: 269–73. Heidelberg: Springer-Verlag. Translated into English by Kalff (1986) and presented to the International Society for Sandplay Therapy. Reprinted (1988c) in English by International Society for Sandplay Therapy.

Kalff, M. (1990). Unpublished letter to the members of the ISST.

Maslow, A.H. (1968). *Toward a Psychology of Being* (2nd ed.). New York: Van Nostrand Reinhold Company.

Montecchi, F. and Navone, A. (1989). "Dora M. Kalff and the Sandplay." In C. Trombetta (ed.) *Psicologia Analitica Contemporanea* (*Contemporary Analytical Psychology*). Milan, Italy: Fabbri Editorial Group.

Neumann, E. (1973). *The Child*. New York: C.G. Jung Foundation for Analytical Psychology, Inc.

Stewart, L.H. (1981). "Play and Sandplay." In K. Bradway *et al.* (eds) *Sandplay Studies: Origins, Theory and Practice*: 21–37. San Francisco: C.G. Jung Institute. Republished (1990) Boston: Sigo Press.

Weinrib, E.L. (1983). *Images of the Self: The Sandplay Therapy Process*. Boston: Sigo Press.

Chapter 7

Laura Ruth Bowyer (Pickford)
Major contributor to sand tray research

Laura Ruth Bowyer (Pickford), who served on the academic staff of the University of Bristol and later in the psychology department at the University of Glasgow in Scotland, made significant contributions to the research literature using Lowenfeld's World Technique. She was born in 1907 in the town of Brechin, Scotland, daughter of Laura and Harry Bowyer. In 1971 she married Dr Ralph W. Pickford, head of the Department of Psychology, University of Glasgow. In addition to being colleagues, they conducted research together in India and Africa on color vision. In 1973 they both retired from full-time teaching, but she continued teaching a few courses until late 1992. Ralph Pickford died in 1986.

Bowyer's contributions include:

1 developing scoring categories to better analyze trays (Bowyer 1956);
2 generating developmental norms for children and adults from both clinical and non-clinical populations (Bowyer 1956);
3 examining the Worlds made by mentally retarded subjects in order to determine the influence of intelligence on sand tray creations and to explore the value of the sand tray as a projective instrument for this special population (Bowyer 1958);
4 researching the importance of the use of sand in the World Technique (Bowyer 1956, 1959a);
5 investigating the deaf population using the World Technique (Bowyer and Gillies 1972; Bowyer, Gillies and Scott 1966; Bowyer and Gilmour 1968; Bowyer, Marshall and Weddell 1963).

It was in her role as an educational psychologist in 1945, when Bowyer first used the World Technique with children in a child guidance clinic in Scotland. Later, as an academician, she studied the World Technique and used it in her research, as well as in play therapy (Bowyer 1959b; Pickford 1973, 1975). This fostered connections with Lowenfeld, and with Lowenfeld's encouragement, Bowyer decided to write a book summarizing the fairly extensive literature on the World Technique. Her book, *The Lowenfeld World Technique* (1970), covers the history of the technique as well as its applications to personality diagnosis, psychotherapy, and research; it also evaluates the World Technique in relation to other projective methods. With its publication, professionals at last had easy access to forty years of thinking and research on Lowenfeld's approach.

RESEARCH CONTRIBUTIONS

The findings of Bowyer's developmental study of sand trays were first presented before the British Psychological Society and later published in its *Bulletin* (Bowyer 1956). The most accessible summary of this study is found in Bowyer's book, *The Lowenfeld World Technique* (1970). Bowyer's research was unique, as it was the only developmental study up to that time that had used sand (the earlier developmental studies of van Wylick [1936] and Bühler [1951] had not used sand). Bowyer's study included 76 subjects spanning 2- to 50-year-olds (50 children, 26 adults); some of the children were clinical cases while others were "normal" (i.e., not referred for clinical treatment). All subjects made a minimum of three trays (unlike van Wylick's [1936] and Bolgar and Fischer's [1947] studies, which required only one tray).

Evaluation criteria

Bowyer used five criteria in evaluating the trays: (1) area of tray used, (2) themes of aggression, (3) control and coherence of tray, (4) use of sand, and (5) content. Her findings were:

1 *Area of tray used.* In the "Worlds" of her normal subjects, Bowyer found that, with increasing age, a greater area of the tray was used. In addition, older children evidenced a firmer sense of boundaries by staying within the edges of the tray more clearly. For example, the youngest subjects, aged two to three, used only a small portion of the tray and ignored the boundaries completely, sometimes placing small heaps of toys outside of the tray. Four- to five-year-olds seemed to be in transition, with some children using a small portion of the tray and others placing toys at intervals throughout the tray. After the age of five, the "Worlds" of the normal population appeared to extend to most of the area of the tray, while the clinical population sometimes used only a portion of the tray.

2 *Themes of aggression.* Bowyer studied themes of aggression at various ages. In the youngest age-group (two to three years old), toys were most often poked, flung, and buried. Four- to six-year-olds used dramatic activity, moving toys in the tray while making noises. After seven years of age, children were able to arrange toys to represent aggressive action in the tray, rather than having to actually move the toys around. After twelve

years of age and through adulthood, the difference was that subjects seemed to be *cognitively* aware of their aggressive feelings and appeared content to depict these feelings in the tray.

A particularly interesting finding was that the trays of children of the same age showed great similarities below eight years; it was not until after eight years of age that the individual differences in the trays became increasingly apparent.

3 *Control and coherence of tray.* Bowyer found that control and coherence increased with age in the "Worlds" of normal subjects. Little or no control was shown by the two- to three-year-olds, whose "Worlds" were chaotic. Some three- to four-year-olds managed coherent detail in separate areas within the tray. From five to ten years of age, fencing increased; ten was the peak age for fencing. After eleven years, there was less use of literal controls (i.e., fences) and more conceptual and symbolic controls (e.g., policemen). Issues of control were also observed in the total Gestalt of the tray after eleven years old, in which complex patterns and themes of control were more often integrated into a whole. For example, topological features such as mountains and streams were included to control and unify the scene.

4 *Use of sand.* Bowyer discussed the use of sand by two- to four-year-olds and by subjects over the age of seven. She found that the younger group used the sand for pouring, pushing, and burying. After age seven, the constructive use of sand (creating roads, waterways, and paths in the sand) depended on individual personality characteristics more than on age differences and indicated a mature use of imaginative inner resources to find ways of enlarging or restructuring the tray.

5 *Content.* With increasing age, realism increased, the toys were more integrated with the scene, and a time-perspective was often included in the theme.

Developmental norms

Some specific toys and themes were more consistently used at certain ages. For example, people were used throughout all age-groups (except by young children using animals as people or by individuals representing a jungle); topics related to eating were common before five years of age; after five, farm scenes and many animals were used; transport remained a strong interest between five and eight years; from seven years onwards, trees were consistently used.

Bowyer noted three particular types of trays that could suggest the need for therapy:

1 when the subject's "World" does not reflect the appropriate developmental stage;

2 when the subject uses the materials consciously to communicate problems; and
3 when the following signs identified by Charlotte Bühler (1951) are
   present in the tray:
   (a) Empty "Worlds" (except in the case of very young children);
   (b) Disorganized "Worlds" (except those made by young children
       who are playing with the materials);
   (c) Aggressive "Worlds" (except those that show certain kinds of aggres-
       siveness that are common at all ages). Aggressive signs of particular
       concern include themes of aggressive animals or burying in the sand
       (after age five); penning in or crowding toys into a tight mass (after
       age five); a "World" scene devoid of aggression, while the client is
       acting aggressively in other situations or vice versa;
   (d) Over-fenced "Worlds" (i.e., exaggerated fencing);
   (e) Unpeopled "Worlds" (except those made by young children using
       animals to represent people).

In her search for developmental norms, Bowyer studied the "Worlds" of
216 institutionalized mentally-retarded children and adults (IQs from 17
to 88) in order to balance the normative sample which until then had a
preponderance of highly intelligent individuals. Her results indicated a
high correlation with results from Binet and WISC intelligence tests;
however, 36 subjects were "untestable" on the WISC or Binet. Individuals
with low IQs (under 56) produced marked incongruities (i.e., houses or
animals upside down – without any intention) in their trays. As the IQ
level increased, trays reflected more congruent categories and added
complexity. Further, members of the hospital nursing staff were able to
identify accurately particular patients from thumb-nail descriptions of
personality and behavior given by Bowyer from her observations of the
sand trays.

The use of sand

As part of her normative research, Bowyer made a significant contribution to the sand tray literature by researching the use of sand in the
tray. During the mid-1930s and 1940s many clinicians and researchers
disregarded Lowenfeld's strong emphasis on the use of sand (Bolgar and
Fischer 1940, 1947; Bühler 1951, 1952) probably as a result of a pilot study
conducted by van Wylick (a student of Bühler's) in 1934, in which it was
found that the use of sand made no difference in her experimental results
(Bowyer 1970). Therefore, van Wylick omitted sand from the research
study she conducted two years later, which produced her developmental
norms (van Wylick 1936).

   Bowyer analyzed van Wylick's results twenty years later, believing
that the findings may have been invalidated by the small sample size

n = 50) and/or by the subjects' young ages (all were under ten years old). These possible methodological weaknesses prompted Bowyer to conduct additional research to determine if sand was an important element. In her study of 50 children and 26 adults, aged 2 to 50, Bowyer (1956) found that the constructive use of sand (i.e., the movement of sand by the client in order to build a creative product) added important dimensions: increased the richness of expression, expanded available information for analysis of the production, and gave added depth to the experience of creating the World. The medium of sand provided the opportunity for subjects to experience and express a large range of emotion through pouring, burying, and hitting the sand. Making their own constructions of hills, valleys, roads, rivers, waves, furrows, etc., deepened and enriched both the experience and interpretation. In a later study, Bowyer (1959a) also found that the constructive use of sand suggested average or above-average intelligence (most often after the age of twelve), as well as the availability of inner imaginative resources.

Comparison of World Technique with other projective approaches

In 1965 Bowyer and Huggan conducted two studies to determine if the World Technique and the Village Test were equivalent and, thus, could substitute for each other; or if they provided different information and could be used in a complementary way. The report of their findings was read in shortened form at the International Rorschach Congress in Paris (Bowyer and Huggan 1965). The full report is presented in Bowyer's (1970) *The Lowenfeld World Technique*.

For the first study, Bowyer and Huggan compared the "Worlds" and "Villages" made by each of thirty-three graduate students in psychology. The second study compared these productions to "Villages" made by twelve hospitalized neurotic patients that were similar in age to the students. Bowyer and Huggan found that both the World Technique and the Village Test have the capacity to discriminate between a clinical group and a non-clinical group; essentially, the two tests can substitute for each other when the presence or absence of a disturbance is being diagnosed. However, for deeper understanding of an individual person, they felt that both approaches should be used, for each offers opportunities for the expression of different aspects of the personality, as well as confirms or contradicts the severity of the problem.

Bowyer, Gillies and Scott (1966) reviewed the use of several projective tests with 100 deaf children: the World Technique (Lowenfeld 1979), Village Test (Arthus 1949; Mabille 1950; Mucchielli 1960), Lowenfeld Mosaic Test (Lowenfeld 1954), and two forms of Human Figure Drawing (i.e., "Draw a boy or girl" and "Draw yourself"). They found that, of the two Lowenfeld techniques (i.e., the World Technique and the Mosaic

Test), the sand tray was highly motivating with young deaf children, while the mosaics were less interesting. They further indicated that, although the World Technique was an excellent instrument for determining the emotional adjustment of deaf children, the bulk and heavy weight of its materials was a drawback to easy transport. They found that the Village Test was less heavy (light wood miniatures are placed on a square piece of felt with no sand) and can be carried by one person in a small cardboard box. In addition the same scoring principles used for the World Technique can be used with the Village Test. However, important diagnostic information is lost when sand is not used.

With regard to Human Figure drawings, the deaf children easily drew a boy or girl, but had great difficulty in drawing themselves. The authors concluded:

> In theory, the usual Human Figure drawing produces self-identification at the unconscious level; the relative ease with which our subjects undertook this task emphasizes the advantage of the true projective technique in stimulating expression, in contrast to the inhibiting effect of a direct request for a self-portrait.
>
> (Bowyer, Gillies and Scott 1966: 6)

Assessment of special populations

After many years of research on the World Technique, Bowyer was convinced that the sand tray was an excellent diagnostic instrument. She then turned to using the sand tray to assess the social and emotional adjustment of deaf and impaired-hearing children (Bowyer and Gillies 1972; Bowyer, Gillies and Scott 1966; Bowyer and Gilmour 1968; Bowyer, Marshall and Weddell 1963). Bowyer, Marshall and Weddell (1963) used the Lowenfeld World materials, along with the Lowenfeld Mosaic Patterns (Lowenfeld 1954) and the qualitative features of the Draw-A-Man test (Goodenough 1926), in a pilot study in Bristol to determine the adjustment of ten partially deaf and ten profoundly deaf children when compared to each other and to ten normal hearing children (8–10 years old). They found that these profoundly deaf children were significantly above average in adjustment when compared to normal hearing children, while the adjustment of the partially deaf children was not significantly below the normal hearing children. They concluded that further research on a larger population was necessary; this was carried out in a series of studies in Glasgow.

Bowyer and Gillies (1972) further investigated the hypothesis that partially deaf children are less well adjusted than profoundly deaf children, again using the Lowenfeld World Test and Mosaic Pattern Test to assess emotional adjustment; teacher ratings measured social behavior. A larger sample size of sixty profoundly deaf children and sixty partially deaf children (8–14 years old) was investigated. The researchers found no significant differences between the profoundly and partially deaf children. Thereafter, an in-depth study of forty of the partially deaf children, who were mainstreamed in regular elementary schools, was conducted. It was concluded that they were able to adjust comparably with hearing children, when regular contact with specialist staff was maintained.

Bowyer and Gilmour (1968) reported a study devised and carried out by Gilmour of forty deaf children in pairs (8–14 years old) and a control group of forty-one hearing children (also paired) making a Village in order to test their ability to interact and communicate. They found that the Village offered opportunities to study personal leadership and dominance in both groups. The deaf children had a larger repertory of nonverbal modes of communication, while the hearing group used almost no other mode than verbal.

CONCLUSION

Bowyer's book, *The Lowenfeld World Technique*, was a landmark contribution, chronicling most of the work that had emanated from Lowenfeld's original contribution through the late 1960s. Bowyer herself was a major contributor to this surprisingly large body of research on the sand tray. Her research results on developmental norms, evaluating trays, and special populations have provided a foundation for understanding trays and continuing research. Even today, Bowyer's interest in the sand tray continues. Her most recent publication (Pickford 1992), written in her mid-eighties, is an update of sand tray literature.

REFERENCES

Arthus, H. (1949). *Le Village: Test d'activité créatrice.* Paris: Presses Universitaires de France.

Bolgar, H. and Fischer, L.K. (1940). "The toy test: A psychodiagnostic method." *Psychological Bulletin* 37: 517–18.

—— (1947). "Personality projection in the World Test." *American Journal of Orthopsychiatry* 17: 117–28.

Bowyer, L.R. (1956). "A normative study of sand tray worlds." *Bulletin of British Psychological Society.* Summarized (1970) in L.R. Bowyer, *The Lowenfeld World Technique.* Oxford: Pergamon Press.

—— (1958). "The sand tray world as a projective technique with mental defectives." *Journal of the Midland Mental Deficiency Society* 4: 44–55.

—— (1959a). "The importance of sand in the World Technique: An experiment." *British Journal of Educational Psychology* 29: 162–4.

—— (1959b). "Two cases illustrating the emotional effects of encephalitis and meningitis in early childhood." *Scottish Medical Journal* 4: 379–85.

—— (1970). *The Lowenfeld World Technique.* Oxford: Pergamon Press.

Bowyer, L.R. and Gillies, J. (1972). "The social and emotional adjustment of deaf and partially deaf children." *British Journal of Educational Psychology* 42(3): 305–8.

Bowyer, L.R., Gillies, J. and Scott, J. (1966). "The use of projective techniques with deaf children." *Rorschach Newsletter* 11: 3–6.

Bowyer, L.R. and Gilmour, R. (1968). "Interpersonal communication of deaf children using the Village Test." In A. Friedemann, H. Phillipson, B. Scott and C. Williams (eds) *Rorschach Proceedings: VIIth International Congress of Rorschach and Other Projective Techniques, London*: 315–18. Bern, Germany: Hans Huber Publishers.

Bowyer, L.R. and Huggan, R. (1965). "A comparative study of the World and Village Techniques." *Actes du VI Congrès International du Rorschach et des Méthodes Projectives. (Proceedings of the VIth International Congress of the Rorschach and Other Projective Techniques.)* Paris. (Full report given in: Bowyer, L.R. (1970). *The Lowenfeld World Technique*. Oxford: Pergamon.)

Bowyer, L.R., Marshall, A. and Weddell, K. (1963). "The relative personality adjustment of severely deaf and partially deaf children." *British Journal of Educational Psychology* 33: 85–7.

Bühler, C. (1951). "The World Test: A projective technique." *Journal of Child Psychiatry* 2: 4–23.

—— (1952). "National differences in World Test projective patterns." *Journal of Projective Techniques* 16(1): 42–55.

Gillies, J. (1982). "The role of communicative abilities and field dependence/independence in the social adjustment of deaf children." Unpublished doctoral dissertation, University of Glasgow.

Gilmour, R. (1971). "Communication and social adjustment in young deaf children." Unpublished master's thesis, University of Glasgow.

Goodenough, F.L. (1926). *Measurement of Intelligence by Drawings*. Chicago: World Book Co.

Lowenfeld, M. (1954). *The Lowenfeld Mosaic Test*. London: Newman Meane.

—— (1979). *The World Technique*. London: George Allen & Unwin.

Mabille, P. (1950) *La Technique du Test du Village*. Paris: Presses Universitaires de France. (Reprinted: Dufour, 1970.)

Mucchielli, R. (1960) *Le Jeu du Monde et le Test du Village Imaginaire*. Paris: Presses Universitaires de France. (First chapter translated by John Hood-Williams.)

Pickford, R. (1973) (a.k.a. Ruth Bowyer). "The versatility of the World Technique." *Projective Psychology* 18: 21–31.

—— (1975) (a.k.a. Ruth Bowyer). "Expression of thoughts by means of the Lowenfeld sand tray 'World' material." In I. Jakab (ed.) *Transcultural Aspects of Psychiatric Art*: 188–92. Basel, Switzerland: Karger.

—— (1992) (a.k.a. Ruth Bowyer). "The sand tray: Update 1970–1990." *British Journal of Projective Psychology* 37(2): 26–32.

van Wylick, M. (1936). *Die Welt des Kindes in seiner Darstellung*. Vienna: Josef Eberle. (Summarized in Bowyer, L.R. (1970). *The Lowenfeld World Technique*. Oxford: Pergamon.)

Margaret Lowenfeld

Charlotte Bühler

Hedda Bolgar

Dora Maria Kalff

H. G. Wells

Erik Erikson

Laura Ruth Bowyer (Pickford)

H. G. Wells and his wife Jane, with their two young sons playing *Floor Games*

Doorway backing into
Dora Kalff's historic home

Dora Kalff's Sandplay room in her home

Margaret Lowenfeld

Liselotte Fischer

Chapter 8

Current trends

By the early 1970s many of the originators and early leaders of the sand tray movement were no longer actively working in the field. Some were elderly; others (Bolgar, Fischer and Erikson) were pursuing different interests. Lowenfeld was ill, and by this time she seldom lectured or supervised clinicians (Urwin and Hood-Williams 1988). Bühler was retired, but would occasionally lecture to graduate students (personal communication, Allen Webb, December, 1990). Both died within a few years of one another. Lowenfeld's work was continued by John Hood-Williams, who had taken over the directorship of the Institute of Child Psychology (ICP), as well as the Lowenfeld Trust; however, interest in the Lowenfeld approach had diminished; Bühler left no legacy of researchers to continue her research with the World Test.

As these prominent early pioneers in sand tray began to fade from the scene, Dora Kalff's Jungian-symbolic approach to Sandplay took center stage. Indeed, the popularity of the sand tray approach dramatically increased during the decade of the seventies due, in part, to the dedication, influence, and talents of Dora Kalff. Kalff interpreted sand tray images to therapists in a way that touched their imaginations and inspired them to pursue this work themselves. Her understanding of and ability to communicate the symbolic Jungian approach added a deeper healing dimension to the Sandplay experience. Through the impact of Kalff's worldwide presentations, her book *Sandplay* (1980), originally published in 1971, and her film *Sandspiel* (c1972), a large following of committed Sandplay therapists emerged, who continued to incorporate Sandplay into their clinical work, teaching, and writing.

Contemporary clinicians resonated to Kalff's message about the need to reconnect to forgotten aspects of the psyche. Kalff's Sandplay presentations vividly displayed the human suffering in our extraverted, technological, and materialist world in which inner experience (as well as unconscious and irrational) are attributed little space and value. Kalff's presentations showed how the spontaneous, immediate, and emotional aspects of Sandplay provided an opportunity for these neglected sides to emerge in therapy. The physical engagement with the sand (i.e., Mother Earth), as well as the opportunity to connect to the symbolic world, balanced the verbal and rational dimensions in traditional therapy. Kalff's presentations also illustrated how the Sandplay technique could heal early, preverbal wounds at any juncture of life for those who had been abused, traumatized, or neglected, while eliciting observable and tangible data (personal and archetypal) for both therapist and client.

The publication of Ruth Bowyer's book, *The Lowenfeld World Technique* (1970), also contributed to the growing professional awareness of sand tray techniques. This book, which synthesized over forty years of research and publications in the field, demonstrated a considerable worldwide interest in sand tray by both clinicians and researchers from a variety of different theoretical orientations. The publication of Bowyer's book marked the end of the early era of sand tray and passed on the legacy work of these early pioneers to the next generation.

Ironically, one of the first and most eloquent voices in sand tray technique was the last to be heard in book form. Lowenfeld's book, *The World Technique* (1979), was published after her death, at last providing easy access to her creative thinking about the World Technique.

The convergence of these three factors – the spirit and depth of Kalff's work, the foundation that Bowyer's book established, and Lowenfeld's timely book – continued to influence the popularity of the sand tray, propelling this method into the next era. Over the past twenty years, further clinical, theoretical, and research work has evolved, mainly on the Jungian Sandplay approach, rather than on the World Technique or the other sand tray methods. The following sections of this chapter present the current literature on:

1 Expansion of Kalffian Sandplay Theory;
2 Current Practice;
3 Empirical Research;
4 Use of Sandplay with Special Groups;
5 Use of Sandplay in Schools.

Some additional information is included on the current leadership of the Kalffian Sandplay Organization.

EXPANSION OF KALFFIAN SANDPLAY THEORY

Since the 1970s, theoretical emphasis has focused on consolidating, deepening, and teaching Kalff's theory. There have been several short overviews of her theoretical approach and its application (Kahn 1989; Kalff 1991; Mitchell 1987; Reed 1980; Spare 1984; Stewart 1977, 1982; Sullwold 1977, 1982; Weinrib 1991). Her basic theory has also been expanded in relation to: (a) the healing process, (b) the therapeutic power of Sandplay from a Jungian perspective, (c) the role of the therapist, (d) transference, and (e) delayed interpretation. Kalff (1980) viewed the Sandplay process as a natural therapeutic modality that facilitated the expression of the archetypal, symbolic, and intrapersonal worlds as well as addressing everyday concerns of outer reality. (See Chapter 6.) Such multi-level expression, within a free and protected space created by the therapist, promoted the manifestation of the Self through images of wholeness. Kalff believed that if the constellation of the Self did not occur in the early years (due to neglect, overanxious mothering, abusive treatment, or external influences such as war, illness, or other environmental disturbances), it could be activated at any juncture of life. It was her belief that Sandplay could facilitate this constellation. Manifestation of the Self through Sandplay trays was seen by Kalff as serving as a base for the development and strengthening of the ego–Self connection which would help the child or adult function in a more balanced and natural manner. Through Kalff's many years of observing the process, she realized that the manifestation of the Self could be activated by using Sandplay with adults as well as with children in an ongoing therapeutic process.

The healing process

Kalff considered the constellation of the Self to be a central principle in the healing process. She believed that "a healthy development of the ego can take place only as a result of manifestation of the Self, whether as a dream symbol or as a depiction in the sandbox. Such a manifestation of the Self seems to guarantee the development and consolidation of the personality" (Kalff 1980: 29). In a lecture to the Sixth International Congress of Sandplay Therapy in Japan (1988a), Kalff showed a series of slides depicting integration of the shadow and constellation of the Self through the theme of a circle (expressing totality). Other identifying aspects of these "Self Trays" included: a religious theme, a circular mandala shape, concentration of the figures in the center of the tray, and/or a union of opposites in the center of the tray. Kalff explained that, when the Self is constellated, it is accompanied by a feeling of inner harmony and a transformation of energies that evokes a numinous quality. Often, behavioral changes occur soon after a "Self Tray" as the transformed negative energies are now available to be used in developing a more integrated personality.

In other communications (1987, 1988b), Kalff cautioned that this time of the constellation of the Self is a particularly vulnerable one and she warned against termination of therapy at this particular juncture. She also noted that, after the constellation of the Self and the emergence of a renewed and strengthened ego, a shift occurs in the Sandplay process: the child or adult becomes more verbal and the sand trays become more progressive in character, suggesting a more capable and independent stance in the outer world as well as a feeling of increased centeredness internally. The client is then ready to participate in the individuation process in a more verbal and direct way.

Refining this aspect of Kalff's theory, both Weinrib (1989) and Ammann (1991) have made clear distinctions between the healing process and the process of transformation. Ammann stated that the healing process occurs within persons who have sustained a preverbal injury,

> originating before birth or in early childhood. These people suffer from a so-called disturbance of the primary relationship with the mother or mother-figures, which makes it impossible for them to grow up with a healthy trust in the world or in their own life process. The pictures and powers of undisturbed wholeness are animated and become effective through Sandplay and a healthy foundation is formed on which the new structure of the personality is built.
>
> (Ammann 1991: 4)

The process of transformation, by contrast, applies to individuals who have a fundamentally healthy and stable ego, but whose worldview is too narrow and one-sided. They may feel restless or depressed, sensing that an expansion of consciousness is necessary. Confronting the shadow, the feminine and the masculine, and encountering the Self in the sand tray disrupts old patterns and creates movement toward psychic development and individuation (Ammann 1991).

Therapeutic power of Sandplay from a Jungian perspective

Kalff's Jungian orientation allowed her to view Lowenfeld's World Technique from a deeper perspective. In addition to using it as a communication technique with children, she also saw its potential to give form to the symbolic images of the unconscious. Stewart (1982) views Kalffian Sandplay as an experiential extension of Jungian psychology. He connects Sandplay to Jung's own experiences with play, which were pivotal to Jung's discovery of the unconscious. Jung viewed his play experiences as a vast creative source of symbolic resources. Stewart likens the Sandplay experience to dream interpretation and active imagination in that they all promote the individuation process.

In giving visual shape to the images during Sandplay, the healing energies are activated. Jung himself emphasized the importance of the role symbols play in the healing process. Symbols (or miniatures in Sandplay) are reflections of images from both the personal and collective unconscious. Jung speaks extensively of the healing power of symbols: "development of the individual can be brought about only by means of symbols which represent something far in advance of himself" (Jung

1961: 293). The power of the symbol can be seen in Sandplay, as well as in dreams, fantasies, myths, and religion.

Weinrib (1983a) points out that the pictures in the tray are not only reflections of inner images, but the use of tangible images (miniatures) in turn affects the unconscious as well. Addressing the interrelationship between the conscious and the unconscious, Adams (1991) says, "Sandplay is . . . a unique process because it combines consciousness and the unconscious in the field of concrete reality" (p. 19). Working interactively with both the conscious and the unconscious contributes to the powerful force of this technique.

Bradway (1987) also analyzed the effectiveness and power of Sandplay from a Jungian perspective to ascertain those critical elements that make it effective and powerful therapeutically. Bradway, like Stewart, agrees that Sandplay is a form of active imagination, but Bradway emphasizes that the images are concrete and immediate in contrast to dream images and active imagination. According to Bradway, the critical therapeutic elements that make Sandplay a powerful tool are:

1 the use of concrete materials, such as sand, water, and miniatures;
2 the coagulative potential of these materials;
3 the freedom to be creative;
4 the feeling of being protected by a trusted, non-intrusive therapist.

Bradway explains that Sandplay provides an opportunity for the client to experience and transcend the opposites, as well as to see order emerging out of chaos. She points out that to experience one's moods and affects through Sandplay in a visible and tangible way can help to objectify and depotentiate negative images leading to a healing experience.

The power of the Sandplay technique is well recognized by those who have participated in the process of creating their own series of sand tray pictures. However, it is hard to capture the numinosity of this experience in words. The clinicians quoted above have all attempted to speak to the powerful experience of Sandplay through identifying some of its therapeutic components: expression through symbols, imaginative use of concrete materials, creation of a free and protected space by a non-intrusive therapist. With the convergence of these components, the Self – a manifestation of one's inner order – can result. Such a manifestation of the Self leads to transcendence into a new stage of development and an increased sense stability of the personality.

Role of the therapist

The importance of establishing positive therapist–client rapport has been discussed and expanded by several Sandplay clinicians. Kalff (1980) emphasized the need for the therapist to create a "free and protected" space in order for clients to express themselves in the sand. To achieve this goal, the therapist must hold two parallel attitudes: one of open- ness and acceptance (non-judgmental understanding), so that self- expression is safe; the other attitude must be protective, so that clients stay within their own natural limits (Kalff 1988b). Weinrib added that the "free and protected" space has both physical and psychological dimen- sions. The physical dimensions are the sand tray itself, which is both limited and contained, along with the finite number of miniatures. The "emotional and psychological free and protected space is provided by the personality of the therapist as the psychological container and protector of the process" (Weinrib 1983a: 29).

Kalff maintains that the therapeutic process is directed by the Self, and that these processes are largely unconscious. Therefore, it is the principal focus of the therapist to organize the environment to facilitate and support the Self in initiating its own renewal. Kiepenheuer likens this space created by the therapist – where individuals play, create, and reveal – to the alchemist's term *vas hermeticum*, suggesting an environment where there is "loving harmony, but also . . . strong confrontations with oneself" (Kiepenheuer 1991: 47).

The process tends to choose its own direction, to have its own goals, and to take its own time. The role of the therapist is to support the process, not lead or direct it anywhere in particular. Kalff writes that the analyst follows the game of the child. To follow this game requires that the therapist have some knowledge and awareness of the symbolic world as well as the external world of the client. "Among the various activities of the therapist . . . is the understanding of those processes, expressed sym- bolically in the material produced by the child, which are 'aiming at wholeness'" (Carmody 1985: 81).

The importance of the feeling connection between therapist and client has been discussed from several different perspectives. Kalff (1987) spoke of it as the "synchronistic moment," in which there is an intuitive link between the therapist and the client through which they both simul- taneously experience the client's inner situation as it is revealed in the tray. This synchronistic moment is one of deep recognition (the aha moment) and one of nonverbal knowing. Bradway (1979b: 37) views this as the "ultimate therapeutic moment."

Hayao Kawai, a Japanese Jungian analyst and Professor at Kyoto University, speaks of the connection between therapist and client in terms of transference that occurs on the Hara level (Kawai 1985) by which direct, nonverbal communication passes from the center (Hara) of one person to the center of the other person. In the Japanese view, Hara is a continuous, nonverbal process, while Kalff's synchronistic moment is a series of separate moments, each generating its own awareness. Although Kalff viewed the Hara process as a valuable concept, she believed that the

Western psyche needed more cognitive awareness than the Hara process provided (Kalff 1983).

Transference

The issue of transference in child therapy has historically been exceedingly controversial. Anna Freud believed that, since the child was in the process of developing a mother–child relationship, transference (i.e., transferring of client's feelings and behavior that have been generated by early experiences with significant others onto the therapist) was not a central issue in the therapeutic process with young children. Melanie Klein, on the other hand, believed that the analysis of transference was critical in understanding infantile traumas and deprivations and that children were ripe for analysis of the transference because the child was currently in the grip of the living experience of the mother–child interaction.

Lowenfeld held yet another view on transference. She wanted the client's central transference to be to the sand tray and the materials themselves. She felt that the client–therapist transference relationship interfered with this. In order to minimize personal transference to the therapist and maximize the transference to the materials, Lowenfeld regularly reassigned children to a different therapist in the midst of treatment (Urwin and Hood-Williams 1988). Lowenfeld viewed the therapist's role to be one of facilitating the child's own personal understanding of his or her sand tray creation; transference to the therapist rather than to the materials thus interfered with the child's understanding of the tray (Lowenfeld 1939). Lowenfeld believed that what the child created in the sand tray was a direct confrontation with him/ herself; therefore, there was little need for therapist interpretation, although the therapist might ask questions to elicit the child's understanding of the drama being enacted in the sand. Yet, as unwavering as Lowenfeld appeared to be on this subject, when she was confronted by Klein (Lowenfeld 1939) regarding her view on transference, Lowenfeld responded in a conciliatory manner by acknowledging that child–therapist transference did take place and had a part in the therapeutic process.

Dora Kalff's attitude toward transference was influenced by Jung's view of analysis, which was as a "dialectical process," implying that both participants (client and therapist) were involved in a two-way interaction in which the therapist could not come from a position of authority for she or he was 'in' treatment just as was the client. It was the therapist's development as a person, rather than of their knowledge, that would ultimately be decisive in the treatment (Samuels 1986). Jung also believed that, in the transference, the therapist stands in relation to the client both as a person and as a projection of an inner content.

Bradway (1991) points out that Kalff did not refer to transference in the classical sense of transferring old feelings onto the therapist. For the most part it was only indirectly that Kalff spoke of transference issues. For Kalff, "transference was the providing of space for the realization of one's potential" (Bradway 1991: 25). It was primarily the positive aspect of the transference, rather than the negative one, that received Kalff's attention.

Kalff believed that if a therapist could create a "free and protected space," this would facilitate a positive transference to the therapist which might, in turn, enhance the constellation of the Self. Kalff said:

> It is the therapist's task to give shape to such a space: a free space in which the client feels fully accepted. It is a space protected by the fact that the sandplay therapist recognizes the patient's boundaries. The therapist becomes a trusted person. In this way negative or destructive tendencies are not suppressed but are portrayed and transformed.
>
> (Kalff 1991: 12)

Over time Kalff's ideas on transference evolved to include that the relationship between client and therapist was sometimes directly expressed in the tray. Kalff began to see how the Sandplay creations themselves often directly referred to the client–therapist relationship. For example, a miniature chosen by a client might depict feelings that the client had toward the therapist.

Bradway notes that the placement of significant figures or the orientation of figures in the tray may be related to where the therapist is sitting in relation to the tray. "A journey in the tray may be directed toward that corner or a gun may be aimed in my direction" (1992: 28). More explicit manifestations of transference in Sandplay occur when clients identify a particular object as the therapist or when the therapist is asked to participate and enact a specific role in the Sandplay drama. In addition, some clients may place two similar miniatures together, which could portray feelings about the transference (Friedman 1989).

Among Sandplay therapists, there is an ever widening recognition that other aspects of the Sandplay process allude to the transference. For example, when:

1 the use of Sandplay is either resisted or too easily accommodated;
2 the Sandplay picture is either openly shared or hidden from the therapist's view;
3 the miniatures are treated uniquely (e.g., destroyed, stolen, envied, valued); or
4 the therapist's miniature collection is criticized, praised, or compared to another's collection.

Weinrib (1983a) offers an example of how the sand tray can become a transitional object, as defined by D.W. Winnicott (1975). The sand tray enables the person's development away from the identification with the therapist into a more independent state. She observes:

the transference moves at least partially from the person of the therapist to the sand tray as it (the sand tray) becomes an independent object. Not infrequently patients report that they consciously carry an image of the sand tray in their minds (instead of a picture of the therapist). They may focus on and re-experience some part of a picture they have made, or change it, or they may make imaginary new pictures which they often then create in reality at the next opportunity.

Weinrib continues:

Sometimes the transference seems to include both the person of the therapist and the sand tray. Another patient who lived a long distance away and could fly in for therapy just once a month said, "It's O.K. I carry the tray in my head and play things out in it and I feel better."

(Weinrib 1983a: 52–3)

This discussion encompasses some of the current views regarding transference in the sand tray. Understanding these views can widen and deepen awareness of the quality of the work, including an understanding of the underlying relationship between the therapist and the client.

Delayed interpretation

Weinrib (1983b) highlights that aspect of the theory which emphasizes the critical importance of delaying the interpretation of the Sandplay production until there is an internal readiness, even though it may be difficult to remain silent in this case. Weinrib quotes Jung (1953: 51) regarding the difficulty of following this approach: "to let the unconscious go its own way and to experience it as a reality is something beyond the courage and capacity of the average [person]." In discussing the appropriate time for interpretation, Weinrib notes that readiness often is not indicated "until after the Self has been constellated and the renewed ego . . . emerges" (Weinrib 1983b: 127–8). She explains that: "To press for associations would be to encourage cerebral activity, which is not desirable here except in its most spontaneous exercise, because it is a basic premise of sandplay that psychological healing is emotional in nature and not cerebral" (1983b: 121).

For Weinrib, delayed interpretation does not mean that the therapist never comments about the scenes. In fact, the role of the Sandplay therapist is to be an empathic observer and listener who is also familiar with developmental stages as they unfold in the scenes. This knowledge enables the therapist to identify more clearly moments for intervention. The skilled therapist can also use the cues from clients' scenes as an indicator of unconscious themes that need highlighting in the verbal therapy. Since personal associations to symbols are so critical, Sandplay therapists often discuss this area with clients.

When the client is ready to discuss their productions, Ammann (1991: 5) noted that she has had "the impressive experience with many analysands that after the process has run its course – which can, however, take months – they themselves are capable of interpreting their sand pictures meaningfully. They have experienced the healing power which has resulted from their creative activity and this experience has affected inner growth and maturation." This later viewing of the Sandplays is a time of understanding and acceptance of growth and change.

CURRENT PRACTICE

Issues regarding professional/personal develpment, Sandplay environment, introduction of Sandplay to clients, and deciphering the trays have been discussed extensively. The following section surveys each of these issues in light of current practice.

Professional and personal development

There is a strong emphasis on the need for specialized training, both personally and professionally, before using the technique with clients (Kalff 1988c). Experiencing a personal, in-depth Sandplay process with a qualified Sandplay therapist is particularly important in order to have first-hand knowledge of the power of this technique. In fact, founding members of the ISST feel that completing one's own Sandplay process is more important than any other aspect of the training (Kay Bradway, personal communication, January 25, 1993). In addition to having achieved basic professional training and competence in the general practice of psychotherapy, training in Sandplay also involves attending special classes and workshops, as well as participating in consultation groups and individual supervision in this specialized field.

Development of the Sandplay environment

During training in Sandplay, therapists begin to create a Sandplay environment, collecting miniatures, making or buying trays, and organizing space. Following Kalff's model, two trays are usually made available for clients, one with moist sand and the other with dry sand. The interior of both trays is painted blue to give the impression of water or sky when the sand is brushed aside. Many Sandplay therapists use a sand tray that adheres to Kalff's recommended size of 28½ × 19½ inches with a depth of 3 inches; this dimension allows the client to view the tray in one glance without moving the head.

Miniatures are typically displayed on open shelves rather than closeted in cabinet drawers (Hegeman 1992). Therapists are no longer

concerned that clients will become overwhelmed by a vast array of miniatures, as were those in the earlier days of Margaret Lowenfeld's work.
Long experience has proven that clients appear to find value in having a
wide display to survey, and therapists have observed that clients often are
drawn to particular miniatures as well as meaningful themes that emerge
in the moment. Contrary to earlier therapists who often limited their
collections to between 150 and 300 miniatures, contemporary Sandplay
therapists have larger collections which allow opportunity for a greater
variety of symbolic themes.

Introduction of Sandplay to clients

In contrast to Lowenfeld's lengthy introduction of the "World Technique" to
clients, the current trend is toward a brief introduction followed by an
invitation to use the materials. Kalff invites the client to "look over the
shelves until you find something that speaks to you and put it in the tray and
then add to it as you wish" (Bradway 1981b: 134). Bradway (1981b), by
contrast, uses Kalff's instructions occasionally, but more often allows instructions to emerge out of the specific circumstances of each new introduction.
Her goal is to create a relaxed atmosphere that facilitates the creative
imagination while not overstimulating intellectual and verbal capacities.

Children usually respond quite naturally and spontaneously to using
the materials. However, adults may express reluctance and discomfort in
this unfamiliar environment. Understanding and support usually enable
the adult client to relax and participate with greater ease in the Sandplay
process. Teenagers often view the tray with skepticism and/or hostility,
believing that they are being given a child's task of playing with toys.
Reassurance that they are not being treated as children is often necessary.
For example, a therapist might emphasize its beneficial use with adults
while playing down its use as a play therapy technique.

Deciphering of trays

Today the majority of trained therapists using sand trays base their interpretation and understanding of the trays on Kalff's views, which are the
result of many complex factors: her long history of using Sandplay, her
Jungian training, the influence of Neumann's developmental theories, her
work with Lowenfeld, her many years of study of Eastern philosophies,
and her own highly developed intuitive capacities. Kalff's model provides a general theoretical understanding of trays (see Chapter 6), rather
than identifying specific guidelines.

In order to make individualized interpretations, most Sandplay therapists
draw upon all of their psychological training and abilities, including theoretical understanding, knowledge of symbolism, observation of the process,

intuition, and empathy. The current trend seems to be moving away from a rigid reliance on specific rules, which are confining and limiting.

In surveying the current Sandplay literature, five main considerations dominate the field:

1 *How the sand tray is created.* A great deal of therapeutic and diag- nostic information can be gleaned from the manner in which the client creates his or her sand picture.

   a How interested or resistant is the client in making the tray?
   b Is a wet or dry tray chosen (Bradway 1981b; Dundas 1978; Maclay 1970; Thompson 1981)?
   c Where does the client stand in relation to the tray (Weinrib 1987)?
   d How are sand and water used (e.g., is the sand molded or mani- pulated, how much water is added, and what is moistened) (Tatum 1991; Thompson 1981)?
   e In what manner are miniatures placed in the tray (e.g., how decisively, with enthusiasm, reluctance, fast or slow paced, does the client change his/her mind regarding placement of miniatures, does the client continually move objects, which miniatures are not used and replaced on the shelves) (Dundas 1978)?
   f Does the picture come to a conclusion or is it a tray "in process," (i.e., dynamic, constantly changing) (Rhinehart and Engelhorn 1986)?
   g What variations of mood can be observed as the client creates a picture?
   h What verbal comments are made during the experience regarding the final story (if given) and any feeling responses to the tray (Thompson 1981)?

2 *The content of the tray.* The therapist studies a variety of data in order to understand the psychological communication in the tray:

   a The symbolic meaning of the objects (Capitolo 1992; Gradwell 1992; Jackson 1991; Kalff 1980; Millikan 1992). For example, with the placement of a frog in the sand tray, a therapist may consider its transformative aspects (i.e., it lives both on water and land and goes through changes from a tadpole to a frog), in addition to its mytho- logical use in stories (e.g., where a prince changes into a frog and then back again into a prince).
   b Use and placement of miniatures. This includes noticing how few or how many miniatures are used, the direction the miniatures are facing (Bradway 1981b), whether objects are placed close to or far from the client (Aite 1978), incongruities (Furth 1988; Pickford 1975), connections between items in the tray (Bradway 1981b), use of opposites (Bradway 1981b; Stewart 1981), similar placement of the same miniature in subsequent trays.

c Shapes that emerge out of the use of sand and miniatures. This includes noticing shapes that resemble other things (particularly body parts), shapes that isolate one part of a tray, shapes that connect one area or miniature to another, and shapes that are incongruent (Kalff 1979).

d The literal and representational use of the five elements: air, water, earth, fire, and wind (Amatruda 1991; Baldridge 1990; Berry 1989; Bradway 1985; Cunningham 1991; Friedman 1991; Kalff 1987; McNally 1984; Tatum 1991).

e Developmental stage indicated in the tray: for example, Neumann's (1973) vegetative, fighting, and collective stages, Piagetian stages (Jones 1986), Eriksonian stages (1963).

f Overall organization of tray: is the tray used vertically, horizontally, or diagonally; how empty or full is the tray; the use of space; the appearance of organization and chaos; how rigid or fluid is the tray; barriers in the tray; edging and enclosures; consideration of the diagonals, especially in the corners (Kalff 1988b); how is the center of the tray used; use of specific quadrants; balance or imbalance of items; connections between opposites (Bradway 1979a); the depiction of conflict in the tray; odd or unusual organization or representation (Furth 1988); static versus dynamic connotations (Bradway 1992).

3 *Developmental perspective of a series of trays.* In viewing a series of trays the therapist is alert to the evolutionary quality (progressive or regressive) emerging in the trays as well as the level of the unconscious, personal or archetypal that has been evoked (Weinrib 1989). Observing this developmental process with the following questions in mind can be helpful:

a Is movement present in the tray, where previously only a static quality existed?

b Is there an increasing quality of balance and centeredness (Bradway 1987; Bowyer 1970)?

c Is there a change in the placement and role of a central object over time?

d Have one or more themes unfolded?

e Have themes or situations birthed (emerged), transformed (changed), or died (disappeared)?

f Has the symbolic content changed (Bradway 1979a)?

g Is there a perseverating quality about the tray (Bradway 1979a)?

4 *The Sandplay story.* The client may tell a spontaneous story either during the creation of the sand picture or at its conclusion. A careful listening to the symbolic content, emotional overtones, theme, and story resolution may give additional insights to the client's internal process (Kawai 1992).

5 *The therapist's feeling response.* An important aspect to be considered is the therapist's personal feeling response during the creation of the tray. This feeling response can give further depth and information that needs to be considered. The therapist's feeling response, as well as spontaneous images that emerge in the therapist's mind, should be encouraged rather than dismissed, even though to the intellect these may at first seem irrelevant. Kalff consistently asked herself upon viewing a tray: "How does this make me feel?" "What impression does the picture give me, what strikes me first about the tray?" (Kalff 1988b). For example, a therapist may experience feelings of incongruence when watching a client make a "pretty" tray while experiencing it as superficial. The totality of the client's experience may not ring true to the therapist. The reality of these feelings needs to be included in the understanding of the tray.

Currently, there is considerable interest and discussion about the significance of the information gleaned from initial trays (Avrech, in press; Crable 1976). Pickford (1975), a colleague of Lowenfeld, contends that a person's special problem is often stated in his or her first world, although Lowenfeld herself did not accord initial trays any sense of special import. Kalff (1988b) differs from Lowenfeld, contending that a first Sandplay can indicate:

1 how the client feels about therapy;
2 their relation to the unconscious;
3 the personal problem;
4 a possible solution.

Friedman (1987) has suggested the following questions as useful guidelines when viewing a first tray:

1 Where are the energy spots?
2 Where are the trouble spots?
3 What kind of groupings are apparent?
4 What types of problems are indicated in the tray?
5 Are there sources of strength or help in the tray?

Weinrib (1989) warns that sometimes a first tray is "just pretty" (a persona tray), but that the second tray may go "right down." For example, some clients willfully select figures and create a scene that represents specific events or personal characteristics they want the therapist to note. This may continue for a short time; however, usually with the second tray, the descent into the deeper realm of the psyche begins.

One of the current issues under discussion in understanding trays is how much weight to give to quadrant theory. Quadrant theory divides the tray into four parts, which are seen as representing opposites (such as mother/father, conscious/unconscious, personal/collective unconscious). Some therapists (including Kalff in her later years) are increasingly hesitant about dividing the tray into quadrants and categorizing them compartmentally rather than viewing the picture as a unified whole (Furth 1988; Kalff 1988b). It is generally accepted that a full understanding of the tray is not facilitated by a "recipe" approach in which trays are analyzed from such a limited perspective. Several therapists, however, see some value in using quadrant theory as a first step in understanding otherwise overwhelming material (Aite 1978; Ammann 1991; Ryce-Menuhin 1992; Weinrib 1983a; Zeller 1979).

EMPIRICAL RESEARCH

Kalff's long years of dedicated teaching and development of a Sandplay theory have just begun to stimulate interest in empirical research. Until recently, Kalff and her followers have avoided quantitative and controlled methods for understanding the tray, choosing instead a more subjective exploration of the symbolic meaning behind the selected figures and movement in the scenes. No specific or organized guidelines for understanding trays have as yet been developed. However, several studies have begun to address the various issues involved in the Sandplay process; others have sought a diagnostic approach despite the fact that the idea of diagnosis is antithetical to Kalff's approach.

Using a variety of investigative approaches, these studies range from those that are empirically based with large sample size (Jones 1986; Volcani *et al.* 1982) to surveys assessing how Sandplay is used currently (Miller 1982), to idiosyncratic case studies that have been approved for inclusion in the ISST archives. Some researchers have been intrigued by specific symbols or configurations in the sand (Abel 1985; Hedberg 1988). Other researchers focus more on the validity of the sand tray technique itself (Fujii 1979), while yet others are attempting to understand the similarities and differences in a particular population (Bradway 1979b; Stewart 1981).

This section surveys the current empirical research published in English on the sand tray since 1970. The amount of published research in the field is small with only a few studies giving depth consideration to this subject, yet the findings of these few scholarly researchers are significant while also pointing to the need for further research.

Reliability of Sandplay technique

Fujii (1979) posed two questions in conducting a reliability study using the sand tray:

1 Can judges correctly identify which group (i.e., elementary school, junior high school, delinquent, and emotionally disturbed) produced the sand tray pictures?

2 Do sand trays have sufficient reliability so that observers can identify
   which ones are made by the same person over a period of time?

Fujii's subjects were adolescent boys from four groups: elementary school
(12 years old), junior high school (13–14 years old), delinquent (13–15
years old), and emotionally disturbed (10–12 years old). There were five
boys in each of the four groups, all of whom had been randomly selected
from four other larger groups.

Each boy created two sand tray pictures, two to four weeks apart. The
boys were simply instructed to "make anything you like with these toys
and sand in this box. There is no time limit. When you are finished, tell
me" (Fujii 1979: 22). Conventional sand trays and miniatures were available. After the Sandplay was completed, a photograph was taken.

The sand tray pictures were examined by ten judges: five experienced
sand tray therapists and five graduate students majoring in educational
psychology who had no clinical experience with Sandplay. Experienced
judges were able to determine in which of the four groups (elementary,
junior high, delinquent, or emotionally disturbed) the photos belonged
($p < .05$ level of significance), and all five experienced judges and three of
the inexperienced judges were able to match at far beyond chance level
($p < .01$) the initial sand tray with one made two to four weeks later by the
same boy; however, the experienced judges were far better able to match
an initial sand tray with the later one ($p < .05$).

Another test–retest reliability study was conducted by the same
researcher, now using the last name of Aoki (1981). Her methods and
materials were similar to her original 1979 study. She did not use judges
in this study, but instead compared tray-making behavior of the four
groups creating two trays. She found that the juvenile delinquent group
took a significantly ($p < .05$) longer time before starting their tray than the
other groups, while the emotionally disturbed boys took a significantly
($p < .05$) longer period of time in actually making their trays. Her findings
with regard to the use of sand were interesting: none of the boys in the
junior high group used sand, while five boys in the elementary school
group dug sand to the bottom of the tray to make rivers, ponds, and seas.
The two maladjusted groups of boys dug sand or drew boundary lines
only with finger tips and were more hesitant about using sand compared
to the elementary school group. The overall results of the study suggested
that the sand tray technique is reliable, with expressions of the maladjusted groups more stable than the adjusted groups. Aoki hypothesized that the maladjusted groups persisted in their way of expression
because of the overriding urgency to express their problems, which may
have inhibited their creative processes.

The effect of children's age on their use of miniatures

Kamp and Kessler (1970) studied how the chronological and mental ages of children affect the way in which they organized miniatures in a given space. They researched four age-groups (6, 7, 8, and 9), each consisting of 5 normal public school children (n = 20) in Topeka, Kansas. The children were offered a total of 431 miniatures to use on a 36" tall rectangular table with one rounded end (approximately 30" × 47").

The developmental level of each child's "World" was determined by using a scale with four stages. In descending order, these stages were:

1 *Realistic scenes* (more than two types of miniatures arranged in a specific way so they could function in reality in a similar arrangement). For example, a car is depicted driving over a bridge that is placed over water, which leads to a house with a family standing outside.
2 *Depictive configurations* (less realistic connections between miniatures). For example, although the scene contains houses, trees, people, and cars, there are no clearly differentiated streets and the cars are all moving in one direction. The overall configuration is too diffuse to be considered realistic.
3 *Schematic configurations* (elements belonging together in only a general way). These productions are more depictive than those in previous categories; the relationships are less defined, and the miniatures are often lined up in rows. For example, there may be an arrangement of trees representing a forest, but the trees would either be lined up in rows or spread diffusely throughout the tray.
4 *Juxtapositional configurations* (miniatures distributed diffusely over a part or whole of the tray in a non-representational manner). A child may be deliberate or thoughtful in placing and naming the toys, but the arrangement does not seem to be determined by what the toys represent.

Kamp and Kessler (1970) found that although most of the children had elements of all the categories in their productions, the child's age was an indicator of what level was used primarily. The youngest children (age 6) produced scenes in the juxtaposition and schematic categories (none of their scenes was in the realistic category); the oldest children (age 9) produced depictive scenes, with some elements of schematic and realistic categories (none of their scenes reflected the juxtaposition category).

The researchers also found that, even though chronological age was more important than mental age in determining which of the four configurations would be used most in the production, intelligence did influence the type of configuration used. More intelligent children achieved a higher developmental level (i.e., they scored closer to the Realistic Configuration level) than same-aged children who were lower in intelligence.

Kamp and Kessler also found that even with younger children, a great deal of movement in the World (dramatically playing in the sand instead of making a static picture) was related to poor adjustment. Their findings seemed to parallel those of Bühler (1951a); both studies found that enclosure of the World or large areas of the World often indicated emotional maladjustment. In addition, the omission of people seemed to suggest disturbance in interpersonal relationships. Gender differences were also noted: girls used more types of elements than boys (more animals, indoor toys, and people). This finding supports Erikson's observation (1951) that girls are more drawn to elements that represent inner space rather than outer elements.

The effect of children's age and mental health on use of miniatures

Kamp, Ambrosius and Zwaan (1986) were interested in the influence of age differences on the play configurations of normal children (comparison group) and children in psychiatric residential treatment (psychiatric group). They studied 30 children ranging in age from 10.3 to 11.6 years. Fifteen children were under residential psychiatric treatment, while the remaining fifteen were from an elementary school in Topeka, Kansas. The children in the elementary school group were matched with children in the residential treatment group on age and sex.

The equipment consisted of 328 miniature toys. The table was rectangular on one side and round at the other (76 cm × 109 cm long). Each child made one arrangement, which was scored for 15 pathological signs (some of which were similar to Bühler's [1951b] pathological signs).

Results indicated that the psychiatric group had more pathological signs (p < .05) than did the comparison group of children. The psychiatric group used less than 50 elements, had one category of miniatures predominating, used less than five categories, did not use soldiers or people, did not follow the table form, used proximal placements (all elements placed within one-third of the area of table surface), used more fences, and moved toys more than 40 per cent of the time. Children in the comparison group, by contrast, used significantly more human beings, soldiers, animals, buildings, indoor equipment (p < .01), and outdoor equipment (p < .02).

Five children in the comparison group produced one or two pathological signs. In order to better understand the relevance of this particular finding, a sociogram was administered to the comparison group. The significant findings (p < .01) of the sociogram indicated that four out of the five children who had one or two pathological signs were never chosen on any scale by the other children. It appeared that these children had no social role at all, not even a negative one.

Intelligence did not appear to be a significant factor in this study. In comparing children with IQs greater than 100 (n=20) with those having IQs lower than 100 (n=8), no difference was found in the number of pathological signs. Thus, Kamp, Ambrosius, and Zwaan found significant differences between disturbed and normal children with regard to their choice and use of miniatures in the tray. Normal children's trays appeared richer, fuller, and less blocked, while disturbed children's trays were less well defined and seemed incomplete.

Piagetian stages in children's Sandplay

Jones (1986) questioned if a child's age is related to the types of pictures produced. She also questioned the relationships between age differences and their consistency with Piaget's developmental principles and chronological stages.

Jones analyzed the initial sand worlds of 185 children ranging in age from 11 months to 18 years. The sample included 10 children (5 boys and 5 girls) at each age level, except for the one-year-old category in which there were 15 children (6 girls and 9 boys). The children were predominantly Caucasian from middle- and upper-middle-class families.

Traditional Sandplay equipment was used with a wide selection of miniatures. The oldest children were asked to "make a world," while the youngest children were told that they could "play in the sand." The children's play was recorded on the following dimensions: the figures used, the sequence in which they were chosen, comments and actions of the child, movement of the figures, use of the sand, interaction with the observer, and total production (recorded by both diagram and photograph) to later determine if the productions were consistent with Piagetian stages.

Three therapists were trained to score the collected data on scales that measured comprehensive and generalized evaluations of the sand worlds as well as on checklists of more specific evaluations. One checklist evaluated sand use, another focused on sand formations. Other scales and checklists measured the placement and the relationship configurations of the miniatures. In addition, two general scales were used to evaluate the use of sand and figures. The "World View" Scale was used to evaluate the whole sand and miniature structure according to Piaget's cognitive and developmental principles and the percentage of tray used. The scales and checklists all had a high degree of rater reliability. The data were analyzed statistically with regard to age and sex.

The results of this study established a body of evidence that supported the assumption that the structure of children's creative expression in Sandplay is consistent with Piaget's principles and chronological stages of cognitive development. Structural complexity of the sand worlds increased with age in accordance with Piaget's developmental sequences.

Observing sand worlds of children who fell within Piaget's developmental stages, Jones found that in *Stage I (0–1 years)*, children constructed sand worlds with the following similarities:

1 No evidence of a world view or a cohesive perspective, parts and themes are scattered and fragmentary;
2 Worlds extend beyond the boundaries of the tray, few figures (25 per cent or less) are within the tray;
3 Figures are placed side-by-side while orientation is unintentional;
4 Little sense of focus or physical coordination, resulting in figures that are heaped and scattered across the room as well as the tray;
5 Relationship between figures is "bizarre" and "highly subjective";
6 Sand is dropped and thrown inside and outside the tray – figures are plunged in and out of it;
7 No boundaries are created within the tray by groupings of figures.

Stage II (2–4 years old)
1 There is an emerging sense of perspective with the sand world in which momentary situations and partial connections are depicted. However, there is still a chaotic massing of figures;
2 Most of the figures are placed within the boundaries of the tray, but often figures are also placed outside. Most of the tray is generally used in this stage, but it is not uncommon to have only part of the tray used as well;
3 Use and orientation of figures may be either intentional or un-intentional, depending upon involvement in simple dramatic play;
4 Sand is used primarily for burying and unburying figures, which may result in a vague sense of boundary through this simple dramatic play;
5 Although figures are not used explicitly to create boundaries, bound-aries may appear without apparent intentionality.

Stage III (5–7 years old)
1 There is a sense of a partial construction that is neither entirely global nor diffuse and that reflects the beginnings of various relationships;
2 The sand world is generally created within the boundaries of the tray, occupying between 91 per cent to 100 per cent of the tray;
3 Two figures are deliberately oriented as well as interpersonally and functionally related;
4 When there are more than two figures, dramatic grouping is a simple one (such as two witches around a caldron);
5 Dramatic action between figures is clear through placement, action, and relationship between figures;
6 Sand is used to create permanent structures and clear, though diffuse, boundaries, even though somewhat diffuse;
7 Boundaries created by figures are simple ones (such as baby animals grouped together with mothers nearby).

Stage IV (8–12 years old)
1 There is a coherent world view, often with a single concrete theme which brings together simple parts. Objects are grouped in meaningful

relationships that include a sense of symmetry (such as a holiday theme without the complexity and richness that older children and adults might include);

2 The figures are entirely within the tray and 91 to 100 per cent of the tray is used;
3 The orientation of the figures is intentional, and scale and placement become important;
4 Some dramatic play still remains, usually centering around the co-operation between figures;
5 There is increased complexity of classification in which, for example, human neighborhoods are clearly portrayed;
6 There is some simple sand construction, although sand is generally left untouched;
7 Either boundaries are defined by figures that are somewhat clear, or there are no boundary figures present.

Stage V (13–18 years old)
1 Symbolic as well as realistic worlds are formed, characterized by: (a) a single theme encompassing complex parts that may not be completely integrated; (b) an abstract theme uniting seemingly unrelated figures; or (c) a single clear theme with parts exhibiting interdependence and integration;
2 The figures are entirely within the tray and 91 to 100 per cent of the tray is used;
3 Intentional orientation of figures is clear – figures are altered (placed in seated or prone positions to increase the drama, for example) and bridges over water are used;
4 No dramatic play is used; groups of figures are complexly organized in a creative way to show dramatic movement;
5 Figures displaying the human community are clearly established or an integrated, lone figure may be used;
6 Sand is extensively used to create land and water forms, as well as boundaries;
7 Boundaries are also created by well-coordinated groupings of minia-tures, which may relate to a complex world.

Jones' study also suggested that the fundamental process of structuring sand worlds is similar for girls and boys, with two important exceptions. First, fewer boys used the sand, especially between the ages of seven and thirteen, which coincides with the period of peer identification and the beginning of operational thinking. Jones proposed that this finding suggested that the process of separation from the mother is more difficult for boys than for girls – an idea which resonates with Kalff's belief (1980) that work with the sand is related to "Mother Earth," the realm of instinct, nature, and the feminine.

The second important finding was that there is a significant difference between boys and girls in how miniatures were used to display relation-ships in their dramatic play. Boys tended to engage in confron- tative play and to represent that confrontation with a dynamic style (especially in Stages II and III), while girls tended to focus on both dyadic relationships and family interactions emphasizing cooperation (especially beginning in Stage III). There were also indications that boys created fewer bodies of water than girls and, also, in contrast to the girls, the boys created no islands. This male tendency toward aggressive play and the female tendency toward more intimate, cooperative play was consistent with previous findings on children's play constructions by Erikson (1951).

Jones concluded that the results of her study supported both Piaget and Jung's belief that there is a central organizing principle which deter-mines the development of the human psyche.

Comparison of MMPI scores to adult Sandplay products

The aim of Denkers' (1985) research was to test the scoring system developed by Jones for its diagnostic and assessment capabilities in measuring adult Sandplay productions. Using Jones' scale, Denkers analyzed the photographic slides of 74 initial sand worlds made by pre-dominantly Caucasian, college-educated, middle-class subjects ranging in age from 18 to 50 (38 males and 36 females). The scores derived were compared to the same subjects' scores on the clinical scales of the Minne-sota Multiphasic Personality Inventory (MMPI).

Results indicated that Jones' scoring system was a valid diagnostic tool for evaluating adult sand world constructions. Her findings strongly suggested that Sandplay measurement is a highly sensitive barometer of psychological disorders in both males and females. Some of her corre-lations were:

1 Females with a high score on the Depression Scale of the MMPI were significantly ($p < .05$) less likely to create boundaries by figure grouping;
2 Females scoring low on the MMPI Social Introversion Scale (i.e., those who feel comfortable in social participation and emotional expression) used significantly ($p < .05$) more of the sand tray. Denkers suggests that the amount of the sand tray used is a good indicator of psychological well-being;
3 Females with a high Social Introversion score on the MMPI tended to use less than 91 per cent of the space of the tray ($p < .05$);
4 Females with high scores on the MMPI Psychopathic Deviate Scale were significantly more likely to place figures behind one another for protection or concealment ($p < .05$);
5 Contrary to Jones' finding about boys' use of sand (in Piaget's Stage II to Stage IV), Denkers found that the use of sand by adult men did not

differ from adult women. Males who scored high on the Hypochondriasis Scale tended to ignore the sand (p < .05);

6 Females who had low scores (p < .05) on the MMPI Social Introversion Scale (socially extraverted women) were able to depict confrontation in their sand worlds;

7 Males with a significantly high score on the MMPI Paranoia Scale had sand worlds that depicted "implied cooperation" and "complex cooperation," suggesting that these individuals were especially sensitive to interpersonal issues and to detecting complex nuances of social interaction. These characteristics are often associated with people having this personality profile;

8 Males with a high score on the MMPI Schizophrenia Scale depicted a significantly (p < .05) high level of "simple cooperation" in their sand worlds, indicating that males with schizophrenia are able to portray cooperative relationships between the miniature figures in their sand worlds, albeit in a simple manner;

9 Significantly fewer males than females (with the exception of males with high scores on the MMPI Psychopathic Deviate Scale) depicted "complex combinations" of relationships in their sand worlds.

Some interesting findings that were not statistically significant but may be relevant to understanding Sandplay are:

1 More females than males related figures to water. Since water is a symbol of the unconscious realm, this finding suggested that females may find more socially recognized means to access the unconscious realm;

2 The absence of vegetation items may be clinically predictive of psychological distress in females;

3 Females tended to use more figures (including animals, vegetation, and natural elements) in their sand worlds, while males included more humans, although more males than females excluded humans altogether.

Denkers ends her study with the conclusion that "the world of creative expression found in Sandplay is structured by coherent patterns . . . at each stage of development" (Denkers 1985: 176). She asserts her belief that Sandplay is an excellent diagnostic tool for psychological disorders as well as a reliable marker of developmental stages.

Effectiveness of Sandplay in eliciting fantasy play

Volcani, Stollak, Ferguson and Benedict (1982) investigated two pertinent therapeutic questions: Does Sandplay elicit fantasy behaviors that can be measured? Is fantasy play in the sand tray linked to parents' perceptions of their own child-rearing behaviors? Ten normal functioning Caucasian first-born boys (ages 7 to 9) from urban upper-middle-class, two-parent families were individually videotaped making three sandplays over a two-week period. In addition, the children's parents completed two inventories regarding their perceptions of their care-giving behaviors (Child Rearing Concerns and Practices Inventory [Green 1975] and Schaeffer's Children's Report of Parental Behavior Inventory [Schaeffer 1965; Armentrout and Burger 1972]).

Comparisons of Sandplay and the parents' test results showed that behavior could be measured on nine dimensions. These behaviors were: benevolence, adequacy, assertion, construction, dominance, propensity for imaginative play, aggression, dependence, and submission. (Aggression was found to be the most common trait among these boys; therefore, aggressive behavior was not necessarily indicative of any psychological problem.) Findings included:

1 a positive relationship between benevolence (any act of kindness in the sand tray) and fathers who saw themselves as effective in their child-care;
2 boys of mothers who reported being rejecting toward their child demonstrated less benevolent behavior in the sand tray;
3 boys of mothers who reported that they fostered autonomy in their children were found to be more dominant and assertive in their sand trays.

In discussing the results, the authors commented that the high occurrence of aggression in the Sandplay of these normal boys may be due to several factors:

1 there is some evidence that permissiveness of aggression by an adult may increase fantasy aggression (Pintler 1946; Siegel 1957);
2 primitive behaviors may be elicited from this particular modality, since Sandplay touches deep layers of the unconscious;
3 following the eruption of deep, unresolved issues, strong feelings of impotence emerge and aggressive behaviors are used to cope with them.

The researchers found that the sand tray technique is highly conducive to eliciting fantasy play in children. Their scoring system, which involved a detailed analysis of the structure, content, and process of the trays, proved to be both highly reliable and relevant to understanding children's fantasy play.

Sandplays of psychiatric patients

Caprio's (1989) study of initial sand trays of 50 adult patients in a short-term psychiatric facility was undertaken to determine the effect of Sandplay therapy on the patients, to study the structure and content of the trays, and to discover the similarities and differences of the sand trays when compared with the patients' art productions. Of the 50 patients involved in the study, there were 20 males (ages 19–41, with the majority being in the mid-20s), 30 females (ages 18–53, with the majority being in their late-30s). It was a mixed ethnic population with the majority Caucasian (29) and the remaining, Hispanic (8), Afro-American (8), and Asian (5).

Caprio's most striking finding was the absence of extraordinarily bizarre imagery in the sand trays of this group of hospitalized patients. However, only two-fifths of the sand trays exhibited any centering. Many of the sand trays contained elements depicting hopeful themes; there was also a preponderance of religious themes, of outdoor settings rather than indoor scenes, of archetypal rather than everyday people, and of wild animals over tame. The trays were notably lacking in bridges and fencing materials as well as weaponry, and there were few reminders of illness or the hospital. Another finding of interest was that the sand trays of manic patients showed an excessive fullness, while those of depressive patients were empty, colorless, and had fewer home furnishings. Trays by chronic paranoic schizophrenic patients showed fewer people. Caprio also found similarities between the sand trays and art productions of patients with similar diagnoses. However, interestingly, their sand trays were less disorganized than their typical art products.

The trays gave clues for the direction of further treatment when they revealed:

1 traumatic experiences which had not been expressed verbally;
2 developmental arrests, which gave therapists indications of where reparative work might begin;
3 specific areas of strength.

Caprio concluded that there were no negative effects resulting from the use of sand trays with these patients; however, the selection process eliminated patients who were too distraught or violent to attend to this activity, so that no conclusion can be reached about the use of sand trays with these two particular psychiatric groups.

Sandplays of men abused in childhood

Shaia (1991) compared the initial sand trays of 16 men who had experienced childhood molestation with the initial sand trays of 33 men who had not been molested to determine if differences existed in content and form. Both groups averaged 33 years of age; the molested men had undergone 2.6 years in therapy compared to 1.7 for the non-molested men.

Shaia noted that the initial sand trays of the molested group contained bears and wolves, while those of the non-molested group did not (p < .05). Also, there was a smaller number of miniatures of ordinary men in the trays of the molested group (p < .05) and the presence of miniatures of body parts and the use of bathroom objects tended toward statistical significance in the molested group.

Shaia also found a significant absence of touching the sand as well as a significant presence of circles created by objects (p < .05) in the molested group. He hypothesized that reluctance to touch the sand might reflect a patient's anxiety over the use of Sandplay, possibly suggesting loss of boundaries and/or fear of engulfment, while a sand tray containing the presence of one or more circles may signify a readiness to engage in Sandplay.

Archetypal themes in Sandplay

Sandu (1978) conducted a study to investigate the accessibility of archetypal themes through Sandplay. Using the initial Sandplays of 20 women (ages 23–62) from diverse backgrounds, the researcher sought to determine whether or not Sandplay would depict archetypal themes, as defined by Jung. She found that the findings clustered around five major archetypal constellations: the feminine, the masculine, the way (or journey), the Self, and numbers (especially three and four). Sandu's other findings indicated that concretizing the inner archetypal images often led to an insight, a new perspective, and a fresh connection within one's Self. She also confirmed that the "interpretation is not as important as the Sandplay experience itself and that the experience can stand alone, independent of the therapist's amplifications" (Sandu 1978: 97). Sandu's study demonstrated that Sandplay is a viable, projective tool through which to view the archetypal nature of the human psyche.

Sandplay as used by Jungian-oriented therapists

Miller (1982) investigated how Sandplay is conceptualized by Jungian-oriented therapists as a therapeutic tool with adults and what procedural/ technical aspects currently characterize Sandplay (materials involved, administration of the technique, and therapeutic methods). Nine therapists (three men and six women) were selected as interviewees/ subjects on the basis of personal recommendation (a non-random sample). Each had at least one year of experience of using Sandplay in treating adults. Miller used a semi-structured, face-to-face interview, which focused on several research questions.

Interviewed therapists admitted that they take a more active role when an adult finishes making a Sandplay than has been previously reported in the literature. Curious to explore and understand the creation, therapists would ask questions and attempt to discover a personal meaning or interpretation that could be understood from the picture. They emphasized the importance of introducing the tray in a flexible and creative way, in attunement with the individual needs and developmental level of the particular client (thus avoiding the use of standardized procedures in introducing the tray). Interestingly, the therapists used the tray infrequently, as only one of several therapeutic methods, noting that the value of the sand tray depends largely on the individual's willingness to explore and be open to the unconscious. They agreed that no individual should be excluded as a candidate for Sandplay, even though some clients may seem quite resistant. However, they do recommend withholding Sandplay from adult schizophrenics and borderline psychotics while in acute psychotic episodes.

Conclusion

Information gained from research may prove to have value for clinicians. Up to now this research has been widely scattered and hard to access. This chapter attempts to consolidate and summarize the empirical research conducted since 1970. Even though the findings are not definitive and care needs to be taken in applying these results to individual cases, some tentative conclusions can be drawn regarding age and sex differences, the use of space and miniatures, and evaluation of trays.

Age and sex differences

The age of the child influences how miniatures are organized within a given space (Kamp and Kessler 1970). Mental age also influences how miniatures are used, but mental age is less of a determinant than chronological age (Kamp and Kessler 1970). Children's Sandplay worlds become more complex with age in accordance with Piaget's developmental stages (Jones 1986). Sandplay is highly conducive in eliciting fantasy play in children, ages 7–9 (Volcani, Stollak, Ferguson and Benedict 1982).

Researchers found significant differences between boys' and girls' pictures. Girls use a wider range of miniatures than boys (Kamp and Kessler 1970). Fewer boys manipulated the sand in the tray, especially between the ages of 7 and 13 (Jones 1986). Adult men did not differ from adult women in their use of sand (Denkers 1985), except men molested as children tended not to touch the sand (Shaia 1991). Boys engaged in more aggressive play in the sand than girls, while girls tended toward more intimate cooperative play with the miniatures (Jones 1986). Adult females are also more likely to depict relationships in the sand tray than are males (Denkers 1985). Aggressive play in boys is not necessarily indicative of psychological problems (Volcani, Stollak, Ferguson and Benedict 1982). Some women depict the following archetypal themes in their sand trays:

the feminine, the masculine, the journey, the self, and numbers (especially three and four) (Sandu 1978). A similar study has not been conducted with men.

Use of space and miniatures

The use of a small amount of space in the tray is often an indicator of emotional distress (Denkers 1985; Kamp, Ambrosius and Zwaan 1986). Emotionally disturbed children use fewer miniatures and categories of miniatures (including fewer people and soldiers) in a smaller space than do normal children. The enclosure of large areas may indicate emotional maladjustment (Kamp and Kessler 1970; Kamp, Ambrosius and Zwaan 1986).

Evaluation of trays

Experienced judges can differentiate between the sand trays made by normal children, normal adolescents, delinquent adolescents, and emotionally disturbed children (Fujii 1979). Judges can also match an initial sand tray with a sand tray made later by the same child (Fujii 1979). The sand trays of hospitalized psychotic patients are not markedly bizarre (Caprio 1989). Sand trays need to be evaluated on more information (if a tray is strikingly unusual), such as types of figures used (Caprio 1989; Shaia 1991), placement of figures (Denkers 1985), and organization of figures in the tray (Jones 1986). For functioning adults there appears to be a connection between scores on the MMPI and sand tray productions (Denkers 1985).

In addition to the published research documented here, many other studies are currently in process using the sand tray to investigate: the imagination, stages of development, and diagnosis of early trauma (Berman, in preparation). Many clinical case studies have also been presented on such topics as: initial sand trays (Avrech, in press); birth images in Sandplay (Shepherd 1992); the implications of early loss and separation as depicted through Sandplay (Friedman 1989; Burt, in press); alienation and the continuing search for intimacy through Sandplay (Matthews 1989); assessment of a dying child's awareness of death (Amatruda 1984); young children's mourning of parental loss (Mantele, in press); symbolism and imagery in the sand tray, such as the inward spiral (Chambers 1990), the mound as a healing image (Reece, in press), animal symbolism (Hedberg, in press), and spiritual imagery (Caprio, in press).

USE OF SANDPLAY WITH SPECIAL GROUPS

Currently there is a surge of interest in identifying the unique ways in which Sandplay can be used with special populations. Some of the special populations that have attracted interest among sand tray therapists are: grieving children (Mantele, in press), dying child (Amatruda 1984), sexually abused children (Allan and Lawton-Speert 1989; Grubbs 1991a, 1991b), deaf children (Bowyer and Gilmour 1968; Gillies 1975), emotionally disturbed children and adolescents (Carey 1990; Eide-Midtsand 1987; Gabriellini and Nissim 1988; Kiepenheuer 1990; Par 1990; Sullwold 1971), learning disabled children (Reed 1975), addicted adults (Campbell, in press), and men's development (Signell 1981). Some sand tray therapists compare sand tray pictures from a number of clients in a similar population, while others examine one case in depth.

Japanese therapists, in particular, emphasize cases that deal with specific populations. Most of the cases in the series, *Studies of Sandplay Therapy in Japan*, and in their annual journal, *Archives of Sandplay Therapy*, are categorized by an identified problem. Some examples: depression (Yamanaka 1982), enuresis nocturna (Kimura 1982), schizophrenia (Takano 1982), battered isolated child (Takano 1988), and asthma (Toyoshima 1985).

Since it is not possible to review all the papers in this category, a representative sample is provided.

Maternal deprivation

Mills (1990) described the unique ways in which maternally deprived children used sand and water in the process of healing. Through Sandplay, traumas were evoked and transformed: "the mixing of sand and water . . . seemed consistently to lead the child to play out fears or memories of pain." Examples from the play of three of the children illustrated the ritualistic types of play indicative of this special group. For example, Mills observed that water was always added to the dry sand and that repetitive washing of oneself and playroom toys was common.

Sexual abuse

John Allan and Sarah Lawton-Speert (1989) discussed the key function served by sand and water in healing the trauma and wounds of abuse. In their article "Sand and water in the treatment of a profoundly sexually abused preschool boy," they presented the general patterns and stages that children go through in treatment, while emphasizing the importance of sand and water in play therapy with a sexually abused 4½-year-old boy. This child first used the Sandplay environment as a backdrop for acting out the trauma, then later for cleansing and healing. As he grew older and worked through his early trauma, his sand tray work included the use of miniature toys and more stable scenes.

Post-traumatic stress

Kate Amatruda (1989) described her work integrating Sandplay and Chakra therapy with a 7-year-old girl who had witnessed a murder and was suffering from post-traumatic stress disorder. In her article, "Grief Sandplay therapy with child trauma victims," Amatruda illustrated the connection between the development in the Sandplay scenes and the progression of energy through the chakras. In her view, Sandplay provides a place for trauma victims where the "voiceless can find their voice, and in which things too terrible or frightening to tell can be told."

USE OF SANDPLAY IN SCHOOLS

In the last decade, the sand tray technique has been introduced into the school setting by teachers as well as school counselors. In some schools, sand tray technique is openly accepted as an aid to academic development, psychological growth, diagnosis, and therapeutic intervention. The challenge and benefits of adapting and implementing sand tray into the schools have been well described in a number of school and counseling journals (Allan and Berry 1987; Currant 1989; Vinturella and James 1987; Watson n.d.).

The sand tray has been more easily accepted into the school system than have many other psychological techniques, because educators have long understood that playing in the sand facilitates the developing physical, social, emotional, and academic abilities of children (McIntyre 1982; Frisby 1979). Historically, in every pre-school and elementary school setting, a play area with sand has been available and widely used by young children. Therefore, it has been a natural move to give sand its own space in the classroom and counseling office.

Watson (n.d.) pointed out that "the educator, by making the sand tray available to a child, is not doing therapy, but only facilitating imaginative play. S/he does not interpret or make any emotional demands. In fact, the teacher's task during the sand tray is to observe only" (p.2). In observing, the teacher focuses on educational problems, not emotional disturbances. Watson compared sand tray to the use of art activity in school, which is not considered psychotherapy. She also noted that, since a basic principle of Sandplay therapy is that the experience is complete without interpretation, the sand tray is particularly appealing as a means of evoking the learning potential of students.

As an adjunctive tool, Sandplay technique fits easily into the theoretical framework of many school counselors. This is due to the fact that the training of school counselors is often humanistically oriented, emphasizing the Rogerian view of unconditional positive regard. This attitude is congruent with respectful witnessing inherent in Sandplay. (Kalff [1980] herself warned against the use of interpretation.) In addition,

Kalff's emphasis on establishing a "free and protected space" is similar to the school counselor's attempt to establish a "therapeutic space."

John Allan, Jungian analyst and Professor of Elementary School Counseling at the University of British Columbia, and Pat Berry, a former teacher and current therapist, have discussed the historical development of Sandplay and its application in schools (1987). Like many Sandplay therapists, Allan and Berry define their own process stages, which are based on their observations of the unfolding drama in children's sand trays. They present a case study demonstrating that, as the sand drama unfolds, children tend to portray chaos, struggle (organized fighting), and resolution in recurring cycles. They point out that Sandplay used in schools (as well as in traditional treatment) can be beneficial by releasing blocked energies and activating the self-healing potential.

In "Sandplay: a therapeutic medium with children," doctoral student Lucy Vinturella and Richard James, Professor of Counseling Psychology at Memphis State University, present an eclectic view of the use of sand tray in the school setting (1987). To them Sandplay serves as both a diagnostic tool and as a means of therapeutic intervention. They present the Lowenfeldian view that Sandplay, as a form of play therapy, can facilitate communication and thus be used by counselors from a variety of therapeutic orientations, giving examples of how behaviorists, psychoanalysts, Jungian analysts, and Gestalt therapists might use this technique. They caution that Sandplay should not be used with children who are extremely emotionally disturbed. Also, in their view, a counselor should not adhere to a fixed interpretation of symbols, because symbols can have several subjective meanings which should be respected. They suggest instead that "the counselor could use person-centered techniques, such as restatement of content and reflection of feelings, to identify and clarify the meaning of the sand picture . . . " (p. 232).

Mary Noyes, a former public school teacher and an ISST member, presents her own classroom experiences working with Sandplay in teaching reading (1981). Her article is unique in several ways. The teacher herself conducted the Sandplay on a one-to-one basis within the classroom rather than the child being treated by a school counselor outside of the classroom. Also, her goal was to help the child academically as well as psychologically. Noyes described her Sandplay environment in the classroom and how she structured its use with the children. She reported that the Sandplay experience deepened rapport and intimacy, improved self-esteem, and helped resolve inner conflicts. In addition, the degree of reading improvement shown by her students by the end of the school year was higher than in two previous years when she worked with similar children in the same school without using Sandplay.

Cynthia Belzer (1991), a special education teacher, also designed and implemented a program using Sandplay for her students to encourage receptivity to learning in a public elementary school. Her eleven students were children with special learning needs in the fourth, fifth, and sixth grades, ranging in age from 10 to 13 years old. Within her classroom she arranged a semi-private location which contained two sand trays and shelves with miniatures. Time for the Sandplay was arranged once a week for each child who desired this activity.

Belzer reported that the Sandplay activity promoted a receptivity to learning as evidenced by improved ability to concentrate and become involved in academic tasks. After making a tray, students exhibited a calmer affect, appearing less stressed and better able to function in the classroom. A striking finding was that Belzer became so familiar with each child's style and particular choices of miniatures, she was able to identify which child made the sand picture without first checking the identity of the child. This informal finding is supported by Fujii's (1979) research study, which found that a personal style in Sandplay was consistent over time.

Belzer also found a pattern similar to that reported by Allan and Berry (1987) and Kalff (1980). Initially sand trays displayed chaotic scenes, which lasted a variable time for each student; fluctuation between the stages of chaos, fighting, then chaos again was common. Eventually, one-half of the students were able to reach the resolution stage.

Belzer concluded that Sandplay has an important place in the classroom, provided there is adequate administrative support and psychological consultation to achieve these positive results. Ideally, Sandplay is most effective when used by a trained school counselor.

CURRENT LEADERSHIP

The Sandplay movement is supported by the International Society for Sandplay Therapy (ISST), which was founded by Dora Kalff in 1985. The founding members involved in this endeavor were: Dr Kay Bradway (Sausalito, California); Dr Paola Carducci (Rome, Italy); Prof. Kazumika Higuchi (Kyoto, Japan); Dora M. Kalff (Zollikon, Switzerland); Dr Martin Kalff (Zollikon, Switzerland); Prof. Hayao Kawai (Nara-shi, Japan); Dr Kaspar Kiepenheuer (Zürich, Switzerland); Dr Chonita Larsen (Honolulu, Hawaii); Sigrid Lowen-Seifert (Stuttgart, Germany); Dr Andreina Navone (Rome, Italy); Joel Ryce-Menuhin (London, England); Estelle Weinrib (New York, New York); Prof. Yasuhiro Yamanaka (Kyoto, Japan).

Membership in ISST is open to qualified therapists, and is based on a certification process (Kalff 1988c). There are now approximately sixty members worldwide. Currently, the ISST is led by President Hayao Kawai and a board of delegates from representative countries (Kalff 1988d).

In the United States the members of ISST also belong to the Sandplay Therapists of America (STA). Estelle Weinrib, a Jungian analyst in New York, and Dr Kay Bradway, a Jungian analyst from Northern California, have been particularly strong leaders in the development of the STA. Currently STA is governed by an executive council of four members. STA members present numerous workshops, sponsor a biennial conference, and publish a journal twice yearly, called *Journal of Sandplay Therapy*. Associate status is available for those who have an interest in Sandplay and wish to support the organization. In addition, there are many local organizations that meet on a regular basis. The Hawaii, Northern California, Southern California, and Minnesota groups are especially active. A widely circulated quarterly newsletter, the *Sandplay Events Newsletter*, is published in the United States by Bonnie McLean, listing meetings, conferences, lectures, publications, and workshops worldwide.

Outside of the United States, centers of interest exist in Canada, England, Germany, Italy, Japan, and Switzerland. Currently, groups have formed around the ISST members in their countries presenting workshops, seminars, and lectures.

There continues to be a small group of dedicated people who use the Lowenfeld World Technique approach. Many of these were also influenced by John Hood-Williams, who succeeded Margaret Lowenfeld as Director of the Institute of Child Psychology. He lectured throughout Europe and in the United States in the 1970s and 1980s. Now Northern California Therapist, Dr Robert Royden, who was trained by Margaret Lowenfeld and is a board member of the Lowenfeld Trust, continues to teach this classical style.

REFERENCES

Abel, C. (1985). "Fire: An image of transformation". Unpublished doctoral dissertation, International College, Los Angeles.

Adams, K.E. (1991). "Sandplay: A modern alchemical process." Unpublished master's thesis, Antioch University, Merritt Island, Florida.

Aite, P. (1978). "Ego and image: Some observations on the theme of 'Sandplay'." *Journal of Analytical Psychology* 23: 332–8.

Allan, J. and Berry, P. (1987). "Sandplay" (special issue: counseling with expressive arts). *Elementary School Guidance and Counseling* 21(4): 300–6.

Allan, J. and Lawton-Speert, S. (1989). "Sand and water in the treatment of a profoundly sexually abused preschool boy." *Association for Play Therapy Newsletter* 8(4): 2–3.

Amatruda, K. (1984). "Psychological interventions in physical illness – The Sandplay Test: Assessing a dying child's awareness of death." Unpublished paper for Saybrook Institute. Donated to the C.G. Jung Institute of San Francisco.

—— (1989). "Grief Sandplay therapy with child trauma victims: A psychospiritual somatic treatment model." *Archives of Sandplay Therapy* 2(1): 91–104.

—— (1991, September). "Psyche, soul and body: All the elements." Paper presented at the *Earth, Air, Water, Fire: Transformation in the Sand* Conference, sponsored by the San Francisco C.G. Jung Institute. (Audiotape.)

Ammann, R. (1991). *Healing and Transformation in Sandplay: Creative Processes become Visible*. (W.P. Rainer, trans.) La Salle, IL: Open Court Publishing. Originally published in German as *Heilende Bilder der Seele*.

Aoki, S. (1981). "The retest reliability of the Sandplay technique" (2nd report). *British Journal of Projective Psychology and Personality* 26(2): 25–33.

Armentrout, J. and Burger, C. (1972). "Factor analysis of college students' recall of parental child-rearing behaviors." *Journal of Genetic Psychology* 122: 155–61.

Avrech, G. (in press). "Initial sand trays: Clues to the psyche." In B. Caprio (ed.) *Sandplay: Coming of Age*. Paper presented at the Los Angeles Sandplay Association 1991 Conference.

Baldridge, A.E. (1990). "In a grain of sand." *Northern California Sandplay Society Newsletter* Fall: 3–8.

Belzer, C.A. (1991). "The effects of sandplay in a classroom setting with children identified as learning disabled." Unpublished master's thesis, Pacific Oaks College, Pasadena, CA.

Berman, B. (in preparation). "Diagnosis of early trauma." Doctoral dissertation.

Berry, P. (1989). "The nitty gritty of sand." *Association for Play Therapy Newsletter* 8(4): 4–6.

Bowyer, L.R. (1970). *The Lowenfeld World Technique*. Oxford: Pergamon Press.

Bowyer, L.R. and Gilmour, R. (1968). "Interpersonal communication of deaf children using the Village Test." In A. Friedemann, H. Phillipson, B. Scott and C. Williams (eds) *Rorschach Proceedings: VIIth International Congress of Rorschach and Other Projective Techniques, London*: 315–18. Bern: Hans Huber Publishers.

Bradway, K. (1979a). "Sandplay in psychotherapy." *Art Psychotherapy* 6(2): 85–93.

—— (1979b). "Initial and final Sandplay worlds of married non-career and unmarried career women in analysis." *Professional Reports* 6: 35–41. San Francisco: C.G. Jung Institute. Presented (March, 1979) at the Joint Conference, United States Societies of Jungian Analysts, Asilomar, CA.

—— (1981a). "Developmental stages in children's sand worlds." In K. Bradway *et al.* (eds) *Sandplay Studies: Origins, Theory and Practice*: 93–100. San Francisco: C.G. Jung Institute.

—— (1981b). "A woman's individuation through Sandplay." In K. Bradway *et al.* (eds) *Sandplay Studies: Origins, Theory, and Practice*: 133–56. San Francisco: C.G. Jung Institute.

—— (1985). *Sandplay Bridges and the Transcendent Function*. San Francisco: C.G. Jung Institute.

—— (1987). "Sandplay: What makes it work?" (workshop). In M.A. Mattoon (ed.) *The archetype of shadow in a split world: Proceedings of the Tenth International Congress for Analytical Psychology, Berlin, 1986*: 409–14. Einsiedeln, Switzerland: Daimon Verlag.

—— (1991). "Transference and countertransference in Sandplay therapy." *Journal of Sandplay Therapy* 1(1): 25–43.

—— (1992). "Sun and moon in Sandplay." *Journal of Sandplay Therapy* 1(2): 47–9.

Bradway, K., Signell, K.A., Spare, G.H., Stewart, C.T., Stewart, L.H. and Thompson, C. (1981). *Sandplay Studies: Origins, Theory and Practice*. San Francisco: C.G. Jung Institute.

Bühler, C. (1951a). "The World Test: A projective technique." *Journal of Child Psychiatry* 2: 4–23.

—— (1951b). "The World Test: Manual of directions." *Journal of Child Psychiatry* 2: 69–81.

Burt, J.C. (1991). "Sandplay therapy: A bridge from boyhood to adolescence." Unpublished master's thesis, Pacific Oaks College, Pasadena, CA.

—— (in press). "Early loss and abandonment issues as revealed in adults' Sandplay." In B. Caprio (ed.) *Sandplay: Coming of Age*. Paper presented at the Los Angeles Sandplay Association 1991 Conference.

Campbell, F. (in press). "Transformation in the sand: From addiction to recovery." In B. Caprio (ed.) *Sandplay: Coming of Age*. Paper presented at the Los Angeles Sandplay Association 1991 Conference.

Capitolo, M. (1992). "The dark goddesses: An encounter with the dark feminine." *Journal of Sandplay Therapy* 1(2): 59–69.

Caprio, B. (1989). "The sand tray: An art therapy perspective." Unpublished master's thesis, Loyola-Marymount University, Los Angeles, CA.

—— (in press). "Spiritual imagery in Sandplay." In B. Caprio (ed.) *Sandplay: Coming of Age*. Paper presented at the Los Angeles Sandplay Association 1991 Conference. (Videotape.)

Carey, L. (1990). "Sandplay therapy with a troubled child." *The Arts in Psychotherapy* 17: 197–209.

Carmody, J.B. (1985). "Self-restoration and initiation in analytical child therapy: Observations on Sandplay." *Dissertation Abstracts International* 45(8-B): 2681.

Chambers, L. (1990). "The in-turning spiral: The path to the healing of the feminine." *Northern California Sandplay Society Newsletter* Fall: 1–2.

Crable, P.G. (1976). "Women and self: An initial investigation of the feminine essence using Sandplay." (Doctoral dissertation, United States International University, 1976.) *Dissertation Abstracts International* 37(3-B): 1483-B. (University Microfilms No. 76–19751.)

Cunningham, L. (1991, September). "Fire." Paper presented at the *Earth, Air, Fire, Water: Transformation in the Sand* Conference, sponsored by the San Francisco C.G. Jung Institute. (Audiotape.)

Currant, N. (1989). "Room to breathe." *The American Journal of Art Therapy* 27: 80–6.

Denkers, G.C. (1985). "An investigation of the diagnostic potential of Sandplay utilizing Linn Jones' Developmental Scoring System." Unpublished doctoral dissertation, Psychological Studies Institute, Pacific Grove Graduate School of Professional Psychology, Berkeley, CA.

Dundas, E. (1978). *Symbols Come Alive in the Sand*. Aptos, CA: Aptos Press.

Eide-Midtsand, N. (1987). "Struggles with the 'other one': The reconciliation of a pre-adolescent boy with his masculinity." *Journal of Analytical Psychology* 32: 157–71.

Erikson, E.H. (1951). "Sex differences in the play configurations of pre-adolescents." *American Journal of Orthopsychiatry* 21: 667–92.

—— (1963). *Childhood and Society*. New York: Norton.

Friedman, H.S. (1987). "Los Angeles Sandplay Associations" (Notes of Seminar). Los Angeles: Mitchell.

—— (1989). "Images of childhood loss." Unpublished paper presented at the Analytical Psychology Club Lecture Series, Los Angeles, CA. (Audiotape.) Available from the C.G. Jung Institute, Los Angeles, CA.

—— (1991). "Heritage rediscovered: A journey through the five elements." Unpublished paper presented at the *Earth, Air, Fire, Water: Transformation in the Sand* Conference, San Francisco, CA. (Audiotape.) Available from the C.G. Jung Institute, San Francisco, CA.

Frisby, D. (1979). *Resource Materials for the Creative Curriculum*. Washington, D.C.: Creative Associates, Inc.

Fujii, S. (1979) (a.k.a. Aoki, S.). "Retest reliability of the Sandplay technique (lst report)." *British Journal of Projective Psychology and Personality Study* 24: 21–5.

Furth, G. (1988). *The Secret World of Drawings*. Boston: Sigo Press.

Gabriellini, G. and Nissim, S. (1988). "Sand play therapy with a psychotic child." In M. Sidoli and M. Davies (eds) *Jungian Child Psychotherapy: Individuation in Childhood*: 221–30. London: Karnac Books.

Gillies, J. (1975). "Personality and adjustment in deaf children." *British Journal of Projective Psychology and Personality Study* 20(1): 33–4.

Gradwell, L.E. (1992). "The mermaid." *Journal of Sandplay Therapy* 1(2): 93–100.

Green, R.J. (1975). "Child-rearing attitudes and perception of children's behavior across two generations in families." Unpublished doctoral dissertation, Michigan State University.

Grubbs, G.A. (1991a). "A categorical and comparative analysis of the Sandplay process of abused and nonabused children." Unpublished doctoral dissertation, California Graduate School of Family Psychology.

—— (1991b). "A categorical and comparative analysis of the Sandplay process of abused and nonabused children." *Northern California Sandplay Society Newsletter*, Fall: 1–2.

Hedberg, T.M. (1988). "Respect for the animal kingdom: A Jungian approach." Unpublished doctoral dissertation, Sierra University, Costa Mesa, CA.

Hegeman, G. (1992). "The Sandplay collection." *Journal of Sandplay Therapy* 1(2): 101–6.

Jackson, B. (1991). "Before reaching for the symbols dictionary." *Journal of Sandplay Therapy* 1(1): 55–8.

Jones, L.E. (1986). "The development of structure in the world of expression: A cognitive-developmental analysis of children's 'sand worlds'." Unpublished doctoral dissertation, Pacific Graduate School of Psychology, Menlo Park, CA. (University Microfilms No. 83–03178.)

Jung, C.G. (1953). *Psychology and Alchemy.* (R.F.C. Hull, trans.). New York: Pantheon Books. (Originally published [1944] in German as: *Psychologie und Alchemie.* Zürich: Rascher Verlag.)

—— (1961). "Freud and psychoanalysis." *Collected Works, IV.* Princeton: Princeton University Press.

Kahn, J. (1989). *The Use of the Sandtray in Psychotherapy with Children and their Parents.* Petaluma, CA: Playrooms.

Kalff, D. (1979). "Sandplay: Mirror of the child's psyche." (Audiotape.) Los Angeles: C.G. Jung Institute.

—— (1980). *Sandplay: A Psychotherapeutic Approach to the Psyche* (W. Ackerman, trans.). Santa Monica: Sigo Press. (Originally published [1966] in German as *Sandspiel.* Zürich: Rascher.) (First published [1971] in English as *Sandplay: Mirror of a Child's Psyche.* [H. Kirsch, trans.]. San Francisco: Browser Press.)

—— (1983). Foreword in Weinrib, E.L., *Images of the Self: The Sandplay Therapy Process.* Boston: Sigo Press.

—— (1987). "Sandplay with Dora Kalff." (Notes of seminar.) Carmel, CA: University of California at Santa Cruz.

—— (1988a). "Beyond the shadow." *Archives of Sandplay Therapy* 1: 87–97.

—— (1988b). "Sandplay in Switzerland." (Notes of seminar.) Zürich: University of California at Santa Cruz.

—— (1988c). "Guidelines for training for becoming a Sandplay therapist." In D. Kalff, *International Society for Sandplay Therapy.* Zollikon, Switzerland: D. Kalff.

—— (1988d). "Articles of the International Society for Sandplay Therapy." In D. Kalff, *International Society for Sandplay Therapy.* Zollikon, Switzerland: D. Kalff.

—— (1991). "Introduction to Sandplay therapy." *Journal of Sandplay Therapy* 1(1): 7–15. Originally published in German by Kalff (1978) as "Eine kurze Einführung in die Sandspieltherapie." *Praxis der Psychotherapie* 23: 269–73. Heidelberg: Springer-Verlag. Translated into English by Kalff (1986) and presented to the International Society for Sandplay Therapy (July, 1988).

Kamp, L.N.J., Ambrosius, A.M. and Zwaan, E.J. (1986). "The World Test: pathological traits in the arrangement of miniature toys." *Acta Psychiatrica Belgica* 86(3): 208–19.

Kamp, L.N.J. and Kessler, E.G. (1970). "The World Test: Developmental aspects of a play technique." *Journal of Child Psychology and Psychiatry* 11: 81–108. Reprinted (1971) in French as "Test du Monde: Aspects développementaux d'une technique de jeu." *Revue de Neuropsychiatrie Infantile* 19(6): 295–322.

Kawai, H. (1985). "Introduction: On transference in Sandplay therapy." In H. Kawai and Y. Yamanaka (eds) *Studies of Sandplay Therapy in Japan* II: iii–xi. Tokyo: Seishin-Shoboh.

—— (1992). "Sandplay and relation." Unpublished paper presented at *Sand, Psyche and Symbol* Conference, San Rafael, CA.

Kiepenheuer, K. (1990). *Crossing the Bridge* (K.R. Schneider, trans.). La Salle, IL: Open Court. Originally published in German as *Geh über die Brücke*.

—— (1991). "The witch's house: A free and protected place for 'bewitched' children." *Journal of Sandplay Therapy* 1(1): 45–7.

Kimura, H. (1982). "Enuresis nocturna, 11-year-old girl." In H. Kawai and Y. Yamanaka (eds) *Studies of Sandplay Therapy in Japan* I: 86–106. Commentator: A. Miki. Tokyo: Seishin-Shoboh.

Lowenfeld, M. (1939). "The World pictures of children: A method of recording and studying them." *British Journal of Medical Psychology* 18 (pt.1): 65–101. Presented to the Medical Section of the British Psychological Society, March, 1938. Reprinted (1988) in C. Urwin and J. Hood-Williams, *Child Psychotherapy, War and the Normal Child*: 265–309. London: Free Association Books.

—— (1979). *The World Technique*. London: George Allen & Unwin.

McIntyre, M. (1982). "Discovery through Sandplay." *Science and Children* 19(6): 36–7.

Maclay, D.T. (1970). *Treatment for Children: The Work of a Child Guidance Clinic*. New York: Science House.

McNally, S.P. (1984). "Sandplay: A sourcebook for psychotherapists." Unpublished manuscript.

Mantele, O. (in press). "A child's grief process through Sandplay." In B. Caprio (ed.) *Sandplay: Coming of Age*. Paper presented at the Los Angeles Sandplay Association 1991 Conference.

Matthews, M.A. (1989). *Alienation and the Continuing Search for Intimacy*. (Audiotape.) Available from the C.G. Jung Institute, Los Angeles, CA.

Miller, C. and Boe, J. (1990). "Tears into diamonds: Transformation of child psychic trauma through Sandplay and storytelling." *The Arts in Psychotherapy* 17: 247–57.

Miller, R.R. (1982). "Investigation of a psychotherapeutic tool for adults: The sand tray." Doctoral dissertation, California School of Professional Psychology, Fresno. *Dissertation Abstracts International* 43(1-B): 257. (University Microfilms No. 82–07557).

Millikan, F. (1992). "Hestia: Goddess of hearth and fire." *Journal of Sandplay Therapy* 1(2): 71–91.

Mills, B. (1990). "The therapeutic use of sand and water play with maternally deprived preschool children." *Association for Play Therapy Newsletter* 9(1): 1–4.

Mitchell, R.R. (1987). "Overview of the Sandplay technique." *Western ACES Newsletter* 25: 5–6.

Neumann, E. (1973). *The Child*. New York: G.P. Putnam's Sons.

Noyes, M. (1981). "Sandplay imagery: An aid to teaching reading." *Academic Therapy* 17(2): 231–7.

Par, M.A. (1990). "Sand and water play: A case study." *Association for Play Therapy Newsletter* 9(1): 4–6.

Pickford, R. (1975). "Expression of thoughts by means of the Lowenfeld sand tray 'World' material." In I. Jakab (ed.) *Transcultural Aspects of Psychiatric Art*: 188–92. Basel, Switzerland: Karger.

Pintler, H.H., Phillips, R. and Sears, R.R. (1946). "Sex differences in the projective doll play of preschool children." *Journal of Psychology* 21: 73–80.

Reece, S.T. (in press). "Symbolic expression in Sandplay: The mound as healing image." In B. Caprio (ed.) *Sandplay: Coming of Age*. Paper presented at the Los Angeles Sandplay Association 1991 Conference.

Reed, J.P. (1975). *Sand Magic Experience in Miniatures: A Non-verbal Therapy for Children*. Albuquerque: JPR Press.

—— (1980). *Emergence: Essays on the Process of Individuation through Sand Tray Therapy, Art Forms and Dreams*. Nehalem, OR: self-published.

Rhinehart, L. and Engelhorn, P. (1986). "The sand tray dialog: The sand tray as an adjunctive tool." Seminar presented at the Annual Conference of the American Association of Art Therapy, Los Angeles, CA.

Ryce-Menuhin, J. (1992). *Jungian Sandplay: The Wonderful Therapy*. London: Routledge.

Samuels, A. (1986). *A Critical Dictionary of Jungian Analysis*. London: Routledge & Kegan Paul.

Sandu, M. (1978). "Feminine psyche: An initial investigation of archetypal constellations as projected in Sandplay." Unpublished master's thesis, United States International University.

Schaeffer, E. (1965). "Children's reports of parental behavior: an inventory." *Child Development* 36: 413–24.

Shaia, A. (1991). "Images in the sand: The initial sand worlds of men molested as children." Unpublished doctoral dissertation, California Institute of Integral Studies, San Francisco, CA.

Shepherd, S.T. (1992). "The birth of the dark child." *Journal of Sandplay Therapy* 1(2): 51–7.

Siegel, A.E. (1957). "Aggressive behavior of young children in the absence of an adult." *Child Development* 26: 371–6.

Signell, K.A. (1981). "The Sandplay process in a man's development: The use of Sandplay with men." In K. Bradway *et al.* (eds) *Sandplay Studies: Origins, Theory and Practice*: 101–31. San Francisco: C.G. Jung Institute. Republished (1990) Boston: Sigo Press.

Spare, G.H. (1981). "Are there any rules? (Musings of a peripatetic Sandplayer)." In K. Bradway *et al.* (eds) *Sandplay Studies: Origins, Theory and Practice*: 195–208. San Francisco: C.G. Jung Institute. Republished (1990) Boston: Sigo Press.

Stewart, C.T. (1981). "The developmental psychology of Sandplay." In K. Bradway *et al.* (eds) *Sandplay Studies: Origins, Theory and Practice*: 39–92. San Francisco: C.G. Jung Institute. Republished (1990) Boston: Sigo Press.

Stewart, L.H. (1977). "Sandplay therapy: Jungian technique." In B. B. Wolman (ed.) *International Encyclopedia of Psychiatry, Psychology, Psychoanalysis, and Neurology* 6: 9–11. New York: Aesculapium.

—— (1981). "Play and Sandplay." In K. Bradway *et al.* (eds) *Sandplay Studies: Origins, Theory and Practice*: 21–37. San Francisco: C.G. Jung Institute. Republished (1990) Boston: Sigo Press.

—— (1982). "Sandplay and Jungian analysis." In M. Stein (ed.) *Jungian Analysis*: 204–18. La Salle, IL: Open Court.

Sullwold, E. (1971). "Eagle eye." In H. Kirsch (ed.) *The Well-tended Tree*: 235–52. New York: G.P. Putnam's Sons.

—— (1977). "Jungian child therapy." In B. Wolman (ed.) *International Encyclopedia of Psychiatry, Psychology, Psychoanalysis, and Neurology* 6: 242–6. New York: Aesculapium.

—— (1982). "Treatment of children in analytical psychology." In M. Stein (ed.) *Jungian Analysis*: 235–55. La Sall, IL: Open Court.

Takano, S. (1982). "Schizophrenia, 21-year-old male." In H. Kawai and Y. Yamanaka (eds) *Studies of Sandplay Therapy in Japan* I: 164–84. Commentator: H. Nakai. Tokyo: Seishin-Shoboh.

—— (1988). "On the process of Sandplay therapy of the case of a battered isolated child." *Archives of Sandplay Therapy* 1 (1): 47–60.

Tatum, J. (1991). "Water." Unpublished paper presented at the *Earth, Air, Fire, Water: Transformation in the Sand* Conference, San Francisco, CA.

Thompson, C.W. (1981). "Variations on a theme by Lowenfeld: Sandplay in focus." In K. Bradway *et al.* (eds) *Sandplay Studies: Origins, Theory and Practice*: 5–20. San Francisco: C.G. Jung Institute. Republished (1990) Boston: Sigo Press.

Toyoshima, K. (1985). "Asthma as an attachment disorder, 8-year-old male." In H. Kawai and Y. Yamanaka (eds) *Studies of Sandplay Therapy in Japan* 11: 31–52. Commentator: H. Kohno. Tokyo: Seishin-Shoboh.

Urwin, C. and Hood-Williams, J. (1988). *Child Psychotherapy, War and the Normal Child*. London: Free Association Books.

Vinturella, L. and James, R. (1987). "Sandplay: A therapeutic medium with children." *Elementary School Guidance and Counseling* 21(3): 229–38.

Volcani, Y., Stollak, G., Ferguson, L. and Benedict, H. (1982). "Sandtray play: Children's fantasy play and parental caregiving perceptions." Paper presented at the Annual Meeting of the American Psychological Association (90th). Washington, DC.

Watson, M. (undated). "Sandtray in education." Unpublished paper, San Francisco, CA.

Weinrib, E.L. (1983a). *Images of the Self: The Sandplay Therapy Process*. Boston: Sigo Press.

—— (1983b). "On delayed interpretation in Sandplay therapy." In *Arms of the Windmill*: 119–29. New York: C.G. Jung Foundation.

—— (1987). "Sandplay: The shadow and the cross." In M.A. Mattoon (ed.) *The archetype of shadow in a split world: Proceedings of the Tenth International Congress for Analytical Psychology, Berlin, 1986*: 415–529. Einsiedeln, Switzerland: Daimon Verlag.

—— (1989). Sandplay Workshop. (Notes.) Phoenix: Friends of C.G. Jung.

—— (1991). "Diagram of the psyche." *Journal of Sandplay Therapy* 1(1): 48–53.

Winnicott, D.W. (1975). "Transitional objects and transitional phenomena." In D.W. Winnicott, *Pediatrics to Psychoanalysis*. New York: Basic Books, Incorporated.

Yamanaka, Y. (1982). "Depressive hypochondriasis, 72-year-old female." In H. Kawai and Y. Yamanaka (eds) *Studies of Sandplay Therapy in Japan* 1: 205–22. Tokyo: Seishin-Shoboh.

Zeller, D. (1979). "The sand tray." Unpublished master's thesis, California State University, Sonoma.

Chapter 9

The future of Sandplay

It is our strong belief that knowledge of the past history and present status of sand tray technique will facilitate conscious choices about the future directions of Sandplay. By identifying emerging issues and their implications in this chapter, we hope to highlight a viable path of progression that will move Sandplay through this decade and into the twenty-first century.

QUESTIONS FOR THE FUTURE

Before a clear path can be determined, several core issues and concerns remain to be considered: What is the role of empirical research in the future of Sandplay? Should the sand tray be used as a diagnostic instrument or solely as a clinical technique? Besides the sand picture, what other elements need to be considered to further psychological integration? How can the sand tray be better integrated into clinical practice? In what settings, under what conditions, and with what types of clients will the sand tray be used? Can the present structure of the International Society for Sandplay Therapy (ISST) meet training needs of therapists interested in Sandplay? What are the future challenges for effective training? These issues and concerns will be considered in the following sections.

What is the role of empirical research in the future of Sandplay?

In order to answer this question adequately, it is necessary to reiterate the past role of research in Sandplay. Lowenfeld was very familiar with research methods (Lowenfeld 1927, 1928) because of her training as a pediatrician and researcher. Others, including Bühler, also recognized the potential of the sand tray for research purposes. Indeed, it was this mutual interest in research that initially brought Lowenfeld and Bühler together; eventually, Bühler developed her "signs" of emotional disturbance based on patterns Lowenfeld had observed in sand trays. Ironically, some years later a theoretical disagreement arose between these two women: should the tray be used mainly as a diagnostic and research instrument? (Bühler's view) or mainly as a therapeutic instrument? (Lowenfeld's position). Lowenfeld was concerned that Bühler's diagnostic work would be confused with her clinical work. Dora Kalff also recognized patterns in the sand; however, she preferred to use her intuitive capacities, rather than research methods, to explore and understand those patterns. She was not drawn to the scientific, rational approach.

Today, the historical pull between the intuitive and rational polarities still exists. Some believe that a scientific research approach would impose rigidity upon the therapeutic environment and interfere with Sandplay's natural function of evoking unconscious processes. Others increasingly value research as a means of better understanding the patterns of the psyche as they unfold in the sand tray and legitimizing the integration of Sandplay into mainstream psychology. It is interesting to note that, currently, there is a heightened interest in Sandplay research, indicating, perhaps, some preliminary bridging between the intuitive and the rational. The question then becomes, what type of Sandplay research is needed and how can it best be integrated into the current body of knowledge? As Sandplay acquires a stronger research base, even more research projects and dissertations examining Sandplay will become available.

Historically, the effectiveness of Sandplay has been demonstrated by analysis of individual case studies, along with a few studies (noted in Chapter 8) that have examined the sand trays of small populations. Larger, more comprehensive studies are now needed to determine the validity of Sandplay as a healing technique. Specifically, several categories of research are recommended. *Replication studies* of historical research findings need to be conducted to determine if these findings are still applicable today. *Outcome research* would be important in addressing such questions as: In what types of settings should Sandplay be used (institutions, schools, hospitals, couples work, group work, private practice)? At what point in the therapeutic process should it be introduced? With what types of client is Sandplay indicated? With what types of client is Sandplay most effective? *Process studies* addressing the Sandplay experience might investigate:

1 In addition to the "free and protected space," are there other critical and identifiable conditions in the Sandplay setting that facilitate change?
2 Do changes in the therapeutic environment (where the therapist sits, where the tray is placed, where miniatures are displayed) affect the therapeutic outcome?
3 Is it valid to use quadrants for understanding the tray?
4 How do client characteristics (age, gender, ethnic background, educational level) affect the Sandplay creation?
5 How do the sand trays of non-clinical populations differ from those of clinical populations?

6 Are archetypal factors deterministic and/or predictable in relation to patterns in the trays? For example, how does the Sandplay process of boys differ from girls? Are there typical sand tray patterns that characterize various developmental stages?
7 What meaning(s) do specific symbols have when used in the Sandplay process?
8 Does the placement of a specific symbol make a difference in the understanding of trays?
9 What effects do verbal and physical interventions of the therapist have on the immediate Sandplay creation as well as the eventual outcome of the treatment?
10 What are the effects of transference and countertransference on sand tray productions?
11 Are there cross-cultural differences in effects of Sandplay as a facilitating factor in the therapeutic process of clients?

The case studies donated to the Archives of the Dora Kalff International Society for Sandplay Therapy in Zürich, Switzerland are a rich resource for those wishing to pursue research interests.

Over the past twenty years the popularity of the sand tray has steadily increased. However, the sand tray will continue to thrive only if it is accepted into mainstream psychotherapy. In all likelihood, this acceptance will result from Sandplay being viewed as facilitating the therapeutic process, providing a unique access to the unconscious, having a sufficient research base that supports the efficacy of Sandplay, and for being easily integrated into verbal therapy. Without these underpinnings, this valuable technique could be relegated to a small, esoteric group of professionals with a highly specialized interest. While safeguarding the fundamental and vital essence of what Dora Kalff contributed to this technique, it is also important to remain open to incorporating yet new possibilities for depth of understanding.

Future research should extrapolate on Sandplay's already established research foundation. Tomorrow's research goal should be to expand the knowledge base that underlies the Sandplay approach, as well as to contribute to the resolution of the struggle between the intuitive and rational that has dichotomized the therapeutic methods and techniques of Sandplay since its inception. Historically, sand tray approaches have reflected the personality typologies of its creators: some approaches were intuitive and soulful, others were theoretically oriented, while still others emphasized the empirical and the scientific. Hopefully, the time has come to integrate all these perspectives.

Sand tray as diagnostic instrument or clinical technique?

Originally, Lowenfeld developed the "World Technique" as a clinical technique to facilitate communication. A decade later Bühler, then Bolgar and Fischer, adapted it as a diagnostic instrument, hoping that it would have the ability to diagnose pathology with a reliability comparable to the Rorschach and other established projective techniques. In the early days of their work, both the diagnostic and therapeutic approaches began to find a place in the psychotherapeutic community. Later in the 1960s, however, as Dora Kalff began to teach her symbolic approach, the emphasis shifted to the therapeutic applications of the sand tray.

Traditionally, the ISST has strongly supported the psychotherapeutic application of the sand tray, not the diagnostic one. This attitude reflects a basic Jungian perspective which views the psyche as having the capacity to promote wholeness, rather than viewing the psyche from a medical model in which behavior is labeled by an outside authority for treatment purposes. Kalff herself used the client's initial tray to help her better understand the direction from which the healing might occur; however, she did not use this information to diagnose the disorders of her clients.

Currently several theses and dissertations have investigated the types of trays made by certain groups of people, seeking a correlation that clearly leans in the diagnostic direction (Grubbs 1991; Shaia 1991). There now seems to be increasing support for this type of research within the ISST; indeed, Professor Kawai, President of the ISST, has endorsed the need for objective as well as subjective evaluation of the trays (personal communication, May 10, 1992).

It would appear that, in the future, there will be a movement toward using the diagnostic/objective methodology to support the intuitive/subjective approach in the service of improved clinical skills. However, it is unlikely that the sand tray will be used for labeling purposes (as part of a test battery) or as a tool to demonstrate environmental circumstances (in court cases of child abuse) in the near future as the prevailing attitude is against using the sand tray in this way, and there is not a sufficient research base to justify its use as a diagnostic instrument. Fundamentally, the concern is that an overly diagnostic attitude could overshadow the awesome and powerful healing energies that can be evoked by Sandplay experiences.

Besides the sand picture, what other elements need to be considered to further psychological integration?

Historically, Kalff emphasized the critical importance of understanding the sand picture itself (the product), including the organization and the symbolic content of the miniatures used. In contrast, Lowenfeld paid close attention to the client's experience in creating the tray, with emphasis on what and how the child verbally communicated while making the tray. Since Lowenfeld saw the tray as a means of both verbal and nonverbal communication, she sat near to the child and was verbally responsive to the child's verbalizations and actions. Kalff, on the other hand, sat further from the client and tended to remain quiet during the experience, in order to allow the unconscious to unfold in a serene space without outer distractions.

Noting the dominance of Kalff's approach, DeDomenico (1991), who studied the Lowenfeld technique under John Hood-Williams, complained that:

> most sand tray therapists appear to neglect the World Technique's unique value as a communication tool. . . . Sand tray play as a uniquely individual language has remained relatively unexplored.
>
> (DeDomenico 1991: 1–2)

Although it is accurate that Kalff did not emphasize the tray-making experience or the clients' comments, many contemporary Sandplay therapists have begun to include the clients' behaviors in their interpretations (Ammann 1991; Kiepenheuer 1990).

In addition to observing the clients' processes and the symbolic content of final pictures, Kawai (1992) has stressed the importance of including the clients' stories and/or comments about their finished sand pictures in the interpretation of the tray. At the conclusion of the tray-making process, a client may either spontaneously volunteer a story or tell one in response to the therapist's inquiry about the tray. The client's comments need to be understood at three levels: the personal level (what does this story represent in the client's life?); the archetypal level (what are the underlying motifs?); and the cultural level (what cultural issues are seen as motivating factors in the story?).

It appears that future emphasis will be placed on viewing the entire Sandplay process from a broader perspective that includes not only an understanding of the final production in the sand, but also considers the client's process in making the tray as well as the stories or associations arising from the sand tray experience.

How can the sand tray be better integrated into clinical practice?

Both Lowenfeld and Kalff highlighted the sand tray along with their verbal therapeutic work, combining both verbal communication and nonverbal sand tray. Kalff stated that she did not consider Sandplay an adjunct to verbal analysis; however, she also indicated that the use of Sandplay could further verbal therapeutic work (Bradway et al. 1981). In addition, her written case studies (Kalff 1980) indicate that play therapy was integrated with Sandplay. Possibly, because Lowenfeld and Kalff both emphasized their work with the sand tray in their presentations and teachings, the impression arose that they used only this technique.

We believe that in the future there will be a continual integration of Sandplay into the techniques used in a traditional clinical practice. For example, Miller and Boe (1990) have reported the successful integration of Sandplay into a treatment program for psychically abused children. They studied children's sand pictures in order to understand their symbolic expressions and to help them (the therapists) select a story that would touch similar archetypal themes. The Sandplay experiences together with the telling of the story evoked the healing energies for these children in the program. It is this type of model that facilitates our understanding of how Sandplay can be integrated with particular techniques aimed at special populations.

In what settings, under what conditions, and with what types of clients will the sand tray be used?

For the most part, it appears that this is a time of widening exploration and experimentation – sometimes divergent from the Kalffian approach. Many of these experimenters use the sand tray with a different theoretical approach (Oaklander 1978). For example the sand tray is being used in retreat settings as a means of evoking personal and spiritual expression and direction. Also, some therapists are using the sand tray with couples (DeDomenico 1993; Gold 1993), with families, and in therapy groups (using one joint tray or separate trays). Sandplay theory contends that the sand tray picture contains an expression of the individual's psyche. Therefore, having several or many psyches converging in the sand creates a more complex dynamic in which the interaction of the clients becomes central, while the symbolic content displayed in the tray may become unclear and chaotic. Since there are no guidelines as yet or standards for understanding the sand tray pictures that emerge in these new settings, the future of these approaches is hard to predict. Further research and understanding of group applications of Sandplay may represent one of the many "growing-edges" of the field.

Sand tray is currently used in schools by teachers to facilitate learning as well as by school counselors for therapy. (The recent availability of lightweight sand tray materials increases its adaptability to this specific setting.) Counselors also find that the sand tray is a helpful technique with the large populations of non-English-speaking children in the schools, as it is one of the very few modalities that does not require language. The sand tray will continue to be used in the educational environment as long as there is administrative support for it as well as the availability of necessary training for school counselors.

Due to the pioneering work of clinicians and researchers who used Sandplay with positive results in clinics and hospitals, traditional views of its applications continue to expand. These inroads into unknown territory hopefully will encourage other clinicians to use the sand tray with non-traditional populations such as developmentally disabled clients, people coping with terminal illnesses, and those encountering a developmental life passage. Another non-traditional application is using Sandplay in short-term therapy. Bradway (1990, 1992) reported the successful use of Sandplay in time-limited situations (including a woman facing terminal illness), noting that the person is able to access at least a portion of the needed unconscious processes within the time allotted.

Can the present structure of ISST meet training needs of therapists interested in using Sandplay?

Sandplay is a complex therapy that requires much study and commitment to one's own personal and professional development. Only through a strong organization can significant training goals be formulated and implemented.

Currently the International Society for Sandplay Therapists (founder: Dora Kalff) has approximately sixty members worldwide. The ISST is governed by the founding members and a board of representatives from the constituency. Training standards for certification and membership in ISST have been developed separately by the various national associations. Only experienced practitioners who have been licensed to practice psychotherapy are accepted into training programs. In order to be admitted into membership of the ISST, a candidate in the United States must complete: one's own Sandplay process, a specified number of hours in Sandplay workshops and in supervision of individual cases, papers demonstrating a depth of understanding of symbols and the Sandplay process, a personal interview, and a written case study displaying solid clinical skills and extensive insight into the Sandplay process.

Members of the ISST who have fulfilled the certification standards are able to use the term "Sandplay" in describing their work with the sand tray. In the United States, therapists having Associate status of the Sandplay Therapists of America (STA) are those who use the sand tray, desire a professional affiliation with ISST, want to take advantage of training, workshops, and publications, and have not fulfilled certification standards. Some of these Associates will choose to fulfill the certification standards for membership in the ISST in the future. Others will choose to remain Associates, receiving the *Sandplay Journal* (published by the STA) and special financial considerations at STA/ISST conferences. For the majority of skilled, clinically trained psychotherapists using the sand tray, the Associate category of STA provides sufficient affiliation.

In the current structure of the ISST, several issues need to be addressed in order to meet the needs of the large number of therapists who desire training in Sandplay (Friedman and Mitchell 1992). Some of these issues are:

1 Given the limited number of ISST members, how can the ISST organization meet the considerable demand for training, particularly in
   remote areas?
2 How can the ISST better co-exist with those practitioners outside of the
   organization who are competently using the sand tray but choose not
   to affiliate with the organization?
3 Can the ISST find increasing ways to recognize and integrate the
   expertise of those individuals who qualify for the Associate category?
4 Should there be an approved curriculum for teaching Sandplay?
5 How can opportunities be provided for meaningful dialogue between
   Kalffian Sandplay therapists, Lowenfeldians, and others using the
   sand tray?

What are the future challenges for effective training?

Because of the cross-cultural popularity of the sand tray and the broad
range of professional people who are drawn to use it, training becomes a
challenging, complex issue. One group of practitioners drawn to Sandplay has a strong background in Jungian clinical theory as well as a deep
understanding of symbolic material. A second group has strong clinical
skills and an openness to learn more about Kalffian Sandplay therapy
with its emphasis on Jungian concepts. A third group has adapted the
sand tray to fit their own clinical training, often using non-traditional
materials and directive interventions that influence the placement and
movement of the miniatures. (In all probability, this third group would
not participate in Sandplay training.)

Another challenge in adequately meeting training needs is geographical: clinicians are widely dispersed around the globe. This situation
causes particular difficulty for those who want to be trained in the
"Kalffian mode," which requires therapists to complete their own
personal Sandplay work as well as attend workshops and supervision
seminars. Not only is training expensive and time-consuming, but it is
extremely difficult to complete one's own Sandplay process when there is
no other Sandplay therapist or supervisory group nearby. In the past,
therapists wanting training in Sandplay traveled to Switzerland to work
with Dora Kalff, sometimes remaining there for many months to complete their own process and comprehensive study. For the majority of
people today, however, this model is impractical. Judging from the growing number of therapists completing ISST requirements, there will soon
be enough trained teachers (ISST members) to sustain a meaningful training program even in remote areas of the United States and Canada. In
addition, ISST members will probably begin to offer training at conferences that traditionally attract a more general professional audience
(e.g., school counselors and art therapists). Local, small groups could be

established to provide a sense of continuity and collegial interaction that is necessary for the continued use of this technique. At present the *Sandplay Events Newsletter* communicates information about workshops, conferences, and publications presented by ISST members. Other newsletters, such as the *Northern California Sandplay Society Newsletter* and *Small Talk*, offer information about miniatures, photography, symbolism, and the Sandplay process.

It is clear that, in addition to trained teachers, supplementary resources will be needed to teach the growing body of knowledge about sand tray; journals, books, and audio- and video-tapes will be in increasing demand. Perhaps in time, a training curriculum with a comprehensive reading list will be developed to assure competency in Jungian theory, knowledge of symbols, and an in-depth study of the Sandplay process.

THE PLACE OF SANDPLAY WITHIN EMERGING THERAPEUTIC AND WORLD TRENDS

Historically, as we have seen, Sandplay has been one of the few therapeutic techniques to be used globally. As a result of global telecommunications and international travel, exchange among Sandplay therapists living in Europe, North America, and the Pacific rim is occurring at an unparalleled pace. This vigorous networking capability has enhanced and intensified research opportunities, and collaboration is now taking place on an international level. In addition, the increasingly sophisticated capabilities of computers to translate from one language to another will widen and quicken the possibilities of exchange. However, it will be the living image in the sand tray that continues to have the most profound impact, facilitating yet a further sense of community among peoples.

One of the consequences of worldwide economic and political change has been mass global patterns of emigration. Our cities are increasingly populated by diverse, cross-cultural groups – a situation which brings both enrichment and misunderstanding. For psychotherapists, the challenge is unique, for they must be able to understand cultural issues as well as transcend language barriers and facilitate acculturation. Because Sandplay is one of the few therapeutic techniques in which language skills are not essential in evoking healing energies, it is distinctly suited for use with multi-cultural populations.

Within this ever-shrinking world, Sandplay offers us a unique opportunity to view universal archetypal patterns as well as observe the unfolding development of the individual psyche. By carefully observing universal patterns in the sand pictures, a feeling of deep connection and a sense of unity among humankind emerges. From this sense of unity, a new world vision is possible – that we are *one*.

Sandplay provides an opportunity for connection to one's own internal natural balance, thus facilitating a personal sense of groundedness and stability in these turbulent times. Naisbitt and Aburdene (1990) have suggested that the need to re-examine the meaning of life will occur through a renaissance in the arts. Sandplay offers an opportunity for personal creative expression that facilitates a renaissance of the psyche. In the future, more people will seek the experience of Sandplay, not just for resolution of neurotic conflicts, but for a source of meaningful reconnection to their own creative and spiritual expressions.

Sandplay is indeed one of those powerful facilitators that reaches into the deepest levels of the unconscious to access healing energies. Jung succinctly addressed our personal responsibility in the healing of this alienated world when he said: "the world hangs by a thin thread and that thread is the human psyche" (Evans 1977: 303). In choosing to make a deep connection to our own psyches and struggling to heal ourselves, we can strengthen that thin thread and become part of the healing fabric of this fragmented world.

REFERENCES

Ammann, R. (1991). *Healing and Transformation in Sandplay: Creative Processes become Visible* (W.P. Rainer, trans.). La Salle, IL: Open Court Publishing. Originally published in German as *Heilende Bilder der Seele*.

Bradway, K. (1990). "Sandplay journey of a 45-year-old woman in five sessions." *Archives of Sandplay Therapy* 3 (1): 68–74.

—— (1992). "Sandplay in preparing to die." *Journal of Sandplay Therapy* 2(1): 13–37.

DeDomenico, G.S. (1991). "Applications of the Lowenfeld World Technique." *Association for Play Therapy Newsletter* 10(2): 1–4.

—— (1993). "Sand tray world play: A psychotherapeutic technique for individuals, couples and families." *The California Therapist* 5(1): 56–61.

Evans, R.I. (1977). "Interview with C.G. Jung: August, 1957." In W. McGuire and R.F.C. Hull (eds) *C.G. Jung Speaking: Interviews and Encounters*. Princeton, N.J.: Princeton University Press.

Friedman, H.S. and Mitchell, R.R. (1992). "Future of Sandplay: Responses from the Sandplay community." *Journal of Sandplay Therapy* 2(1): 77–90.

Gold, J. (1993). "Sandplay with couples." *The California Therapist* 5(1): 53–5.

Grubbs, G.A. (1991). "A categorical and comparative analysis of the Sandplay process of abused and nonabused children." Unpublished doctoral dissertation, California Graduate School of Family Psychology.

Journal of Sandplay Therapy. Lauren Cunningham (ed.) 331 Thistle Circle, Martinez, CA 94553.

Kawai, H. (1992). "Sandplay and relation." Presentation at ISST Conference, *Sand, Psyche and Symbol*, May 16, San Rafael, CA.

Kiepenheuer, K. (1990). *Crossing the Bridge*. La Salle, IL: Open Court.

Lowenfeld, M. (1927). "Organization and the rheumatic child." *Lancet* June 4: 1177.

—— (1928). "Researches in lactation." *Journal of Obstetrics and Gynaecology of the British Empire* 35(1): 114–30.

McGuire, W. and Hull, R.F.C. (eds) (1977). *C.G. Jung Speaking: Interviews and Encounters*. Princeton, N.J.: Princeton University Press.

Miller, C. and Boe, J. (1990). "Tears into diamonds: Transformation of child psychic trauma through Sandplay and storytelling." *The Arts in Psychotherapy* 17: 247–57.

Naisbitt, J. and Aburdene, P. (1990). *Megatrends 2000: Ten New Directions for the 1990's*. New York: Avon Books.

Northern California Sandplay Society Newsletter. 3490 Buskirk Ave., Suite A, Pleasant Hill, CA 94523.

Oaklander, V. (1978). *Windows to our Children*. Moab, UT: Real People Press.

Sandplay Events Newsletter. Bonnie Arendt (ed.) P.O. Box 925, Little Compton, RI 02837.

Shaia, A. (1991). "Images in the sand: The initial sand worlds of men molested as children." Unpublished doctoral dissertation, California Institute of Integral Studies, San Francisco, CA.

Small Talk. Kathie Carr (ed.) 1647 Willow Pass Rd., Suite 163, Concord, CA 94520.

Bibliographies

SANDPLAY AND OTHER RELATED TECHNIQUES

English language

This bibliography includes sand tray citations published in English. In order to be included in this listing, the article, book, or thesis/dissertation had to explore a technique(s) that uses the placement of three-dimensional miniatures and objects within a specified space, such as within a container (e.g., the sand tray), on a table top, or within a specified floor space. Articles that are exclusively devoted to Sandplay are designated by an asterisk (*).

*Abel, C. (1985). "Fire: An image of transformation." Unpublished doctoral dissertation, International College, Los Angeles.
*Adams, K.E. (1991). "Sandplay: A modern alchemical process." Unpublished master's thesis, Antioch University, Merritt Island, Florida.
*Aite, P. (1977a). "Communication through imagination." *Annual of Italian Analytical Psychologists* 1: 105–30.
*—— (1977b). "The activity of the ego and the image: Observations on the theme of 'Sandplay'." Paper presented at the Seventh International Congress of Analytical Psychology, Rome.
*—— (1978). "Ego and image: Some observations on the theme of 'Sandplay'." *Journal of Analytical Psychology* 23: 332–8.
Albino, R. (1954). "Defenses against aggression in the play of young children." *British Journal of Medical Psychology* 27: 61–71.
*Allan, J. (1988). *Inscapes of the Child's World: Jungian Counseling in Schools and Clinics.* Dallas: Spring Publications, Inc.
*Allan, J. and Berry, P. (1987). "Sandplay" (special issue: counseling with expressive arts). *Elementary School Guidance and Counseling* 21(4): 300–6.
*Allan, J. and Lawton-Speert, S. (1989). "Sand and water in the treatment of a profoundly sexually abused preschool boy." *Association for Play Therapy Newsletter* 8(4): 2–3.
*Amatruda, K. (1984). "Psychological interventions in physical illness – The Sandplay Test: Assessing a dying child's awareness of death." Unpublished paper for Saybrook Institute. Donated to the C.G. Jung Institute of San Francisco.

*—— (1989). "Grief Sandplay therapy with child trauma victims: A psychospiritual somatic treatment model." *Archives of Sandplay Therapy* 2(1): 91–104.

*Ammann, R. (1991). *Healing and Transformation in Sandplay: Creative Processes become Visible* (W.P. Rainer, trans.). La Salle, IL: Open Court Publishing. Originally published in German as *Heilende Bilder der Seele*.

Andersen, V. (1979a). "Historical note on the manuscript." In M. Lowenfeld, *The World Technique*: xi–xii. London: George Allen & Unwin.

—— (1979b). "Origin of the 'World'." In M. Lowenfeld, *The World Technique*: 278–81. London: George Allen & Unwin.

Anderson, H.H. and Anderson, G.L. (eds) (1951). *An Introduction to Projective Techniques*. Englewood Cliffs, NJ: Prentice-Hall, Inc.

*Aoki, S. (1981). "The retest reliability of the Sandplay technique" (2nd report). *British Journal of Projective Psychology and Personality* 26(2): 25–33.

*Avrech, G. (in press). "Initial sand trays: Clues to the psyche." In B. Caprio (ed.) *Sandplay: Coming of Age*. Paper presented at the Los Angeles Sandplay Association 1991 Conference.

Baker, C. (1993). "Healing in sand: Navajo sand painting and Sandplay." *Journal of Sandplay Therapy* 2(2): 89–112.

*Baldridge, A.E. (1990). "In a grain of sand." *Northern California Sandplay Society Newsletter* Fall: 3–8.

Bell, J.E. (1948). *Projective Techniques*. New York: Longmans, Green & Co.

*Belzer, C.A. (1991). "The effects of sandplay in a classroom setting with children identified as learning disabled." Unpublished master's thesis, Pacific Oaks College, Pasadena, CA.

Bender, L. and Woltmann, A. (1941). "Play and psychotherapy." *Nervous Child* 1: 17–42.

*Berry, P. (1989). "The nitty gritty of sand." *Association for Play Therapy Newsletter* 8(4): 4–6.

Bolgar, H. and Fischer, L.K. (1940). "The toy test: A psychodiagnostic method." *Psychological Bulletin* 37: 517–18.

—— (1947). "Personality projection in the World Test." *American Journal of Orthopsychiatry* 17: 117–28.

Bowyer, L.R. (1956). "A normative study of sand tray worlds." *Bulletin of British Psychological Society*. Summarized (1970) in L.R. Bowyer, *The Lowenfeld World Technique*. Oxford: Pergamon Press.

—— (1958). "The sand tray world as a projective technique with mental defectives." *Journal of the Midland Mental Deficiency Society* 4: 44–55.

—— (1959). "The importance of sand in the World Technique: An experiment." *British Journal of Educational Psychology* 29: 162–4.

—— (1970). *The Lowenfeld World Technique*. Oxford: Pergamon Press.

Bowyer, L.R. and Gillies, J. (1972). "The social and emotional adjustment of deaf and partially deaf children." *British Journal of Educational Psychology* 42(3): 305–8.

Bowyer, L.R., Gillies, J. and Scott, J. (1966). "The use of projective techniques with deaf children." *Rorschach Newsletter* 11: 3–6.

Bowyer, L.R. and Gilmour, R. (1968). "Interpersonal communication of deaf children using the Village Test." In A. Friedemann, H. Phillipson, B. Scott and C. Williams (eds) *Rorschach Proceedings: VIIth International Congress of Rorschach and Other Projective Techniques*, London: 315–18. Bern: Hans Huber Publishers.

Bowyer, L.R. and Huggan, R. (1965). "A comparative study of the World and Village Techniques." *Proceedings of the VIth International Congress of the Rorschach and Other Projective Techniques*, Paris.

Bowyer, L.R., Marshall, A. and Weddell, K. (1963). "The relative personality adjustment of severely deaf and partially deaf children." *British Journal of Educational Psychology* 33: 85–7.

*Bradway, K. (1978). "Hestia and Athena in the analysis of women." *Inward Light* 41: 28–42.

*—— (1979a). "Sandplay in psychotherapy." *Art Psychotherapy* 6(2): 85–93.

*—— (1979b). "Initial and final Sandplay worlds of married non-career and unmarried career women in analysis." *Professional Reports* 6: 35–41. San Francisco: C.G. Jung Institute. Presented (March, 1979) at the Joint Conference, United States Societies of Jungian Analysts, Asilomar, CA.

*—— (1981a). "Developmental stages in children's sand worlds." In K. Bradway *et al.* (eds) *Sandplay Studies: Origins, Theory and Practice*: 93–100. San Francisco: C.G. Jung Institute. Republished (1990) Boston: Sigo Press.

*—— (1981b). "A woman's individuation through Sandplay." In K. Bradway *et al.* (eds) *Sandplay Studies: Origins, Theory and Practice*: 133–56. San Francisco: C.G. Jung Institute. Republished (1990) Boston: Sigo Press.

*—— (1985). *Sandplay Bridges and the Transcendent Function*. San Francisco: C.G. Jung Institute.

*—— (1987). "Sandplay: What makes it work?" In M.A. Mattoon (ed.) *The archetype of shadow in a split world: Proceedings of the Tenth International Congress for Analytical Psychology, Berlin, 1986*: 409–14. Einsiedeln, Switzerland: Daimon Verlag.

*—— (1990). "Sandplay journey of a 45-year-old woman in five sessions." *Archives of Sandplay Therapy* 3(1): 68–78.

*—— (1991). "Transference and countertransference in Sandplay therapy." *Journal of Sandplay Therapy* 1(1): 25–43.

*—— (1992a). "Sun and moon in Sandplay." *Journal of Sandplay Therapy* 1(2): 47–9.

*—— (1992b). "Sandplay in preparing to die." *Journal of Sandplay Therapy* 2(1): 13–37.

*Bradway, K., Signell, K.A., Spare, G.H., Stewart, C.T., Stewart, L.H. and Thompson, C. (1981). *Sandplay Studies: Origins, Theory and Practice*. San Francisco: C.G. Jung Institute. Republished (1990) Boston: Sigo Press.

Brun, G. (1948). "Report on the work of the department of child psychiatry of Bispebjerg Hospital, Copenhagen." In M. Lowenfeld (ed.) *On the Psychotherapy of Children*: 94–106. London: E.T. Heron & Co. Ltd.

Bühler, C. (1941). "Symbolic action in children." *Transactions of the New York Academy of Science* 17: 63.

—— (1951a). "The World Test: A projective technique." *Journal of Child Psychiatry* 2: 4–23.

—— (1951b). "The World Test: Manual of directions." *Journal of Child Psychiatry* 2: 69–81.

—— (1952). "National differences in World Test projective patterns." *Journal of Projective Techniques* 16(1): 42–55.

Bühler, C. and Carrol, H.S. (1951). "A comparison of the results of the World Test with the teachers' judgment concerning children's personality adjustment." *Journal of Child Psychiatry* 2: 36–68.

Bühler, C. and Kelly, G. (1941). *The World Test: A measurement of emotional disturbance*. New York: Psychological Corporation.

*Burt, J.C. (1991). "Sandplay therapy: A bridge from boyhood to adolescence." Unpublished master's thesis, Pacific Oaks College, Pasadena, CA.

*—— (in press). "Early loss and abandonment issues as revealed in adults' Sandplay." In B. Caprio (ed.) *Sandplay: Coming of Age*. Paper presented at the Los Angeles Sandplay Association 1991 Conference.

*Campbell, F. (in press). "Transformation in the sand: From addiction to recovery." In B. Caprio (ed.) *Sandplay: Coming of Age*. Paper presented at the Los Angeles Sandplay Association 1991 Conference.

*Capitolo, M. (1992). "The dark goddesses: An encounter with the dark feminine." *Journal of Sandplay Therapy* 1(2): 59–69.

*Caprio, B. (1989). "The sand tray: An art therapy perspective." Unpublished master's thesis, Loyola-Marymount University, Los Angeles, CA.

*—— (ed.) (in press). *Sandplay: Coming of Age*. Proceedings of the Los Angeles Sandplay Association 1991 Conference.

*—— (in press). "Spiritual imagery in Sandplay." In B. Caprio (ed.) *Sandplay: Coming of Age*. Paper presented at the Los Angeles Sandplay Association 1991 Conference.

*Caprio, B. and Hedberg, T. (1986). *Coming Home: A Manual for Spiritual Direction*. Mahwah, NJ: Paulist Press.

*Carey, L. (1990). "Sandplay therapy with a troubled child." *The Arts in Psychotherapy* 17: 197–209.

*—— (1991). "Family Sandplay therapy." *Arts in Psychotherapy* 18: 231–9.

*Carmody, J.B. (1985). "Self-restoration and initiation in analytical child therapy: Observations on Sandplay." *Dissertation Abstracts International* 45(8-B): 2681. (University Microfilms No. 84–25701.)

Cashore, S. (1992). "Sand and water play: Three brief examples." *Association for Play Therapy Newsletter* 9(2): 4–5.

*Chambers, L. (1990). "The in-turning spiral: The path to the healing of the feminine." *Northern California Sandplay Society Newsletter* Fall: 1–2.

Clegg, H.D. (1981). "The reparative motif in expressive play therapy." Unpublished doctoral dissertation. Berkeley, CA: The Wright Institute.

—— (1984). *The Reparative Motif in Child and Adult Therapy*. New York: Jason Aronson.

*Crable, P.G. (1976). "Women and self: An initial investigation of the feminine essence using Sandplay." (Doctoral dissertation, United States International University.) *Dissertation Abstracts International* 37(3-B): 1483-B. (University Microfilms No. 76–19751.)

Cramer, P. and Hogan, K.A. (1975). "Sex differences in verbal and play fantasy." *Developmental Psychology* 11: 145–54.

*Creadick, T.A. (1985). "The role of the expressive arts in therapy." *Journal of Reading, Writing and Learning Disabilities International* 1(3): 55–60.

*Currant, N. (1989). "Room to breathe." *The American Journal of Art Therapy* 27: 80–6.

Dahlgren, B. (1957). *Research Bulletin No. 11*. Stockholm: University Institute of Education.

DeDomenico, G.S. (1986a). "The Lowenfeld World apparatus: A methodological contribution towards the study and the analysis of the sand tray play process." Doctoral dissertation, Pacific Graduate School of Psychology, Menlo Park, CA.) *Dissertation Abstracts International*. (University Microfilms No. 87–17059.)

—— (1986b). *Applications of the Lowenfeld World Technique: A comparative illustration of the analysis of the final world and the analysis of the sand tray play process in clinical practice*. Oakland, CA: Vision Quest into Symbolic Reality.

—— (1988). *Sand Tray World Play: A comprehensive guide to the use of sand tray in psychotherapeutic transformational settings*. Oakland, CA: Vision Quest into Symbolic Reality.

—— (1991a). "Applications of the Lowenfeld World Technique." *Association for Play Therapy Newsletter* 10(2): 1–4.

—— (1991b). "The Lowenfeld World Technique: A clinical example." *Association for Play Therapy Newsletter* 10(3): 1–4.

—— (1993). "Sand tray world play: A psychotherapeutic technique for individuals, couples and families." *The California Therapist* 5(1): 56–61.

*Denkers, G.C. (1985). "An investigation of the diagnostic potential of Sandplay utilizing Linn Jones' Developmental Scoring System." Unpublished doctoral dissertation, Psychological Studies Institute, Pacific Grove Graduate School of Professional Psychology, Berkeley, CA.

*Dukes, S.D. (1992). "The significance of play." *Journal of Sandplay Therapy* 2(1): 53–7.

*Dundas, E. (1978). *Symbols Come Alive in the Sand.* Aptos, CA: Aptos Press.

*—— (1992). "Sandplay therapy." *Association for Play Therapy Newsletter* 3(11): 1–3.

*Dunn-Fierstein, P. (1993). "Exploring the egg: The creative center." *Journal of Sandplay Therapy* 2(2): 59–73.

Eickhoff, L.F.W. (1952). "Dreams in sand." *British Journal of Psychiatry* 98: 235–43.

—— (1993). "The development of masculine power in one example of Sandplay therapy." *Journal of Sandplay Therapy* 2(2): 75–87.

*Eide-Midtsand, N. (1987). "Struggles with the 'other one': The reconciliation of a pre-adolescent boy with his masculinity." *Journal of Analytical Psychology* 32: 157–71.

Erikson, E.H. (1951). "Sex differences in the play configurations of pre-adolescents." *American Journal of Orthopsychiatry* 21: 667–92.

—— (1963). *Childhood and Society.* New York: Norton.

—— (1964). "Inner and outer space: Reflections on womanhood." *Daedalus* 93: 582–97.

—— (1968). *Identity: Youth and Crisis.* New York: Norton.

Fischer, L.K. (1950a). "The World 'Test'." In W. Wolff (ed.) *Personality Symposia on Topical Issues: Projective and Expressive Methods of Personality Investigation ("Diagnosis"):* 62–76. New York: Grune & Stratton.

—— (1950b). "A new psychological tool in function: Preliminary clinical experience with the Bolgar–Fischer World Test." *American Journal of Orthopsychiatry* 20: 281–92.

*Friedman, H.S. (in press). "A heritage rediscovered: A case history." In B. Caprio (ed.) *Sandplay: Coming of Age.* Paper presented at the Los Angeles Sandplay Association 1991 Conference.

*Friedman, H.S. and Mitchell, R.R. (1991). "Dora Maria Kalff: Connections between life and work." *Journal of Sandplay Therapy* 1(1): 17–23.

*—— (1992). "Future of Sandplay: Responses from the Sandplay community." *Journal of Sandplay Therapy* 2(1): 77–90.

Fujii, S. (1978) (a.k.a. Aoki, S.). "Research note on Lowenfeld's World Technique in Japan: Test–retest reliability of the Sandplay 'world' expression by children." *British Journal of Projective Psychology and Personality Study* 23: 27.

*—— (1979). "Retest reliability of the Sandplay technique (1st report)." *British Journal of Projective Psychology and Personality Study* 24: 21–5.

*Gabriellini, G. and Nissim, S. (1988). "Sandplay therapy with a psychotic child." In M. Sidoli and M. Davies (eds) *Jungian Child Psychotherapy: Individuation in Childhood:* 221–30. London: Karnac Books.

Gillies, J. (1975). "Personality and adjustment in deaf children." *British Journal of Projective Psychology and Personality Study* 20(1): 33–4.

—— (1982). "The role of communicative abilities and field dependence/independence in the social adjustment of deaf children." Unpublished doctoral dissertation, University of Glasgow.

Gilmour, R. (1971). "Communication and social adjustment in young deaf children." Unpublished master's thesis, University of Glasgow.

Gitlin, K. (1988, June). "The World Technique: A review." *Association for Play Therapy Newsletter* 7(2): 1–3, 6.

—— (1988, September). "The World Technique: A review." *Association for Play Therapy Newsletter* 7(3): 1–4.

Gold, J. (1993). "Sandplay with couples." *The California Therapist* 5(1): 53–5.

*Gradwell, L.E. (1992). "The mermaid." *Journal of Sandplay Therapy* 1(2): 93–100.

*Grubbs, G.A. (1991). "A categorical and comparative analysis of the Sandplay process of abused and nonabused children." Unpublished doctoral dissertation, California Graduate School of Family Psychology.

*—— (1991). "A categorical and comparative analysis of the Sandplay process of abused and nonabused children." *Northern California Sandplay Society Newsletter* Fall: 1–2.

Harding, G. (1948). "Themes with variations." In M. Lowenfeld (ed.) *On the Psychotherapy of Children*: 82–93. London: E.T. Heron & Co. Ltd.

*Hedberg, T.M. (1988). "Respect for the animal kingdom: A Jungian approach." Unpublished doctoral dissertation, Sierra University, Costa Mesa, CA.

*—— (in press). "Animal symbolism in Sandplay." In B. Caprio (ed.) *Sandplay: Coming of Age*. Paper presented at the Los Angeles Sandplay Association 1991 Conference.

*Hegeman, G. (1992). "The Sandplay collection." *Journal of Sandplay Therapy* 1(2): 101–6.

Henry, W.E. (1960). "Projective techniques." In P. Mussen (ed.) *Handbook of Research Methods in Child Development*: 603–44. New York: Wiley & Sons.

Homberger, E. (1937) (a.k.a. Erik Erikson). "Configurations in play – clinical notes." *Psychoanalytic Quarterly* 6: 139–214.

—— (1938) (a.k.a. Erik Erikson). "Dramatic productions test." In H.A. Murray (ed.) *Explorations in Personality*: 552–82. New York: Oxford University Press.

Honzik, M. P. (1951). "Sex differences in the occurrence of materials in the play constructions of preadolescents." *Child Development* 22(1): 15–35.

Hood-Williams, J. (1987, October). "A window on the child's unconscious: A reunion of the four great schools of thought on entering the child's inner world." Paper presented at International Congress of Child Psychotherapy, San Francisco.

Irwin, E. C. (1983). "The diagnostic and therapeutic use of pretend play." In C.E. Schaefer and D.J. O'Connor (eds) *Handbook of Play Therapy*: 148–73. New York: John Wiley.

*Jackson, B. (1991). "Before reaching for the symbols dictionary." *Journal of Sandplay Therapy* 1(1): 55–8.

*Jones, L.E. (1986). "The development of structure in the world of expression: A cognitive-developmental analysis of children's 'sand worlds'." (Doctoral dissertation, Pacific Graduate School of Psychology, Menlo Park, CA.) *Dissertation Abstracts International*. (University Microfilms No. 83–03178.)

*Kahn, J. (1989). *The Use of the Sandtray in Psychotherapy with Children and their Parents*. Petaluma, CA: Playrooms.

*Kalff, D. (1957). "The significance of the hare in Reynard the Fox." *Journal of Analytical Psychology* 2(2). Reprinted (1992) in *Journal of Sandplay Therapy* 1(2): 13–26.

*—— (1966a). "Symbolism and Child Analysis." Unpublished transcription of seminar conducted at Footlighters' Child Guidance Clinic, Hollywood Presbyterian Hospital, Hollywood, CA.

*—— (1966b). "The archetype as a healing factor." *Psychologia* 9: 177–84. Originally printed (1962) in German in A. Guggenbühl-Craig (ed.) *The Archetype: Proceedings of the 2nd International Congress for Analytical Psychology*: 182–200. Basel, Switzerland: S. Karger.

*—— (1971). "Experiences with far eastern philosophers." In J.B. Wheelwright (ed.) *The Analytic Process: Aims, Analysis, Training*: 56–7. The Proceedings of the Fourth International Congress for Analytical Psychology. New York: G.P. Putnam's Sons.

*—— (1980). *Sandplay: A Psychotherapeutic Approach to the Psyche* (W. Ackerman, trans.). Santa Monica: Sigo Press. Originally published (1966) in German as *Sandspiel*. Zurich: Rascher. First published (1971) in English as *Sandplay: Mirror of a Child's Psyche* (H. Kirsch, trans.). San Francisco: Browser Press.

*—— (1981). Foreword. In K. Bradway, *et al.*, *Sandplay Studies: Origins, Theory and Practice*. San Francisco: C.G. Jung Institute. Republished (1990) Boston: Sigo Press.

*—— (1982). Preface. In H. Kawai and Y. Yamanaka (eds) *Studies of Sandplay Therapy in Japan* I: 227–9. Tokyo: Seishin-Shoboh.

*—— (1983). Foreword. In E.L. Weinrib, *Images of the Self: The Sandplay Therapy Process*. Boston: Sigo Press.

*—— (1987). "Sandplay with Dora Kalff." (Notes of seminar.) Carmel, CA: University of California at Santa Cruz.

*—— (1988a). "Beyond the shadow." *Archives of Sandplay Therapy* 1: 87–97.

*—— (1988b). "Sandplay in Switzerland." (Notes of seminar.) Zürich: University of California at Santa Cruz.

*—— (1988c). *International Society for Sandplay Therapy* (Founder: Dora M. Kalff). (Information booklet.) Zollikon, Switzerland: Dora Kalff.

*—— (1991). "Introduction to Sandplay therapy." *Journal of Sandplay Therapy* 1(1): 7–15. Originally published (1978) in German as "Eine kurze Einführung in die Sandspieltherapie." *Praxis der Psychotherapie* 23: 269–73. Heidelberg: Springer-Verlag. Translated into English by Kalff (1986) and presented to the International Society for Sandplay Therapy. Printed (1988c) in English by *International Society for Sandplay Therapy*.

—— (1992). "Steps of the emotional changes in prepuberty." *Archives of Sandplay Therapy* 5(1): 3–16.

*—— (1993). "Twenty points to be considered in the interpretation of a Sandplay." *Journal of Sandplay Therapy* 2(2): 17–35.

Kamp, L.N.J., Ambrosius, A.M. and Zwaan, E.J. (1986). "The World Test: pathological traits in the arrangement of miniature toys." *Acta Psychiatrica Belgica* 86(3): 208–19.

Kamp, L.N.J. and Kessler, E.G. (1970). "The World Test: Developmental aspects of a play technique." *Journal of Child Psychology and Psychiatry* 11: 81–108. Reprinted (1971) in French as "Test du Monde: Aspects développementaux d'une technique de jeu." *Revue de Neuropsychiatrie Infantile* 19(6): 295–322.

*Kiepenheuer, K. (1990). *Crossing the Bridge* (K.R. Schneider, trans.). La Salle, IL: Open Court. Originally published in German as *Geh über die Brücke*.

*—— (1991). "The witch's house: A free and protected place for 'bewitched' children." *Journal of Sandplay Therapy* 1(1): 45–7.

*Kosirog, A. and Mahdi, L. (1983). "Sandplay in America." *Association for Play Therapy Newsletter* 2(2): 5–6.

*Larsen, C. (1991). "Puer-senex paper." *Archives of Sandplay Therapy* 4(1): 59–73.

*Lenhart, D. (1989). "The children of Ganymede: An investigation into the symbolic language of gay men through the use of Sandplay therapy."

(Doctoral dissertation, Union for Experimenting Colleges and Universities.) *Dissertation Abstracts International* (University Microfilms No. 59-04B).

Lowenfeld, M. (1931). "A new approach to the problem of psychoneurosis in childhood." *British Journal of Medical Psychology* 1(3): 194–227. Presented to the Medical Section of the British Psychological Society, March 15, 1931. Reprinted (1988) in C. Urwin and J. Hood-Williams, *Child Psychotherapy, War and the Normal Child*: 177–214. London: Free Association Books.

—— (1934). "Psychogenic factors in chronic disease in childhood." *Medical Women's Federation Newsletter* July: 1–18. Reprinted (1988) in C. Urwin and J. Hood-Williams, *Child Psychotherapy, War and the Normal Child*: 215–34.

—— (1935). *Play in Childhood*. London: Victor Gollancz. Reprinted (1976) New York: John Wiley & Sons. Reprinted (1991) London: Mac Keith Press.

—— (1937a). "The value of direct objective record of children's phantasies with special reference to ideas of movement." *Proceedings of the International Congress of Psychology* 8: 396.

—— (1937b). "A thesis concerning the fundamental structure of the mento-emotional processes in children." Unpublished paper presented at the annual meeting of the General Section of the British Psychological Society in Manchester on April 18. Printed (1988) in C. Urwin and J. Hood-Williams, *Child Psychotherapy, War and the Normal Child*: 247–64. London: Free Association Books.

—— (1938). "The theory and use of play in psychotherapy of childhood." *Journal of Mental Science* 84: 1057–8.

—— (1939). "The World pictures of children: A method of recording and studying them." *British Journal of Medical Psychology* 18 (pt.1): 65–101. Presented to the Medical Section of the British Psychological Society, March, 1938. Reprinted (1988) in C. Urwin and J. Hood-Williams, *Child Psychotherapy, War and the Normal Child*: 265–309. London: Free Association Books.

—— (1944). "Direct projective therapy." Unpublished paper presented to the General Section of the British Psychological Society in Glasgow, April. Printed (1988) in C. Urwin and J. Hood-Williams, *Child Psychotherapy, War and the Normal Child*: 315–23. London: Free Association Books.

—— (1946). "Discussion on the value of play therapy in child psychiatry." *Proceedings of the Royal Society of Medicine* 39: 439–42.

—— (ed.) (1948a). *On the Psychotherapy of Children*. London: E.T. Heron & Co. Ltd.

—— (1948b). "The nature of the primary system." In M. Lowenfeld (ed.) *On the Psychotherapy of Children*: 31–48. London: E.T. Heron & Co. Ltd. Reprinted (1988) in C. Urwin and J. Hood-Williams, *Child Psychotherapy, War and the Normal Child*: 325–45. London: Free Association Books.

—— (1950). "The nature and use of the Lowenfeld World Technique in work with children and adults." *The Journal of Psychology* 30: 325–31.

—— (1951). "Principles of psychotherapy applied to the situation of the withdrawn child." Compilation of two unpublished papers ("Some principles of child psychotherapy" and "The problem of the withdrawn child") both presented at the International Congress for Psychotherapeutics, Leiden-Oegstgeest, September 5–8. Printed (1988) in C. Urwin and J. Hood-Williams, *Child Psychotherapy, War and the Normal Child*: 351–62. London: Free Association Books.

—— (1952). "Training seminars for child therapists at the Institute of Child Psychology." Unpublished transcripts, London.

—— (1954). *The Lowenfeld World Technique*, Memorandum from the Institute of Child Psychology, 6 Pembridge Villas, Bayswater, London.

—— (1955). "The structure of transference." *Acta Psychotherapeutica Psychosomatica et Orthopaedagogica* 3: 502–7. Paper presented at the International Congress of Psychotherapy, Zürich, July 20–24, 1954. Partially reprinted (1988) in C. Urwin and J. Hood-Williams, *Child Psychotherapy, War and the Normal Child*: 363–7. London: Free Association Books.

—— (1960). "The World Technique." *Topical Problems in Psychotherapy* 3: 248–63.

—— (1964a). "The non-verbal 'thinking' of children." In M. Lowenfeld, P. Traill and F. Rowles (eds) *The Non-verbal 'Thinking' of Children and its Place in Psychotherapy*. London: Institute of Child Psychology Ltd.

—— (1964b). "The study of preverbal thinking and its relation to psychotherapy." Paper presented at the Sixth International Congress of Psychotherapy, London.

—— (1966). "The adolescent's search for identity." Unpublished paper presented at the Sixth International Congress on Child Psychiatry in Edinburgh, July 24–29. Printed (1988) in C. Urwin and J. Hood-Williams, *Child Psychotherapy, War and the Normal Child*: 371–3. London: Free Association Books.

—— (1967a). "Communication with children." *Revue de Neuropsychiatrie Infantile* 5: 431–45. Printed (1988) in C. Urwin and J. Hood-Williams, *Child Psychotherapy, War and the Normal Child*: 375–87. London: Free Association Books.

—— (1967b). "On normal emotional and intellectual development of children." Lecture presented at St Edmund's College, Ware, England.

—— (1970). "The Lowenfeld technique." In R. Bowyer (ed.) *The Lowenfeld World Technique*. Oxford: Pergamon Press.

—— (1979). *The World Technique*. London: George Allen & Unwin.

Lumry, G.K. (1951). "Study of World Test characteristics as a basis for discrimination between various clinical categories." *Journal of Child Psychiatry* 2: 24–35.

Maclay, D.T. (1970). *Treatment for Children: The Work of a Child Guidance Clinic*. New York: Science House.

*McNally, S.P. (1984). "Sandplay: A sourcebook for psychotherapists." Unpublished manuscript.

*Mantele, O. (in press). "A child's grief process through Sandplay." In B. Caprio (ed.) *Sandplay: Coming of Age*. Paper presented at the Los Angeles Sandplay Association 1991 Conference.

Mead, M. (1979). Foreword. In M. Lowenfeld, *The World Technique*. London: George Allen & Unwin.

Michael, J.C. and Bühler, C. (1945). "Experiences with personality testing in a neuropsychiatric department of a public general hospital." *Diseases of the Nervous System* 6(7): 205–11.

*Miller, C. and Boe, J. (1990). "Tears into diamonds: Transformation of child psychic trauma through Sandplay and storytelling." *The Arts in Psychotherapy* 17: 247–57.

*Miller, R.R. (1982). "Investigation of a psychotherapeutic tool for adults: The sand tray." (Doctoral dissertation, California School of Professional Psychology, Fresno.) *Dissertation Abstracts International* 43(1-B): 257. (University Microfilms No. 82–07557.)

*Millikan, F. (1992a). "Hestia: Goddess of hearth and fire." *Journal of Sandplay Therapy* 1(2): 71–91.

*—— (1992b). "Relationship and process in Sandplay: A self psychology perspective." *Journal of Sandplay Therapy* 2(1): 39–51.

Mills, B. (1990). "The therapeutic use of sand and water play with maternally deprived preschool children." *Association for Play Therapy Newsletter* 9(1): 1–4.

*Mitchell, R.R. (1987). "Overview of the Sandplay technique." *Western ACES Newsletter* 25: 5–6.

*—— (in press). "A survey of Sandplay history." In B. Caprio (ed.) *Sandplay: Coming of Age*. Paper presented at the Los Angeles Sandplay Association 1991 Conference.

*Mitchell, R.R. and Friedman, H.S. (1992). "Sandplay: Overview of the first sixty years." *Journal of Sandplay Therapy* 1(2): 27–38.

*Mizushima, K. (1971/72). "Art therapies in Japan." *Interpersonal Development* 2: 213–21.

Morris, W.W. (1951). "Other projective methods: The World Test." In H.H. Anderson and G.L. Anderson (eds) *An Introduction to Projective Techniques*: 524–6. New York: Prentice-Hall.

Murphy, L.B. (1956a). *Personality in Young Children: Methods for the Study of Personality in Young Children* (Volume I). New York: Basic Books.

—— (1956b). *Personality in Young Children: Colin – a Normal Child* (Volume II). New York: Basic Books.

*Noyes, M. (1981). "Sandplay imagery: An aid to teaching reading." *Academic Therapy* 17(2): 231–7.

*Nyman, N.W. (1984). "An exploration of non-verbal expression in childhood: Child art and sandplay." Paper prepared for School of Social Welfare, University of California, Berkeley.

Oaklander, V. (1978). *Windows to Our Children*. Moab, UT: Real People Press.

Par, M.A. (1990). "Sand and water play: A case study." *Association for Play Therapy Newsletter* 9(1): 4–6.

Pascal, G. (1952). "Gestalt functions: The Bender-Gestalt, Mosaic and World Tests." In D. Brower and L. Abt (eds) *Progress in Clinical Psychology* 1: 185–90.

Pickford, R. (1959). "Two cases illustrating the emotional effects of encephalitis and meningitis in early childhood." *Scottish Medical Journal* 4: 379–85.

—— (1973). "The versatility of the World Technique." *Projective Psychology* 18: 21–3.

—— (1975). "Expression of thoughts by means of the Lowenfeld sand tray 'World' material." In I. Jakab (ed.) *Transcultural Aspects of Psychiatric Art*: 188–92. Basel, Switzerland: Karger.

—— (1992). "The sand tray: Update 1970–1990." *British Journal of Projective Psychology* 37(2): 26–32.

*Reece, S.T. (in press). "Symbolic expression in Sandplay: The mound as healing image." In B. Caprio (ed.) *Sandplay: Coming of Age*. Paper presented at the Los Angeles Sandplay Association 1991 Conference.

*Reed, J.P. (1975). *Sand Magic Experience in Miniatures: A Non-verbal Therapy for Children*. Albuquerque: JPR Press.

*—— (1980). *Emergence: Essays on the Process of Individuation through Sand Tray Therapy, Art Forms and Dreams*. Nehalem, OR: self-published.

Rhinehart, L. and Engelhorn, P. (1986). "The sand tray dialog: The sand tray as an adjunctive tool." Seminar presented at the Annual Conference of the American Association of Art Therapy, Los Angeles, CA.

Rosenzweig, S., Bundas, L.E., Lumry, K. and Davidson, H.W. (1944). "An elementary syllabus of psychological tests." *The Journal of Psychology* 18: 9–40.

Rosenzweig, S. and Kogan, K. (1949). *Psychodiagnosis: An Introduction to the Integration of Tests in Dynamic Clinical Practice*. New York: Grune & Stratton.

Rosenzweig, S. and Shakow, D. (1937). "Play technique in schizophrenia and other psychoses." *American Journal of Orthopsychiatry* 7: 32–47.

*Ryce-Menuhin, J. (1983). "Sandplay in an adult Jungian psychotherapy." *British Journal of Projective Psychology and Personality Study* 28(2): 13–21.

*—— (1988). *The Self in Early Childhood*. London: Free Association Books.

*—— (1992). *Jungian Sandplay: The Wonderful Therapy*. London: Routledge.

*Sandner, D. (1991). Preface. In R. Ammann, *Healing and Transformation in Sandplay*. La Salle, IL: Open Court.

*Sandu, M. (1978). "Feminine psyche: An initial investigation of archetypal constellations as projected in sandplay." Unpublished master's thesis, United States International University.

*Shaia, A. (1991). "Images in the sand: The initial sand worlds of men molested as children." Unpublished doctoral dissertation, California Institute of Integral Studies, San Francisco, CA.

*—— (1992). "When men are missing." *Northern California Sandplay Society Newsletter* Spring: 1–2.

*Shankle, J. (1980). "Brian's development: An application of sand tray therapy." Unpublished master's thesis/project, Pacific Oaks College, Pasadena, CA.

*Shepherd, S.T. (1992). "The birth of the dark child." *Journal of Sandplay Therapy* 1(2): 51–7.

*Sidoli, M. and Davies, M. (eds) (1988). *Jungian Child Psychotherapy: Individuation in Childhood*. London: Karnac Books.

*Signell, K.A. (1981). "The Sandplay process in a man's development: The use of Sandplay with men." In K. Bradway *et al.* (eds) *Sandplay Studies: Origins, Theory and Practice*: 101–31. San Francisco: C.G. Jung Institute. Republished (1990) Boston: Sigo Press.

Sjolund, M. (1981). "Play-diagnosis and therapy in Sweden: The Erica-method." *Journal of Clinical Psychology* 37(2): 322–5.

—— (1983). "A 'new' Swedish technique for play diagnosis and therapy: The Erica method." *Association for Play Therapy Newsletter* 2(1): 3–5.

*Spare, G.H. (1984) "Are there any rules? (Musings of a peripatetic Sandplayer)." In K. Bradway *et al.* (eds) *Sandplay Studies: Origins, Theory and Practice*: 195–208. San Francisco: C.G. Jung Institute. Republished (1990) Boston: Sigo Press.

*Stewart, C.T. (1981). "The developmental psychology of Sandplay." In K. Bradway *et al.* (eds) *Sandplay Studies: Origins, Theory and Practice*: 39–92. San Francisco: C.G. Jung Institute. Republished (1990) Boston: Sigo Press.

*Stewart, L.H. (1977). "Sandplay therapy: Jungian technique." In B.B. Wolman (ed.) *International Encyclopedia of Psychiatry, Psychology, Psychoanalysis, and Neurology* 6: 9–11. New York: Aesculapium.

*—— (1981). "Play and Sandplay." In K. Bradway *et al.* (eds) *Sandplay Studies: Origins, Theory and Practice*: 21–37. San Francisco: C.G. Jung Institute. Republished (1990) Boston: Sigo Press.

*—— (1982). "Sandplay and Jungian analysis." In M. Stein (ed.) *Jungian Analysis*: 204–18. La Salle, IL: Open Court.

Stewart, L.H. and Stewart, C.T. (1981). "Play, games and affects: A contribution toward a comprehensive theory of play." In A. Cheska (ed.) *Play as Context*: 42–52. West Point, NY: Leisure Press.

*Stone, H. (1980). Prologue. In D. Kalff, *Sandplay*. Santa Monica: Sigo Press.

Stone, L.J. (1959). "The Toy World Test." In O.K. Buros (ed.) *The Fifth Mental Measurements Yearbook*: 168–9. Highland Park, NJ: Gryphon.

*Sullwold, E. (1971). "Eagle eye." In H. Kirsch (ed.) *The Well-tended Tree*: 235–52. New York: G.P. Putnam's Sons.

*—— (1977). "Jungian child therapy." In B. Wolman (ed.) *International Encyclopedia of Psychiatry, Psychology, Psychoanalysis, and Neurology* 6: 242–6. New York: Aesculapium.

*—— (1982). "Treatment of children in analytical psychology." In M. Stein (ed.) *Jungian Analysis*: 235–55. La Salle, IL: Open Court.

*——— (1989). "Clouds and the creative imagination." *Psychological Perspectives* 21: 12–29.

*——— (1990). Foreword. In K. Kiepenheuer, *Crossing the Bridge: A Jungian Approach to Adolescence.* La Salle: IL: Open Court.

*Sweig, T. (1988, November). "Is showing telling? Art therapy and Sandplay as treatment for dissociative disorders." Paper presented at the meeting of the American Art Therapy Association, Chicago, IL.

*Talamini, M. (1992). "Geometric forms in Sandplay therapy." *Archives of Sandplay Therapy* 5(2): 38–52.

*Tatum, J. (1991). Preface to Dora Kalff's "Introduction to Sandplay Therapy." *Journal of Sandplay Therapy* 1(1): 7–8.

*——— (1992a). Preface to Dora Kalff's "Significance of the hare in Reynard the Fox." *Journal of Sandplay Therapy* 1(2): 11–12.

*——— (1992b). "Clare Thompson: Reflections on the 'Sandtray World'." *Journal of Sandplay Therapy* 2(1): 67–74.

*Thompson, C.W. (1981). "Variations on a theme by Lowenfeld: Sandplay in focus." In K. Bradway *et al.* (eds) *Sandplay Studies: Origins, Theory and Practice*: 5–20. San Francisco: C.G. Jung Institute. Republished (1990) Boston: Sigo Press.

Traill, P. (1948). "Experiences with the use of the World Technique in clinical work with children." In M. Lowenfeld (ed.) *On the Psychotherapy of Children*: 74–8. London: E.T. Heron & Co. Ltd.

Traill, P. and Rowles, F. (1964). "Non-verbal 'thinking' in child psychotherapy." In M. Lowenfeld, P. Traill, and F. Rowles (eds) *The Non-verbal 'Thinking' of Children and its Place in Psychotherapy.* London: Institute of Child Psychology Ltd.

Tremlin, B. (1970). "From custodial care to therapeutic play." *Nursing Times* 66: 1144.

Ucko, L.E. (1967). "Early stress experiences mirrored in World Play Test at five years." *Human Development* 10: 107–27.

Urwin, C. and Hood-Williams, J. (1988). *Child Psychotherapy, War and the Normal Child.* London: Free Association Books.

Van-Zyl, D. (1977). "Traumatic birth symbolized in play therapy." *Journal of Primal Therapy* 4(2): 154–8.

*Vinturella, L. and James, R. (1987). "Sandplay: A therapeutic medium with children." *Elementary School Guidance and Counseling* 21(3): 229–38.

Volcani, Y., Stollak, G., Ferguson, L. and Benedict, H. (1982). "Sandtray play: children's fantasy play and parental caregiving perceptions." Paper presented at the Annual Meeting of the American Psychological Association (90th). Washington, DC.

*Watson, M. (undated). "Sandtray in education." Unpublished paper, San Francisco, CA.

*Weinrib, E.L. (1983a). *Images of the Self: The Sandplay Therapy Process.* Boston: Sigo Press.

*——— (1983b). "On delayed interpretation in Sandplay therapy." In *Arms of the Windmill*: 119–29. New York: C.G. Jung Foundation.

*——— (1987). "Sandplay: The shadow and the cross." In M.A. Mattoon (ed.) *The archetype of shadow in a split world: Proceedings of the Tenth International Congress for Analytical Psychology, Berlin, 1986*: 415–529. Einsiedeln, Switzerland: Daimon Verlag.

*——— (1989). "Sandplay Workshop." (Seminar notes.) Phoenix: Friends of C.G. Jung.

*——— (1991). "Diagram of the psyche." *Journal of Sandplay Therapy* 1(1): 48–53.

Wells, H.G. (1911). *Floor Games.* London: Palmer. Reprinted (1976) New York: Arno Press.

Wenar, C. (1954). "The effects of a motor handicap on personality: II. The effects on integrative ability." *Child Development* 25: 278–94.

—— (1956). "The effects of a motor handicap on personality: III. The effects on certain fantasies and adjustive techniques." *Child Development* 27: 9–15.

*Zappacosta, J.D. (1992). "Healing our children: Divine energies in play." *Journal of Sandplay Therapy* 2(1): 59–65.

*Zarrow, S.D. (in press). "Taking the initiative in a less than perfect sandworld." In B. Caprio (ed.) *Sandplay: Coming of Age*. Paper presented at the Los Angeles Sandplay Association 1991 Conference.

*Zeller, D. (1979). "The sand tray." Unpublished master's thesis, California State University, Sonoma.

Non-English language

This bibliography includes sand tray citations published in a language other than English. In order to be included in this listing, the article, book, or thesis/dissertation had to explore a technique that uses the placement of three-dimensional miniatures and objects within a specified space, such as within a container (e.g., the sand tray), on a table top, or within a specified floor space. Articles that are exclusively devoted to Sandplay are designated by an asterisk (*). This bibliography does not include journal citations listed in Takahashi *et al.* (1990, 1991a, 1991b).

*Akita, I. (1985). "Human relations disorder, 18-year-old female." In H. Kawai and Y. Yamanaka (eds) *Studies of Sandplay Therapy in Japan* II: 96–117. Commentator: S. Nishimura. Tokyo: Seishin-Shoboh.

*—— (1990a). "Sandplay therapy for a patient with hysteria who exhibited double personality: A case of identical twins." *Archives of Sandplay Therapy* 3(1): 3–13.

*—— (1990b). "Misa and Maria: A drama of an inner world of an 8-year-old girl who suffered from dream walking." *Archives of Sandplay Therapy* 3(1): 37–49.

*—— (1991). "Sandplay therapy without the use of toys: From a case of a girl with anorexia nervosa." *Archives of Sandplay Therapy* 4(2): 49–59.

*Ando, Y. (1990). "The Sandplay process in the case of a neurotic girl, expressed mainly by 'Ie' images" ('Ie': house, home or family in Japanese). *Archives of Sandplay Therapy* 3(2): 68–78.

*Aoki, S. (1982). "Tic, 6-year-old girl." In H. Kawai and Y. Yamanaka (eds) *Studies of Sandplay Therapy in Japan* I: 1–22. Commentator: Y. Okada. Tokyo: Seishin-Shoboh.

*Arakawa, Y. (1988). "On the process of Sandplay therapy for a girl with trichotillomania." *Archives of Sandplay Therapy* 1(1): 38–46.

*Araki, M. (1990). "A thought of traditional Japanese landscape: On movie 'Toki o Kakeru Shojo' (A Time Travelled Girl), and the landscape in Kamiichi and Shimoichi (Takehara-city)." *Archives of Sandplay Therapy* 3(1): 61–7.

Arthus, H. (1949). *Le Village: Test d'Activité créatrice*. Paris: Presses Universitaires de France.

*Baden, R. (1982). "School refusal with night terror, 8-year-old girl." In H. Kawai and Y. Yamanaka (eds) *Studies of Sandplay Therapy in Japan* I: 23–42. Commentator: J. Hayashi. Tokyo: Seishin-Shoboh.

Borecky, V. (1989). *Prostorove vyjadrene egocentrismu v konstruktivri mime-ticke hrs*. Prague: Academie.

*Bradway, K. (1992). "Aspekte der übertragung und co-übertragung in der Sandspieltherapie." *Zeitschrift für Sandspiel Therapie* 1: 12–25.

Bühler, C. (1937). "Mouvement et intelligence." *Proceedings of the International Congress of Psychology* 8: 348–52.

*Burney, C. and Kawai, H. (1987). "Schizophrenic experience of a middle-aged woman." In H. Kawai and Y. Yamanaka (eds) *Studies of Sandplay Therapy in Japan* III: iii–xv. Tokyo: Seishin-Shoboh.

*Fukudome, R. (1992). "The process of changing mental attitude with security in the Sandplay therapy." *Archives of Sandplay Therapy* 5(2): 24–37.

*Haiamatsu, K. (1982). "School maladjustment, 11-year-old female." In H. Kawai and Y. Yamanaka (eds) *Studies of Sandplay Therapy in Japan* I: 65–85. Commentator: Y. Yamanaka. Tokyo: Seishin-Shoboh.

Harding, G. (1950). "Forslag till standardisering av lekmaterial for diagnostiskt och terapeutiskt bruk." *Nordisk Medecin* 43: 619–27.

—— (1965). *Leken son Avslojar*. Stockholm: Naturoch Kultur.

*Hayashi, K. (1987). "A case of aichmophobia, 17-year-old male." In H. Kawai and Y. Yamanaka (eds) *Studies of Sandplay Therapy in Japan* III: 26–47. Commentator: S. Nishimura. Tokyo: Seishin-Shoboh.

*Hayashi, S. (1991). "The study of emotional changes during the menstrual cycle." *Archives of Sandplay Therapy* 4(2): 3–14.

*Higashiyama, H. (1992). "Sandplay, dream, and play." *Archives of Sandplay Therapy* 5: 1–2.

*Hiraguchi, M. (1990). "Mari: A case of tic." *Archives of Sandplay Therapy* 3(1): 50–60.

*Hiramatsu, Y. (1992). "A case of a high school boy with vocal tic disorder." *Archives of Sandplay Therapy* 5(2): 13–23.

Hohn, E. (1964). "Spielerische Gestaltungsverfahren." In R. Heiss (ed.) *Handbuch der Psychologie: Psychologische Diagnostic* VI: 685–705. Gottingen: Verlag für Psychologie, C.J. Hogrefe.

*Hoshi, K. (1992). "Consideration on the expressing images and sex difference: Combativeness vs Pacifism." *Archives of Sandplay Therapy* 5(2): 85–94.

*Ikujima, H. (1982). "Anthropophobia, 20-year-old male." In H. Kawai and Y. Yamanaka (eds) *Studies of Sandplay Therapy in Japan* I: 145–59. Commentator: H. Kawai. Tokyo: Seishin-Shoboh.

*Inoue, K. (1990). "The process of Sandplay therapy of a male with duchenne type muscular dystrophy: Preparation for death." *Archives of Sandplay Therapy* 3(1): 14–25.

*Inoue, Y. (1972). "A case report on psychotherapy of a restless boy." *Archives of Counseling in Kyoto City Counseling Center* 6: 59–75.

*Iri, S. and Ohmori, K. (1990). "Changes of articles in Sandplay technique." *Japanese Bulletin of Art Therapy* 21: 71–80.

*Irie, S. (1987). "Remission process of a schizophrenic patient, 26-year-old male." In H. Kawai and Y. Yamanaka (eds) *Studies of Sandplay Therapy in Japan* III: 190–216. Commentator: H. Naniwa. Tokyo: Seishin-Shoboh.

*Ishikawa, S. (1992). "Cooperative Sandplay for a drug (thinner) abuse juvenile delinquent." *Archives of Sandplay Therapy* 5(2): 3–12.

*Ito, K. (1991). "Sandplay therapy process of a boy with tic." *Archives of Sandplay Therapy* 4(1): 28–37.

*Ito, Y. (1988). "On the depth of Sandplay expression: A sleeping boy." *Archives of Sandplay Therapy* 1(1): 3–16.

*Iwado, M. and Kimura, H. (1971). "A fundamental study on the Sandplay technique (2): Some expressions by gifted children in Sandplay." *Annual Report of the Science of Living* 19: 217–27.

*—— (1972). "A fundamental study on the Sandplay technique (3): Some expressions by the children of 3–5 years old." *Annual Report of the Science of Living* 20: 175–84.

*Iwado, M. and Nabikawa, M. (1970). "A fundamental study on the Sandplay technique." *Annual Report of the Science of Living* 18: 183–92.

*Kalff, D. (1966). *Sandspiel*. Zurich: Rascher. Later published (1972) in Japanese as *Sandplay Therapy of Kalff*. (O. Mitsugu and Y. Yasuhiro, trans., H. Kawai, supv.) Tokyo: Seishin-Shobou.

*—— (1969). "Das Sandspiel: Ein Beitrag aus der Sicht C.G. Jungs zur Kinderpsychotherapie." [The Sandplay: A contribution from C.G. Jung's point of view on child therapy.] In G. Bierman (ed.) *Handbuch der Kinderpsychotherapie*: 451–6. Munich/Basel: Ernst Reinhardt Verlag.

*—— (1978). "Eine kurze Einführung in die Sandspieltherapie." *Praxis der Psychotherapie* 23: 269–73. Heidelberg: Springer-Verlag. Translated into English by Kalff (1986) and presented to the International Society for Sandplay Therapy. Printed in English (1992) as "Introduction to Sandplay therapy." *Journal of Sandplay Therapy* 1(1): 7–15. (Reprinted in German (1992) as "Einführung in die Sandspieltherapie." *Zeitschrift für Sandspiel Therapie* 1: 7–11.)

*Kamei, T. (1982). "PSD; fever, 9-year-old male." In H. Kawai and Y. Yamanaka (eds) *Studies of Sandplay Therapy in Japan* I: 43–64. Commentator: H. Kohno. Tokyo: Seishin- Shoboh.

Kamp, L.N.J. and Kessler, E.S. (1971). "Le Test du Monde: Aspects développementaux d'une technique de jeu." *Revue de Neuropsychiatrie Infantile* 19(6): 295–322. Originally printed in English (1970) as "The World Test: Development aspects of a play technique." *The Journal of Child Psychology and Psychiatry* 11: 81–108.

*Kanno, S. (1982). "Depression, 23-year-old male." In H. Kawai and Y. Yamanaka (eds) *Studies of Sandplay Therapy in Japan* I: 185–204. Commentator: S. Nishimura. Tokyo: Seishin-Shoboh.

*Kataza, K. (1990). "Sandplay drama: The experimental application to a female student." *Archives of Sandplay Therapy* 3(2): 79–91.

*Kawai, H. (ed.) (1969). *Introduction to the Sandplay Technique*. Tokyo: Seishin-Shoboh.

*—— (1975). *Counseling and Humanity*. Tokyo: Sogen-sha.

—— (ed.) (1977). *Practice of Psychotherapy*. Tokyo: Seishin-Shoboh.

*—— (1982). "Introduction: Development of Sandplay therapy." In H. Kawai and Y. Yamanaka (eds) *Studies of Sandplay Therapy in Japan* I: iv–xviii. Tokyo: Seishin-Shoboh.

*—— (1985). "Introduction: On transference in Sandplay therapy." In H. Kawai and Y. Yamanaka (eds) *Studies of Sandplay Therapy in Japan* II: iii–xi. Tokyo: Seishin-Shoboh.

*—— (1988). "On the qualification of psychotherapist." *Archives of Sandplay Therapy* 1(1): 1–2.

*—— (1992). Vorwort. *Zeitschrift für Sandspiel-Therapie* 1(1): 3–5.

*Kawai, H., Nakamura, Y. and Akashi Society for the Study of Sandplay Therapy (1984). *Intellect of topos: The world of Sandplay therapy*, TBS Britannica.

*Kawai, H. and Tarigawa, S. (1979). *You Don't Need a Scalpel for the Soul*. Tokyo: Asahi Shauppan-Sha.

*Kawai, H. and Yamanaka, Y. (eds) (1982). *Studies of Sandplay Therapy in Japan* I. Tokyo: Seishin-Shoboh.

*—— (eds) (1985). *Studies of Sandplay Therapy in Japan* II. Tokyo: Seishin-Shoboh.

*—— (eds) (1987). *Studies of Sandplay Therapy in Japan* III. Tokyo: Seishin-Shoboh.

*Kikuchi, A. (1985). "Homosexual identity disorder, 20-year-old male." In H. Kawai and Y. Yamanaka (eds) *Studies of Sandplay Therapy in Japan* II: 118–38. Commentator: H. Ujihara. Tokyo: Seishin-Shoboh.

*Kimura, H. (1982). "Enuresis nocturna, 11-year-old girl." In H. Kawai and Y. Yamanaka (eds) *Studies of Sandplay Therapy in Japan* I: 86–106. Commentator: A. Miki. Tokyo: Seishin-Shoboh.

*—— (1985). "Research: A study on points of view on Sandplay works." In H. Kawai and Y. Yamanaka (eds) *Studies of Sandplay Therapy in Japan* II: 183–217. Commentator: Y. Okada. Tokyo: Seishin-Shoboh.

*Kita, T. (1992). "Circular motion as the inner stability: The Sandplay therapy process for a young woman who suffered from depressive state." *Archives of Sandplay Therapy* 5(1): 74–84.

*Koume, S. (1990). "An attempt at Sandplay therapy in a psychiatric day care center." *Japanese Bulletin of Art Therapy* 21: 80–98.

*Kusas, M. and Honda, T. (1990). "Sandplay productions of alcoholics." *Japanese Bulletin of Art Therapy* 21: 107–16.

*Lowen-Seifert, S. (1992). "Übertragung–Gegenübertragung im Sandbild." *Zeitschrift für Sandspiel Therapie* 1: 26–37.

Lowenfeld, M. (1953). "Einige Grundzüge einer Kinder-Psychotherapie." *Psyche* 7: 208–16.

—— (1958). "La Tecnica del Mundo: un metodo objetivo para el estudio de la personalidad de ninos y adultos." *Revista de Psiquiatria y Psicologia Medica: IV Congreso Internacional de Psicoterapia*: 509. Barcelona.

—— (1969). "Die 'Welt'-Technik in der Kinderpsychotherapie." In G. Bierman (ed.) *Handbuch der Kinderpsychotherapie*: 442–51. Munich/Basel: Ernst Reinhardt Verlag.

Mabille, P. (1950). *La Technique du Test du Village*. Paris: Presses Universitaires de France. (Reprinted: Dufour, 1970.)

*Maeda, T. (1985). "Fear of death, anxiety, 9-year-old male." In H. Kawai and Y. Yamanaka (eds) *Studies of Sandplay Therapy in Japan* II: 53–73. Commentator: Y. Yamanaka. Tokyo: Seishin-Shoboh.

*Matsumoto, K. (1992). "A Sandplay process of a trichotilomanic girl." *Archives of Sandplay Therapy* 5(1): 51–61.

Meyer, H. (1957). *Das Weltspiel*. Bern: Hans Huber Publisher.

*Miki, A. (1977). *A Path to Self-realization*. Tokyo: Seishin-Shoboh.

*—— (1988). "A long journey with K (a schizophrenic)." *Archives of Sandplay Therapy* 1(1): 61–73.

*Miki, A., Mitsumoto, K. and Tanaka, C. (1991). *Experiences: Sandplay Therapy – Fundamentals and Practice of Sandplay*. Tokyo: Sanou-Shuppan.

*Miura, K. (1990). "A process of a playtherapy of a schoolphobic boy: On the process of 'exertion'." *Archives of Sandplay Therapy* 3(1): 26–36.

*Miyaki, Y. (1991). "On a psychotherapeutic process with a girl suffering from hysteria." *Archives of Sandplay Therapy* 4(1): 16–27.

*Miyashita, H. (1985). "Paralysis of all limbs after eclampsy, 27-year-old female." In H. Kawai and Y. Yamanaka (eds) *Studies of Sandplay Therapy in Japan* II: 139–59. Commentator: K. Higuchi. Tokyo: Seishin-Shoboh.

*Miyazaki, E. (1985). "Psychogenic contraction of visual field, 12-year-old female." In H. Kawai and Y. Yamanaka (eds) *Studies of Sandplay Therapy in Japan* II: 1–30. Commentator: H. Nakai. Tokyo: Seishin-Shoboh.

Monod, M. (1968). "De l'interprétation de la création projective dans le test de Rorschach, le test du Village et les tests thématiques chez l'enfant." In A. Friedemann, H. Phillipson, B. Scott and C. Williams (eds) *Rorschach Proceedings: VIIth International Congress of Rorschach and Other Projective Techniques, London*. Bern: Hans Huber Publisher.

Monod, M. and Bidault, H. (1960). "Test de Rorschach et test du Village, technique d'investigation de la personnalité chez l'enfant." *Rorschachiana: Proceedings of the IVth International Rorschach Congress, Brussels*: 149–50. Bern: Hans Huber Publisher.

*Montecchi, F. and Navone, A. (1989). "Dora M. Kalff and the Sandplay." In C. Trombetta (ed.) *Psicologia Analitica Contemporanea (Contemporary Analytical Psychology)*. Milan, Italy: Fabbri Editorial Group.

*Moritani, H. (1990). "Applications of collage to psychotherapy, with comparisons with Sandplay." *Japanese Bulletin of Art Therapy* 21: 27–37.

Mucchielli, R. (1960). *Le Jeu du Monde et le Test du Village Imaginaire* (The World Game and the Imaginary Village Test). Paris: Presses Universitaires de France. (First chapter translated by John Hood-Williams.)

*Muramoto, K. (1990). "A case of a hysteric woman who produced inaccessible Sandplay works." *Archives of Sandplay Therapy* 3(2): 3–15.

*Murayama, M. (1982). "Adolescent crisis, 15-year-old girl." In H. Kawai and Y. Yamanaka (eds) *Studies of Sandplay Therapy in Japan* I: 128–44. Commentator: K. Higuchi. Tokyo: Seishin-Shoboh.

*Nagasawa, S. *et al.* (1966). *Sandplay Techniques*. Kyoto: Archives of Counseling City Centre.

*Nakano, T. (1987). "A difficult case of asthma bronchiale, 17-year-old male." In H. Kawai and Y. Yamanaka (eds) *Studies of Sandplay Therapy in Japan* III: 171–89. Commentator: H. Kohno. Tokyo: Seishin-Shoboh.

*Naniwa, H. (1969). "Case report of psychotherapy of a school phobia girl." *Archives of Counseling in Kyoto City Counseling Center* 3: 43–64 (English), 44–57 (Japanese).

*Nara, E. (1991). "Sandplay therapy for a junior high school refusal student." *Archives of Sandplay Therapy* 4(1): 38–47.

*Nishimura, S. (1972). "A case report on the play therapy process of a 4-year-old boy with separation anxiety." *Archives of Counseling in Kyoto City Counseling Center* 6: 231–7.

*—— (1992). "The great mother constellation has nourished Sandplay therapy." *Archives of Sandplay Therapy* 5(2): 1–2.

*Nishimura, Y. (1992). "The process of Sandplay therapy for a 12-year-old girl with school refusal and somatic complaints." *Archives of Sandplay Therapy* 5(1): 62–73.

*Oda, T. (1991). "Sandplay therapy and counter-transference." *Archives of Sandplay Therapy* 4(1): 1–2.

*Oda, T. and Okubo, Y. (1987). "A case of conversion hysteria and his nightmare, 10-year-old male." In H. Kawai and Y. Yamanaka (eds) *Studies of Sandplay Therapy in Japan* III: 119–39. Commentator: K. Higuchi. Tokyo: Seishin-Shoboh.

*Ogawa, K. (1991). "From sand tray technique to Sandplay therapy." *Archives of Sandplay Therapy* 4(2): 1–2.

*Oimatsu, K., Hamasaki, Y. and Tanaka, Y. (1991). "The center and the rage, as healing powers." *Archives of Sandplay Therapy* 4(2): 37–48.

*Okada, K. (1988). "Sandplay therapy for a handicapped child." *Archives of Sandplay Therapy* 1(1): 27–37.

*Okada, M. (1991). "A study of the stages of self-expression in the Sandplay works of an asthmatic girl." *Archives of Sandplay Therapy* 4(2): 15–23.

*—— (1984). *Basics of Sandplay Therapy*. Tokyo: Seishin Publications.

*Okada, Y. (1969) "A study of the Sandplay technique by means of the Semantic Differential Method." *The Japanese Journal of Clinical Psychology* 18: 151–63.

*—— (1972). "A study of the Sandplay technique by means of spheres." *Kyoto University Research Studies in Education* 18: 231–44. (Fujii (1979) entitled this article "Studies on the Sandplay technique: A study on the area of the Sandplay picture.")

—— (1984). *Basics of Sandplay Therapy.* Tokyo: Seishin Publications.

*—— (1990). "Primal landscape and Sandplay therapy." *Archives of Sandplay Therapy* 3(2): 1–2.

*Okada, Y., Mori, S., Okudaira, N. and Bansho, A. (1988). "An investigation of inner world of Australian students by using Sandplay." *Archives of Sandplay Therapy* 1(1): 17–26.

*Okudaira, N. (1988). "On the Hakoniwa, the landscape in a box in Japan." *Archives of Sandplay Therapy* 1(1): 74–86.

*Ono, J. (1987). "Trichotillomania and acting out, 14-year-old female." In H. Kawai and Y. Yamanaka (eds) *Studies of Sandplay Therapy in Japan* III: 140–70. Com- mentator: H. Nakai. Tokyo: Seishin-Shoboh.

Pacheco, O. de A. (1951/2). "Os 'pequenos mundos' e o descentio das criancas com alteracoes de comportamento." *A Crianca Portuguesa* 11(1): 333–42.

—— (1951). "The 'Little Worlds' in Portugal." Paper presented at Thirteenth International Congress of Psychology, Stockholm.

*Saitoh, S. (1992). "A nomothetic study of the Sandplay characteristic of the children having difficulty attending school." *Archives of Sandplay Therapy* 5(1): 39–50.

*Sakata, Y. (1987). "A case of maladaptation at school, 7-year-old male." In H. Kawai and Y. Yamanaka (eds) *Studies of Sandplay Therapy in Japan* III: 48–70. Commentator: Y. Okada. Tokyo: Seishin-Shoboh.

*Satoh, M. (1985). "Obsessive compulsive neurosis, 11-year-old male." In H. Kawai and Y. Yamanaka (eds) *Studies of Sandplay Therapy in Japan* II: 74–95. Commentator: H. Naniwa. Tokyo: Seishin-Shoboh.

Segalen, J. (1968). "Développement de l'enfant et test du Village." In A. Friedemann, H. Phillipson, B. Scott and C. Williams (eds) *Rorschach Proceedings: VIIth International Congress of Rorschach and Other Projective Techniques, London*: 286–91. Bern: Hans Huber.

*Shimada, A. and Ishida, M. (1991). "When a psychosomatic patient faces to the sand box in Sandplay therapy." *Archives of Sandplay Therapy* 4(1): 3–15.

*Shimizu, S. (1987). "A case of hysteria, 10-year-old female." In H. Kawai and Y. Yamanaka (eds) *Studies of Sandplay Therapy in Japan* III: 99–118. Commentator: Y. Yamanaka. Tokyo: Seishin-Shoboh.

*Shimoyama, H. (1990). "The therapeutic meaning of the Sandplay therapy in terms of the relation-oriented hypothesis." *Archives of Sandplay Therapy* 3(2): 16–30.

*Suga, S. (1991). "Sandplay for a child of psychogenic visual disturbance." *Archives of Sandplay Therapy* 4(2): 24–36.

*Suga, S. and Hirai, K. (1982). "Elective mutism, 14-year-old male." In H. Kawai and Y. Yamanaka (eds) *Studies of Sandplay Therapy in Japan* I: 107–27. Commentator: H. Naniwa. Tokyo: Seishin-Shoboh.

*Takahashi, M. (1987). "An anthropophobiac 3-year-old girl." In H. Kawai and Y. Yamanaka (eds) *Studies of Sandplay Therapy in Japan* III: 3–25. Commentator: D. Kalff. Tokyo: Seishin-Shoboh.

*Takahashi, M., Okada, Y. and Bansho, A. (1990). "Literature of Sandplay therapy in Japan." *Archives of Sandplay Therapy* 3(2): 92–6.

*—— (1991a). "Literature on Sandplay therapy in Japan, 1978–84." *Archives of Sandplay Therapy* 4(1): 74–8.

*—— (1991b). "Literature on Sandplay therapy in Japan, 1985–8." *Archives of Sandplay Therapy* 4(2): 69–73.

*Takano, S. (1982). "Schizophrenia, 21-year-old male." In H. Kawai and Y. Yamanaka (eds) *Studies of Sandplay Therapy in Japan* I: 164–84. Commentator: H. Nakai. Tokyo: Seishin-Shoboh.

*—— (1985). "Schizophrenic with frame-emphasizing-tray, 28-year-old male." In H. Kawai and Y. Yamanaka (eds) *Studies of Sandplay Therapy in Japan* II: 160–82. Commentator: A. Miki. Tokyo: Seishin-Shoboh.

*—— (1987). "Therapeutic approach to a borderline case, 16-year-old female." In H. Kawai and Y. Yamanaka (eds) *Studies of Sandplay Therapy in Japan* III: 71–89. Commentator: A. Miki. Tokyo: Seishin-Shoboh.

*—— (1988). "On the process of Sandplay therapy of the case of a battered isolated child." *Archives of Sandplay Therapy* 1(1): 47–60.

*Tanaka, S. (1990). "The centralization and reconstitution of the inner cosmology in the Sandplay therapy." *Archives of Sandplay Therapy* 3(2): 57–67.

*Taniguchi, F. (1990). "On the process of Sandplay therapy for the case of alopecia areata, employing hypnosis and autogenic training." *Archives of Sandplay Therapy* 3(2): 31–43.

*Toyoshima, K. (1985). "Asthma as an attachment disorder, 8-year-old male." In H. Kawai and Y. Yamanaka (eds) *Studies of Sandplay Therapy in Japan* II: 31–52. Commentator: H. Kohno. Tokyo: Seishin-Shoboh.

*Tsukada, Y. (1991). "A case of aerophagia." *Archives of Sandplay Therapy* 4(1): 48–58.

van Wylick, M. (1936). *Die Welt des Kindes in seiner Darstellung*. Vienna: Josef Eberle.

von Staabs, G. (1969). "Die Rolle des Scenotests in der Kinderpsychotherapie." In E. Reinhardt (ed.) *Handbuch der Kinderpsychotherapie*: 456–63. Munich/Basel: Ernst Reinhardt Verlag.

*Weinrib, E. (1992). "Der Schatten und das Kreuz." *Zeitschrift für Sandspiel Therapie* 1: 38–45.

*Yamanaka, Y. (1981). "Multi-dimensional expression therapy and its application on a case of anorexia nervosa." In V. Andreori (ed.) *The Pathology of Non-verbal Communications*: 359. Milan: Masson Italia Editori.

*—— (1982). "Depressive hypochondriasis, 72-year-old female." In H. Kawai and Y. Yamanaka (eds) *Studies of Sandplay Therapy in Japan* I: 205–22. Tokyo: Seishin-Shoboh.

*—— (1990). "A great 'psyche' passed away: An essay on the Worldtest–Sandspiel–Hakoniwa-ryoho." *Archives of Sandplay Therapy* 3(1): 1–2.

*—— (1991). "Von der 'Aggressiv-Regression' zur 'Selbstfindung': 'Dota der Hundebeisser,' 8 jahre. alt." *Archives of Sandplay Therapy* 4(2): 60–8.

*Yoshisue, M. (1990). "Sandplay for a neurotic child." *Archives of Sandplay Therapy* 3(2): 44–56.

Zust, R. (1963). *Das Dorfspiel*. Bern, Switzerland: Hans Huber Publisher.

ISST SANDPLAY PAPERS ON SYMBOLS OR THEORY

The following papers have been donated to the International Society for Sandplay Therapy (Founder: Dora Kalff). These papers are accessible only to ISST members. Selected cases are available through the C.G. Jung Institute, San Francisco.

Amatruda, K. (1984). "Psychological interventions in physical illness – The Sandplay Test: Assessing a dying child's awareness of death." Unpublished paper for Saybrook Institute. Donated to the C.G. Jung Institute of San Francisco.

Baum, N. (1987). "The multi-focal approach." Unpublished manuscript donated to the Archives of the Dora Kalff International Society for Sandplay Therapy.
—— (1988a). "The significance of the therapeutee's attitude towards Sandplay therapy." Unpublished manuscript donated to the Archives of the Dora Kalff International Society for Sandplay Therapy.
—— (1988b). "Sandplay with dually diagnosed children: Its validity for the development of the self." Unpublished manuscript donated to the Archives of the Dora Kalff International Society for Sandplay Therapy. Identical manuscript donated to the C.G. Jung Institute of San Francisco as: "Sandplay therapy with mentally retarded individuals with severe emotional or psychiatric disorders (dual diagnosis)."
Bobo, L.V. (1990). "The Heart." Unpublished manuscript donated to the C.G. Jung Institute of San Francisco.
Burney, C. (1983). "Transformation and Sandplay." (Transcribed and edited by S. Shepherd from a tape recording made at the Journey into Wholeness Conference, Saint Simon's Island, Georgia.) Unpublished manuscript donated to the C.G. Jung Institute of San Francisco.
Capitolo, M. (1990). "The dark goddesses: An encounter with the dark feminine." Unpublished manuscript donated to the Archives of the Dora Kalff International Society for Sandplay Therapy.
Dexter, S.S. (1989a). "The child in development process." Unpublished manuscript donated to the Archives of the Dora Kalff International Society for Sandplay Therapy and the C.G. Jung Institute of San Francisco.
—— (1989b). "The importance of play." Unpublished manuscript donated to the Archives of the Dora Kalff International Society for Sandplay Therapy and the C.G. Jung Institute of San Francisco.
Gradwell, L.E. (1989). "The mermaid." Unpublished manuscript donated to the Archives of the Dora Kalff International Society for Sandplay Therapy and the C.G. Jung Institute of San Francisco.
Jackson, B. (1991a). "The symbolism of the candle in Sandplay." Unpublished manuscript donated to the C.G. Jung Institute of San Francisco.
—— (1991b). "Treasure in Sandplay." Unpublished manuscript donated to the C.G. Jung Institute of San Francisco.
Johnson, H.H. (1991). "Sandplay therapy and the autistic child: A research study." Unpublished manuscript donated to the C.G. Jung Institute of San Francisco.
Macnofsky, R.S. (1986). "Jung: The symbol of the mandala: A resource paper for Sandplay." Unpublished manuscript donated to the C.G. Jung Institute of San Francisco.
Miriello, B.A. (1991). "Mirror symbology and Sandplay therapy." Unpublished manuscript donated to the C.G. Jung Institute of San Francisco.
Nyman, N.W. (1984). "An exploration of non-verbal expression in childhood: Child art and Sandplay." Unpublished paper prepared for School of Social Welfare, University of California, Berkeley. Donated to the C.G. Jung Institute of San Francisco.
Rowland, L. (1989a). "Sandplay: A medium for Apollo's gift of wholeness." Unpublished manuscript donated to the Archives of the Dora Kalff International Society for Sandplay Therapy and the C.G. Jung Institute of San Francisco.
—— (1989b). "Sandplay process and the manifestation of wholeness through the archetype of Apollo." Unpublished manuscript donated to the Archives of the Dora Kalff International Society for Sandplay Therapy and the C.G. Jung Institute of San Francisco.

Shepherd, S. (1986). "Tibetan chakras: Patterns of the psyche." Unpublished manuscript donated to the Archives of the Dora Kalff International Society for Sandplay Therapy and the C.G. Jung Institute of San Francisco.

Talamini, M. (1989). "Ricerca teorica su strutture spaziali e forme geometriche nella 'Sandplay Therapy'." Unpublished manuscript donated to the Archives of the Dora Kalff International Society for Sandplay Therapy.

Zarrow, S.D. (1990). "Explication of the Sandplay figure Bodhidarma, its history and meaning: A search for understanding; Why the Bodhidarma figure appeared concurrently in my personal Sandplay work and in the Sandplay of three of my patients." Unpublished manuscript donated to the C.G. Jung Institute of San Francisco.

ISST FINAL CASE REPORTS

The final case reports are submitted to the ISST Archives for partial fulfillment of ISST certification requirements. The case reports are accessible only to ISST members. Selected cases are available through the C.G. Jung Institute, San Francisco.

Amatruda, K. (1986). "Jacqui: Treatment of a young adolescent girl using Sandplay therapy." Unpublished manuscript donated to the Archives of the Dora Kalff International Society for Sandplay Therapy and to the C.G. Jung Institute of San Francisco.

Bath, L. (1986). "Case presentation to the Dora Kalff International Sandplay Society." Unpublished manuscript donated to the Archives of the Dora Kalff International Society for Sandplay Therapy and the C.G. Jung Institute of San Francisco.

Baum, N. (1987). "Sandplay: The therapeutic process of a mentally retarded young woman." Unpublished manuscript donated to the Archives of the Dora Kalff International Society for Sandplay Therapy and the C.G. Jung Institute of San Francisco.

Bayley, A.G. (1988). "Beginning work with Sandplay." Unpublished manuscript donated to the Archives of the Dora Kalff International Society for Sandplay Therapy.

Ben-Yehuda, L. (1991). "The American hero: Sandplay of a 10-year-old boy." Unpublished manuscript donated to the Archives of the Dora Kalff International Society for Sandplay Therapy and the C.G. Jung Institute of San Francisco.

Berghes, A. (1988). "A case study." Unpublished manuscript donated to the Archives of the Dora Kalff International Society for Sandplay Therapy.

Bianchi, F. (1989). "The woman of snakes." Unpublished manuscript donated to the Archives of the Dora Kalff International Society for Sandplay Therapy.

Blotto, W. (1987). "Anxiety neurosis in an 8-year-old girl." Unpublished manuscript donated to the Archives of the Dora Kalff International Society for Sandplay Therapy.

Bobo, L.V. (1989). "Sandplay: Paradise found." Unpublished manuscript donated to the Archives of the Dora Kalff International Society for Sandplay Therapy and the C.G. Jung Institute of San Francisco.

Bradway, K. (1986). "Kathy, a 10-year-old girl with dyslexia." Unpublished manuscript donated to the Archives of the Dora Kalff International Society for Sandplay Therapy. Identical manuscript donated to the C.G. Jung Library in San Francisco as: "Sandplay with a 10-year-old girl with dyslexia."

Capitolo, M. (1992). "Sandplay with a 36-year-old male: A search for the natural self." Unpublished manuscript donated to the Archives of the Dora Kalff International Society for Sandplay Therapy and the C.G. Jung Institute of San Francisco.

Carduccim, P. (1988). "The case of 'J': Alchemical initiation in the realm of matter." Unpublished manuscript donated to the Archives of the Dora Kalff International Society for Sandplay Therapy.

Chambers, L. (1987). "Tommy: A case in Sandplay." Unpublished manuscript donated to the Archives of the Dora Kalff International Society for Sandplay Therapy and the C.G. Jung library in San Francisco.

Cunningham, L. (1986). "A 5-year-old girl's process in Sandplay." Unpublished manuscript donated to the Archives of the Dora Kalff International Society for Sandplay Therapy.

De Darel, C. (1989). "The case study of a 7-year-old boy." Unpublished manuscript donated to the Archives of the Dora Kalff International Society for Sandplay Therapy.

Dexter, S.S. (1989). "Sandplay: Let the silent child speak." Unpublished manuscript donated to the Archives of the Dora Kalff International Society for Sandplay Therapy and the C.G. Jung Institute of San Francisco.

Fluckiger, J. (1990). "Monica: Weibliche Ich-entwicklung im Sandspielprozess." Unpublished manuscript donated to the Archives of the Dora Kalff International Society for Sandplay Therapy.

Friedman, H. (1986). "Sandplay: A rite of passage into womanhood." Unpublished manuscript donated to the Archives of the Dora Kalff International Society for Sandplay Therapy and the C.G. Jung Institute of San Francisco.

Gabriellini, G. (1986). "Case history." Unpublished manuscript donated to the Archives of the Dora Kalff International Society for Sandplay Therapy.

Garzonio, M. (1987). "Salvatore's story: the man who mistook his girlfriend for a rock." Unpublished manuscript donated to the Archives of the Dora Kalff International Society for Sandplay Therapy.

Gassmann, R. (1990). "Marcel: Die Beschreibung einer Sandspieltherapie." Unpublished manuscript donated to the Archives of the Dora Kalff International Society for Sandplay Therapy.

Gradwell, L.E. (1989). "Allison: Treatment of a young girl using Sandplay Therapy." Unpublished manuscript donated to the Archives of the Dora Kalff International Society for Sandplay Therapy and the C.G. Jung Institute of San Francisco.

Jackson, B. (1991). "Sandplay with a 6-year-old girl healing a mother–daughter wound." Unpublished manuscript donated to the Archives of the Dora Kalff International Society for Sandplay Therapy and the C.G. Jung Institute of San Francisco.

Johnson, H.H. (1991). "Sandplay therapy with a 7-year-old boy exhibiting a severe anxiety disorder: A case study." Unpublished manuscript donated to the Archives of the Dora Kalff International Society for Sandplay Therapy.

Kawai, H. (1986). "A case of chronic depression." Unpublished manuscript donated to the Archives of the Dora Kalff International Society for Sandplay Therapy.

Larsen, C. (1983). "Linda W.: Case study of an emotionally disturbed child with symptoms of trichotillomania." Unpublished manuscript donated to the Archives of the Dora Kalff International Society for Sandplay Therapy.

Lowen-Seifert, S. (1986). "Die Therapie eines elektiv mutistischen Mädchens aus symbolischer Sicht." Unpublished manuscript donated to the Archives of the Dora Kalff International Society for Sandplay Therapy.

Macnofsky, R.S. (1986). "Living now: A Sandplay presentation." Unpublished manuscript donated to the Archives of the Dora Kalff International Society for Sandplay Therapy.

Marinucci, S. (1986). "Case history." Unpublished manuscript donated to the Archives of the Dora Kalff International Society for Sandplay Therapy.

Markell, M.J. (1987). "Elizabeth: Sandplay, the process of a 42-year-old woman artist." Unpublished manuscript donated to the Archives of the Dora Kalff International Society for Sandplay Therapy and the C.G. Jung Institute of San Francisco.

Mazzarella, A. (1987). "The story of Bianca." Unpublished manuscript donated to the Archives of the Dora Kalff International Society for Sandplay Therapy.

Miriello, B.A. (1991). "Sandplay series: Case study, Ms Y." Unpublished manuscript donated to the Archives of the Dora Kalff International Society for Sandplay Therapy and the C.G. Jung Institute of San Francisco.

Mitchell, R.R. (1992). "Sandplay: one hero's journey, preadolescent male." Unpublished manuscript donated to the Archives of the Dora Kalff International Society for Sandplay Therapy and the C.G. Jung Institute of San Francisco.

Montecchi, F. (1986). "Silvia's case." Unpublished manuscript donated to the Archives of the Dora Kalff International Society for Sandplay Therapy.

Nagliero, G. (1987). "A clinical case." Unpublished manuscript donated to the Archives of the Dora Kalff International Society for Sandplay Therapy.

Navone, A. (1986). "The case of Giovanna." Unpublished manuscript donated to the Archives of the Dora Kalff International Society for Sandplay Therapy.

Nissim, S. (1990). "Il percorso di Anna." Unpublished manuscript donated to the Archives of the Dora Kalff International Society for Sandplay Therapy.

Noyes, M. (1990). "Fire, blood and sand: A spiritual journey." Unpublished manuscript donated to the Archives of the Dora Kalff International Society for Sandplay Therapy and the C.G. Jung Institue of San Francisco.

Oda, T. (1982). "Sandplay therapy to a female patient who has been suffering from hallucinations." Unpublished manuscript donated to the Archives of the Dora Kalff International Society for Sandplay Therapy.

Rise, C. (1990). "La costruzione della relazione dopo la tossicodipendenza." Unpublished manuscript donated to the Archives of the Dora Kalff International Society for Sandplay Therapy.

Rowland, L. (1989). "Sandplay: A child's path to wholeness." Unpublished manuscript donated to the Archives of the Dora Kalff International Society for Sandplay Therapy and the C.G. Jung Institute of San Francisco.

Ryce-Menuhin, J. (1986). "A sonata in the sand." Unpublished manuscript donated to the Archives of the Dora Kalff International Society for Sandplay Therapy.

Selzam, U. (1988). "Falldarstellung." Unpublished manuscript donated to the Archives of the Dora Kalff International Society for Sandplay Therapy.

Shepherd, S. (1987). "Celina: A Sandplay case study." Unpublished manuscript donated to the Archives of the Dora Kalff International Society for Sandplay Therapy and the C.G. Jung Institute of San Francisco.

Stern, M. (1986). "Verlaufsbericht von einem psychologischen Selbsterfahrungsprozess am Sandkasten." Unpublished manuscript donated to the Archives of the Dora Kalff International Society for Sandplay Therapy.

Talamini, M. (1989). "Processo di un io bisognoso per raggiungere il se originario." Unpublished manuscript donated to the Archives of the Dora Kalff International Society for Sandplay Therapy.

Tortolani, D. (1986). "About the primal mysteries of the feminine in a case of ideopathic obesity." Unpublished manuscript donated to the Archives of the Dora Kalff International Society for Sandplay Therapy.

Weinrib, E.G. (1989). "Sandplay illustrating the resolution of a father complex in an adult male." Unpublished manuscript donated to the Archives of the Dora Kalff International Society for Sandplay Therapy and the C.G. Jung Institute of San Francisco.

Weinrich, A.K.H. (1989). "A woman's intrapsychic search for the masculine." Unpublished manuscript donated to the Archives of the Dora Kalff International Society for Sandplay Therapy.

Weller, B. (1987). "Timmy: Journey of a small hero." Unpublished manuscript donated to the Archives of the Dora Kalff International Society for Sandplay Therapy and the C.G. Jung Institute of San Francisco.

Yamanaka, Y. (1985). "A case study of anorexia nervosa by Sandplay with mutual scribbling." Unpublished manuscript donated to the Archives of the Dora Kalff International Society for Sandplay Therapy.

Zarrow, S.D. (1990). "Funeral face: A Sandplay case study of a 40-year-old man." Unpublished manuscript donated to the Archives of the Dora Kalff International Society for Sandplay Therapy and the C.G. Jung Institute of San Francisco.

VIDEOTAPES AND AUDIOTAPES ON SANDPLAY

Bradway, K. (1979). "The sacred place in Sandplay." (Audiotape) Presentation to Analytical Psychology Club of San Francisco. Available from the C.G. Jung Institute, San Francisco, CA.

—— (1988). *Sandplay* (Videotape). Produced by Paula Kimbro. Available from the C.G. Jung Institute, San Francisco, CA.

—— (1990). *Sandplay turtles and the transitional object* (Videotape). Produced by Paula Kimbro. Available from the C.G. Jung Institute, San Francisco, CA.

Dundas, E. (1991). *Sandplay training, I & II* (Videotapes). Available from Evalyn Dundas, 2315 Gloria St., El Cerrito, CA 94530. (415) 234–9601.

Friedman, H. (1986). "Sandplay: An approach to the child's unconscious." (Audiotape). Available from C.G. Jung Institute, Los Angeles, CA.

—— (1989). "Images of childhood loss" (Audiotape). Available from C.G. Jung Institute, Los Angeles, CA.

—— (1990). "The mother goddess" (Audiotape). Paper presented at the Los Angeles Analytical Psychology Club Lecture Series. Available from C.G. Jung Institute, Los Angeles, CA.

—— (1992). *Young girl's passage into womanhood* (Videotape). Unpublished paper presented at San Rafael Conference. Available from C.G. Jung Institute, Los Angeles, CA.

Henderson, J. (1991). "The alchemy of Sandplay" (Audiotape). San Francisco C.G. Jung Institute Conference: Earth, Air, Fire, Water: Transformation in the Sand. Available from C.G. Jung Institute, San Francisco.

Kalff, D. (c1972). *Sandspiel* (16mm film). Directed and produced by Peter Ammann. Videotaped (1985). Available from C. G. Jung Institute, Los Angeles, CA.

—— (1979). "Sandplay: Mirror of the child's psyche" (Audiotape). Available from C.G. Jung Institute, Los Angeles, CA.

—— (July, 1984). "The four stages of birth" (Audiotapes 1 & 2). Zurich: Unex.

—— (1988). *Beyond the shadow . . . Sandplay therapy* (Videotape). Recorded at the International Transpersonal Conference, Santa Rosa, CA. Produced by Conference Recording Service. Available from C.G. Jung Institute, San Francisco, CA.

Los Angeles Sandplay Association (1991). *First Los Angeles Sandplay Association Conference* (Videotape). Conference proceedings, November 2. Available from C.G. Jung Institute, Los Angeles, CA.

Macnofsky, S. (1987). "Beyond the spoken word: Sandplay and art" (Audiotape). San Diego: Friends of Jung. Available from the C.G. Jung Institute, Los Angeles.

Matthews, M.A. (1989). "Alienation and the continuing search for intimacy" (Audiotape). Available from C.G. Jung Institute, Los Angeles, CA.

Oaklander, V. (1987). *A typical Sandplay session* (Videotape).

San Francisco C.G. Jung Institute (1991). "Earth, Air, Water, Fire: Transformation in the Sand" (Audiotape). Conference proceedings, September 21–2.

The Dr Margaret Lowenfeld Trust (1990). *The legacy of Margaret Lowenfeld* (Videotape). Available from Community Video Productions, 13 Arcadia Rd, Old Greenwich, CT 06870, USA.

Zeller, D. (1986). *On Sandplay* (Videotape). Self-produced. Available from C.G. Jung Institute, Los Angeles, CA.

Index